D0209471

also by dea birkett

Spinsters Abroad: Victorian Lady Explorers

Jella: From Lagos to Liverpool—A Woman
at Sea in a Man's World

ANCHOR BOOKS

*Doubleday*

New York   London   Toronto   Sydney   Auckland

# serpent in paradise

~ ~ ~

## dea birkett

AN ANCHOR BOOK

PUBLISHED BY DOUBLEDAY
a division of Bantam Doubleday Dell Publishing Group, Inc.
1540 Broadway, New York, New York 10036

ANCHOR BOOKS, DOUBLEDAY, and the portrayal of an anchor are
trademarks of Doubleday, a division of Bantam Doubleday Dell
Publishing Group, Inc.

The names of some of the characters and places have been changed.

*Book design by Maria Carella*
*Maps designed by Jackie Aher*

Library of Congress Cataloging-in-Publication Data
Birkett, Dea, 1958–
    Serpent in paradise / Dea Birkett.
        p.  cm.
    1. Pitcairn Island—Description and travel.   2. Birkett, Dea,
1958– —Journeys—Pitcairn Island.   I. Title.
DU800.B53   1997                                    97-10890
919.61'8—dc21                                            CIP

ISBN 0-385-48870-X
Copyright © 1997 by Dea Birkett
All Rights Reserved
Printed in the United States of America
First Anchor Books Edition: September 1997
10   9   8   7   6   5   4   3   2   1

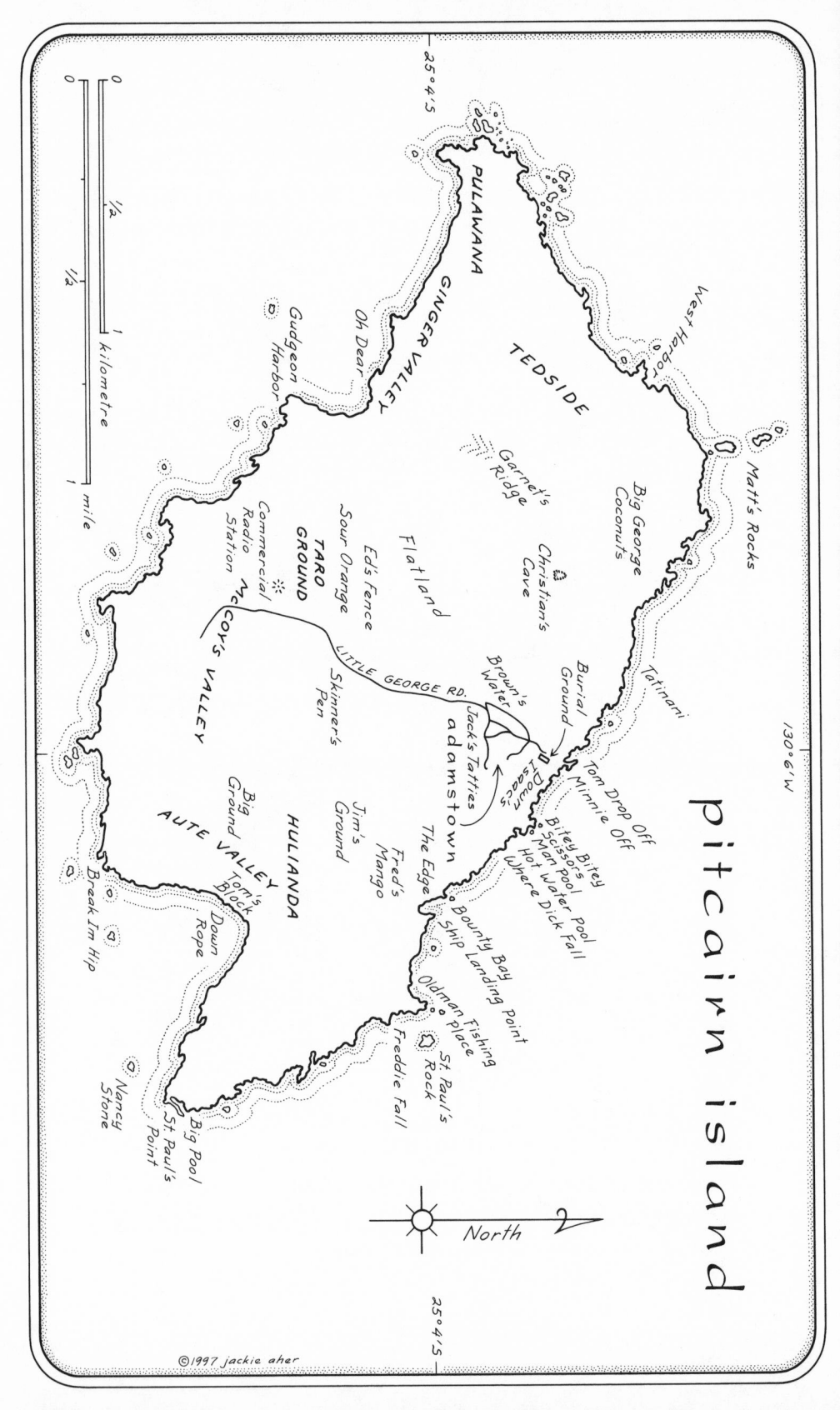

# pitcairn island

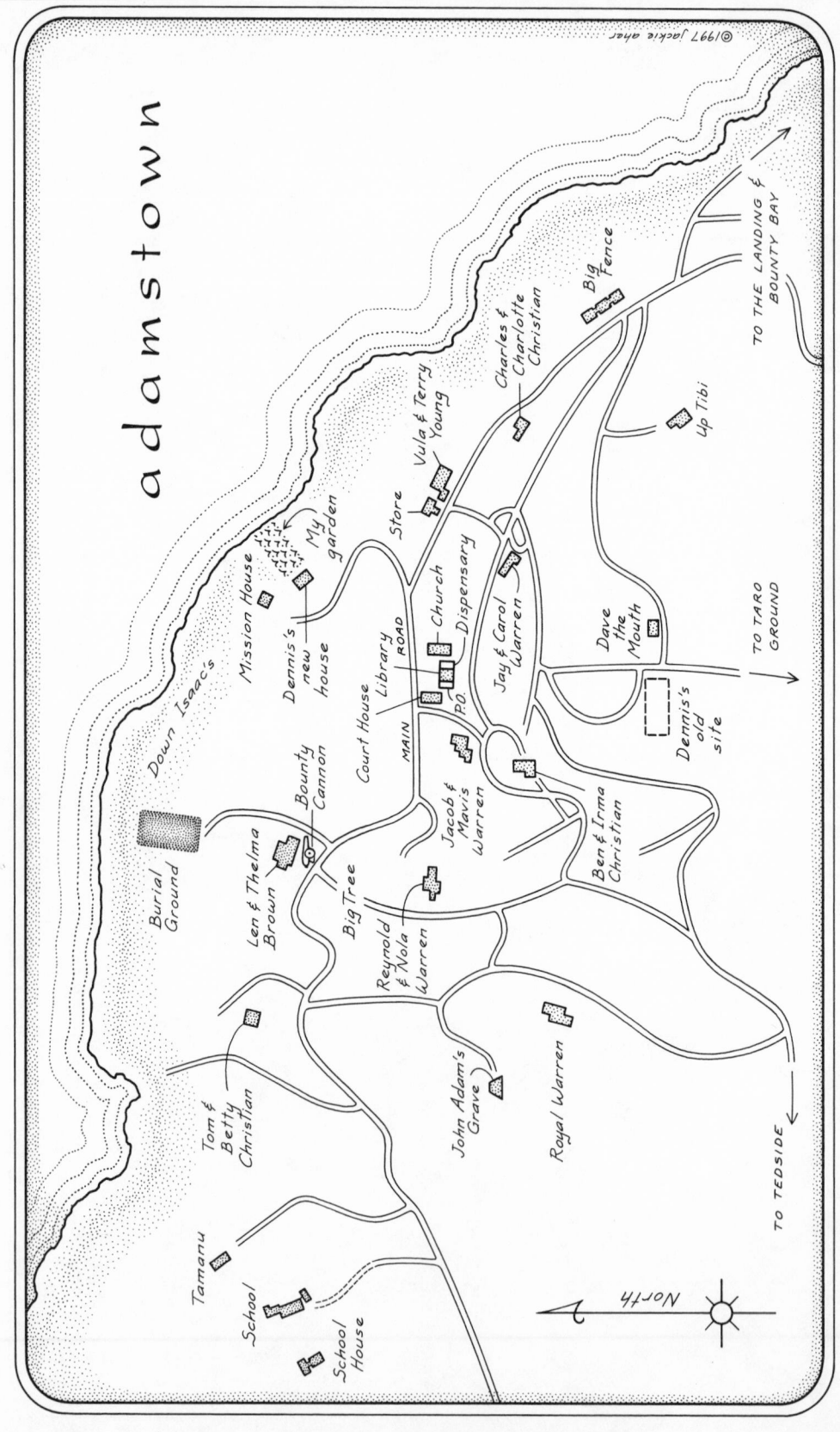

adamstown

© 1997 Jackie aker

North

## the complement of HMAV bounty and their fates following the mutiny

| | | |
|---|---|---|
| Lt. William Bligh | Commander | Cast adrift in launch; survived |
| John Fryer | Master | Cast adrift in launch; survived |
| William Cole | Boatswain | Cast adrift in launch; survived |
| William Peckover | Gunner | Cast adrift in launch; survived |
| William Purcell | Carpenter | Cast adrift in launch; survived |
| Thomas Huggan | Surgeon | Died of drink on Tahiti, 1788 |
| Thomas Ledward | Surgeon's Mate | Cast adrift in launch; probably lost at sea on *Welfare*, c. 1789 |
| Fletcher Christian | Master's Mate | Leader of mutineers; murdered on Pitcairn, c. 1793 |
| William Elphinstone | Master's Mate | Cast adrift in launch; died in Batavia (Djakarta), 1789 |
| Thomas Hayward | Midshipman | Cast adrift in launch; returned to Tahiti as Third Lieutenant on *Pandora*; shipwrecked and rescued |
| John Hallett | Midshipman | Cast adrift in launch; survived |
| George Stewart | Acting Midshipman | Mutineer; drowned on *Pandora*, 1791 |

| Peter Heywood | Acting Midshipman | Loyalist but remained on *Bounty;* returned on *Pandora;* found guilty at court-martial; received the King's pardon |
| Edward Young | Acting Midshipman | Mutineer; died of respiratory disease on Pitcairn, 1800 |
| Peter Linkletter | Quartermaster | Cast adrift in launch; died in Batavia, 1789 |
| John Norton | Quartermaster | Cast adrift in launch; murdered on Tofua, 1789 |
| George Simpson | Quartermaster's Mate | Cast adrift in launch; survived |
| James Morrison | Boatswain's Mate | Loyalist but remained on *Bounty;* returned on *Pandora;* found guilty at court-martial; received the King's pardon |
| John Mills | Gunner's Mate | Mutineer; murdered on Pitcairn, c. 1793 |
| Charles Norman | Carpenter's Mate | Loyalist but remained on *Bounty;* returned on *Pandora;* acquitted at court-martial |
| Thomas McIntosh | Carpenter's Crew | Loyalist but remained on *Bounty;* returned on *Pandora;* acquitted at court-martial |
| Lawrence Lebogue | Sailmaker | Cast adrift in launch; survived |
| Joseph Coleman | Armorer | Loyal to Bligh but remained on *Bounty;* returned on *Pandora;* acquitted at court-martial |
| Charles Churchill | Master-at-Arms | Mutineer; murdered by Matthew Thompson on Tahiti, 1790 |
| John Samuel | Clerk and Steward | Cast adrift in launch; survived |
| Thomas Burkett | Able-bodied Seaman | Mutineer; returned on *Pandora;* found guilty at court-martial; hanged, 1792 |
| Michael Byrne | Fiddler | Loyalist but remained on *Bounty;* returned on *Pandora;* acquitted at court-martial |

| Thomas Ellison | Able-bodied Seaman | Mutineer; returned on *Pandora;* found guilty at court-martial; hanged, 1792 |
| Henry Hillbrant | Able-bodied Seaman (cooper) | Mutineer; drowned on *Pandora,* 1791 |
| Isaac Martin | Able-bodied Seaman | Mutineer; murdered on Pitcairn, c. 1793 |
| William McCoy | Able-bodied Seaman | Mutineer; committed suicide on Pitcairn, c. 1797 |
| John Millward | Able-bodied Seaman | Mutineer; returned on *Pandora;* found guilty at court-martial; hanged, 1792 |
| William Muspratt | Able-bodied Seaman | Mutineer; returned on *Pandora;* found guilty at court-martial; freed on a technicality |
| Matthew Quintal | Able-bodied Seaman | Mutineer; murdered (probably by Adams) on Pitcairn, c. 1799 |
| Richard Skinner | Able-bodied Seaman (barber) | Mutineer; drowned on *Pandora,* 1791 |
| John Adams | Able-bodied Seaman | Mutineer; died on Pitcairn of old age, 1829 |
| John Sumner | Able-bodied Seaman | Mutineer; drowned on *Pandora,* 1791 |
| James Valentine | Able-bodied Seaman | Died at sea, 1788 |
| Matthew Thompson | Able-bodied Seaman | Mutineer; murdered on Tahiti, 1790 |
| John Williams | Able-bodied Seaman | Mutineer; murdered on Pitcairn, c. 1793 |
| Thomas Hall | Able-bodied Seaman (cook) | Cast adrift in launch; died in Batavia, 1789 |
| Robert Lamb | Able-bodied Seaman (butcher) | Case adrift in launch; died on passage from Batavia to Cape Town, 1789 |
| Robert Tinkler | Able-bodied Seaman | Cast adrift in launch; survived |

John Smith          Servant              Cast adrift in launch; survived

David Nelson        Botanist             Cast adrift in launch; died at
                                         Timor, 1789

William Brown       Botanist's Assistant Mutineer; murdered on
                                         Pitcairn, c. 1793

*They say it scares a man to be alone.*
*No such thing . . . What scares him worst is to be right*
*in the midst of a crowd, and have no guess*
*of what they're driving at.*

ROBERT LOUIS STEVENSON
*The Beach of Falesá*

# contents

Pitcairnese is a spoken, not a written language, and there is no agreed form of spelling. This applies to place names as well as ordinary verbs and nouns. I have chosen the spellings that have been most commonly used by those who have studied the language, or which are most phonetic and therefore easiest to read. A Pitcairner would not recognize a spelling as "correct" or "incorrect" but would accept whatever convention the writer chose to follow, as long as the words were pronounced properly. Recently Pitcairnese was recognized as the official language of Pitcairn (along with English) and renamed "Pitkern."

serpent in paradise

≈    ≈

# part one

≈   ≈

## 1 · the elephant

The teenager in the seat beside me scooped up another handful of popcorn and plunged his fingers deep inside his mouth. He stared ahead at the screen, where the toffee-colored breasts of the South Pacific maidens were wobbling like jelly freed from its mold. Captain William Bligh's forehead glistened with sweat. Fletcher Christian, Bligh's master's mate on His Majesty's Armed Vessel *Bounty*, was sitting cross-legged next to Tinah, the Tahitian chief. Fletcher Christian's eyes met those of a young Tahitian woman, then, embarrassed, flicked away.

The teenager took another handful of popcorn, held it close to his lips for a moment, then, transfixed, returned it to the carton. The dance was becoming more frenzied. The men, naked except for a band between their legs, advanced toward the most beautiful woman, thrusting at her.

Her body rippled like a wave, her hips beckoned. The men grasped her, tossed her into the air, caught her, and threw her to the ground. A young man, a tight mesh of dark muscle, fell on top of her, and the crowd began to chant: *"Ver-ruum, ver-ruum, ver-ruum . . ."*

It had been a gray London afternoon. The air was heavy and moist, blanketing the traffic noise to a steady thud. My mood was also dull. I had been out of work for the last week, and had arrived in London to enjoy the city, but found everyone else busy and full of purpose. The afternoons were long, and I had come to watch a film at the Coronet cinema in an area of south London known as the Elephant, in the hope of being transported to another place.

The story on screen continued at a feverish pace. *"Christian's taking the ship. Christian's taking the ship . . . taking the ship,"* the whisper was relayed by the *Bounty's* crew.

The setting switched to the Royal Naval College at Greenwich, where Captain Bligh was defending himself before a panel of inquiry into how his ship, HMAV *Bounty,* came to be seized.

*"What made them so easy to corrupt?"* an admiral asked the captain of his crew.

*"I don't know—it was the place itself,"* he replied.

The scene of temptation rolled up before us—a granite island with lush green valleys and bare brown peaks, skirted by an opal sea. Like its inhabitants, the place itself was gorgeous and succulent. Inside a wooden hut, in a green valley, on this beautiful island, Fletcher Christian was lying with the young Tahitian woman.

Behind me, someone sucked the last drop from his Sunkist orange drink, making the sound of a bath being emptied.

*"I am committed to a desperate enterprise,"* Fletcher Christian entered in his log. *"I have said farewell to everything I have come to regard as indispensable . . . But I have found freedom."*

The *Bounty* weighed anchor and set out to sea, in hope of a haven, *"somewhere the British ships won't find us . . ."* muttered Christian through pursed lips. As the ship bucked over the waves, a swarthy Tahitian stood at her prow, scanning the horizon for the harborless, uninhabited Pitcairn Island, the mutineers' refuge from the gallows.

Back in Greenwich, the Lords of the Admiralty delivered their verdict: *"The court finds that the seizure of His Majesty's Armed Vessel* Bounty *was an act of mutiny by Fletcher Christian and other of her crew, and her captain, Lieutenant William Bligh, is, in the opinion of the court, to be exonerated of all blame."*

Off a small bay on Pitcairn Island, the *Bounty* was burning. Fletcher Christian and his followers watched the flames while Christian's young Tahitian wife stood by his side.

*"We'll never get off this island now, will we, sir? We'll never see England again,"* said seaman Adams.

The credits rolled and the lights went up. By the time the final paragraph scrolled over the screen, the row in front was shuffling out. I just caught the last few words: *". . . his descendants live on Pitcairn Island to this day."*

It was already dark outside. The line for the next showing of

THE BOUNTY
Mel Gibson—Anthony Hopkins
*After 200 Years, the Truth Behind the Legend*

caterpillared out onto the street. The teenager met some friends and they hung about under the lobby lights, passing a cigarette between them.

I walked over to the bus stop. The gorgeous isle still existed, out there, somewhere, and could be visited. The *Bounty* story was not just a myth; the Utopia the mutineers had searched for was a real place, and the inhabitants were the inheritors of this mutinous dream.

It started to rain and the cars switched on their windshield wipers. A dip in the pavement collected water, and pedestrians had to step from the curb into the road, where they were splashed by the cars. There was no sign of a bus.

I hunched against the rain. When, twenty minutes later, the bus still hadn't arrived, I resolved to leave for Pitcairn Island.

# 2 · *p a r a d i s e   i s l e*

The volume of the British Library catalog that included Pitcairn material was marked with the four letters of the first entry—"PISS."

I ordered up all the literature it listed, noting the smallest differences in the accounts of the mutiny and its aftermath, and attempted to construct a coherent story. The Cheerful Visitors' Library Consisting of the Most Choice and Cherished Works of Fiction, Romance, Poetry, and Morals of Our Richly Varied, Popular and Instructive Literature's *The Mutiny of the Bounty; Or, Christian and His Comrades* (1853) came down firmly in support of Fletcher Christian. The mutineers' story was so appealing that in the same year the Permanent Secretary to the Admiralty wrote a *defense* of the mutineers. More scholarly volumes followed. *Who Caused the Mutiny on the Bounty?* (1965) subjected the master's mate to

Freudian analysis, arguing that conflict arose because Christian harbored homosexual lust for his superior officer. *The Wake of the Bounty: A Piece of Literary Reflection* (1953) suggested, with footnotes, that Christian returned to England in secret, where he was spotted strolling along Fore Street, Plymouth, by Peter Heywood, his former midshipman. Fletcher Christian was said to have personally related this marvelous story to William Wordsworth, who passed it on to his friend Samuel Coleridge, who then composed "The Rime of the Ancient Mariner," modeled on Christian's story. Decades later, whether Christian was the inspiration behind this epic poem was still being debated in pages as obscure as the *Dalhousie Review*. A learned journal, *Studia Bountyana*, was launched to trawl over the finer points. Scholars, religious devotees, poets and fanatics all advocated their version of the events that had overtaken the *Bounty* and her crew. What happened, and what we wanted to have happened, were from the very beginning confused.

All that could be agreed upon was this bare skeleton: Lieutenant William Bligh, whose reputation as an outstanding navigator had been established on Captain James Cook's third and final expedition, was appointed to the command of HMAV *Bounty* on August 16, 1787. His orders were to proceed to the South Pacific around Cape Horn, collect breadfruit seedlings and transport them to the West Indies.

Hawkesworth's *An Account of the Voyages Undertaken by the Order of His Present Majesty for Making Discoveries in the Southern Hemisphere*, a copy of which Bligh kept in his cabin, had aroused great interest in the potential of the breadfruit plant. Needing no cultivation, weeding or feeding, its insipid fruit, resembling a large melon with warts, had become a symbol to British botanists of the ease of cultivation in the tropics; it was bread that grew on trees. The white settlers had long lobbied for the introduction of just such a cheap and nutritious staple to feed the slaves working their plantations. Enthusiasm for the project was so great that it was likened in importance to Sir Walter Raleigh's expedition to bring the potato plant from Virginia to Great Britain.

The *Bounty* had been especially equipped for her task, and no expense was spared for this project of imperial proportions. The deck was made waterproof with a lead lining, and fitted with a false floor cut with holes, in which 629 earthenware pots were lodged; the breadfruit does not propagate through seeds but shoots, which had to be accommodated on board. Two skylights brought fresh air into the cabin, and pipes were fixed in each corner to save any fresh water that drained from the plants. The first men assigned to the ship were the breadfruit plants' carers—David Nelson, a botanist, and William Brown, a gardener from the Royal Botanic Gardens at Kew.

All that was left to young Lieutenant Bligh was to choose a working crew. With an obsessional desire for the voyage to succeed, Bligh, by nature very particular, was fastidious in selecting his men, insisting that his ship carry a musician to entertain and exercise the seafarers with dancing, and a second surgeon to oversee their health on the long voyage. For the important post of master's mate, Bligh chose a family friend and former shipmate with whom he had made two passages to the West Indies, twenty-three-year-old Fletcher Christian. Christian, a young gentleman, had less than four years' sea experience; Bligh, a professional seaman ten years his senior, had served with the Royal Navy for almost two decades.

Fitted out with flowerpots and crew, the *Bounty* sailed from Deptford on October 9, 1787, bound for Spithead, where orders would be received to make for Tahiti via Cape Horn. Bad weather dogged the enterprise from the start, and after almost a month of being buffeted about the English Channel they found harbor on the South Coast of England. But the orders to proceed had not yet arrived, and the Lieutenant sat at the dockside for three weeks watching any possibility of a break in the weather blow away before the necessary papers came. On December 3, the *Bounty* at last struck out for Tahiti, but within two days she was forced back. Bligh tried again on December 6, and was forced back once more. He was growing anxious. By December 10 he had recorded in his log, "I suppose my character will be at stake."

Two days before Christmas, the *Bounty* set out for the last time, lashed by heavy seas. Seven barrels of beer were washed overboard, most of the ship's biscuits were destroyed by the salt water, and a seaman fell from a yard while furling a maintop gallant sail, a stay breaking his fall. Two weeks after leaving England, they anchored off Tenerife, resupplying the ship after the losses and repairing the damage.

The port of call also reinvigorated the crew, and when they weighed anchor five days later, Bligh wrote, "our ship's company all in good health and spirits." As the south end of Tenerife passed out of view, Bligh made known to his crew the intent and importance of the voyage, of which they had until this time been ignorant. Promising "the certainty of promotion to everyone whose endeavours should merit it," the lieutenant put the men on two-thirds rations, adding that they would be sailing directly to Tahiti without landfall.

Throughout the first two months of 1789, the ship plowed a south-southwesterly course toward the Horn. Often the becalmed sea and heavy rain made it impossible to dry clothes and bedding, and Bligh, fearing his men would fall sick, ordered all the decks below to be frequently sprinkled with vinegar. At other times, the ship struggled against bad weather and contrary winds. On the last day of March, the wind came round to the north-northeast, and Bligh was confident that the passage around the Horn would be accomplished without difficulty. But within two days, the unpredictable sea had changed once more; Bligh recorded that "the storm exceeded what I had never met with before."

By Saturday April 12, after ten days of unceasingly violent weather, the *Bounty* was having to be pumped out every hour. Not only were the conditions on board intolerable—the cook fell and broke a rib, another man dislocated a shoulder, and the sheep and poultry all perished—they were also losing ground. A few hours of calm on Sunday, April 20, gave them hope; but it was a tease, and by the afternoon there were snow and hail storms accompanying a fierce wind. Weeks went by without their making any headway at all. The men became ill; the ship was sodden. On April 22, after one month's hard work had shown not one mile's progress, Bligh ordered the helm to be put round for the Cape of Good Hope, with pumping continuing hourly all the way. When the *Bounty* anchored in the shadow of Table Mountain, she needed extensive repairs, including a complete recaulking of her hull. This was in preparation for the longest leg of the voyage, to Van Diemen's Land, more than six thousand miles away.

They left Cape Town on July 1, 1788 and, at the end of the month, St. Paul's Island was in sight, just a rock that Bligh had set as a target to test his navigational skills. After spending a few days anchored in Adventure Bay, Van Diemen's Land, the *Bounty* headed for Tahiti with no further landfalls.

Ten months and, according to Bligh's meticulous log, 27,086 nautical miles after leaving the naval dockyard in London, the *Bounty* dropped anchor in Matavai Bay, Tahiti. Gardeners Nelson and Brown set about collecting breadfruit shoots and overseeing the construction of a large hut as a greenhouse. Meanwhile Bligh delegated petty tasks to the rest of the men—patching sails, fetching wood and water, spreading out the moldy ship's biscuits to dry in the sun—although these were no substitute for the absorbing and strict routine while at sea. The lieutenant was occupied in attending to the breadfruit, examining them daily and becoming anxious at the loss of a single shoot.

Freed from the restraints of shipboard discipline, the officers and crew amused themselves wrestling with the island men and flirting with the island women. Christian had his buttocks blackened with a tattoo. Able-bodied seaman Thomas Ellison, still a teenager, simply had a date scratched on his right arm—October 25, 1788. It was the day they had first sited Oro-Hena, the highest peak of Tahiti, which shadows Matavai Bay. After the freedom of an island with woods, beaches and an abundance of fresh water, the specter of returning to the conditions on board a claustrophobic British vessel must have seemed intolerable, and three men attempted to desert.

After five idyllic months on Tahiti, all cats were put ashore, a stowaway search was made, and the breadfruit-laden *Bounty* at last set out for the West Indies. Despite all the setbacks, "The voyage had advanced in a course of uninterrupted prosperity, and had been attended with many circumstances equally pleasing and satisfactory," wrote Bligh. By this time, half the ship's company had been treated for venereal disease.

On April 28, 1789, just before sunrise, Master's Mate Fletcher Christian, Master-at-Arms Charles Churchill, Gunner's Mate John Mills and Able-bodied Seaman Thomas Burkett entered Captain Bligh's cabin as he slept and tied him up. Three weeks after leaving behind the temptations of Tahiti, the discontented crew of HMAV *Bounty* were mutinying. Captain William Bligh and eighteen loyal followers were forced over the side into a launch; more would have liked to join their commander, but the twenty-three-foot launch could not carry them. Fletcher Christian assumed command of HMAV *Bounty*.

The new commander's first order was to head for Tubuai, an island three hundred and fifty miles south of Tahiti's elysian fields. Although sighted by Captain Cook, with poor anchorage and only one narrow passage through the encircling reef, it was unlikely to be visited. Here, Christian hoped to found a South Pacific settlement; but the mutinous crew were not welcomed by the Tubuaians, and there was no meat on the island. One month after the mutiny, the *Bounty* set out to sea again, bound for Tahiti, in search of pigs, goats, chickens and, most important, women. Christian's own favorite, Mauatua, was loaded on board along with 38 goats, 96 chickens, 312 pigs and a bull and cow left behind by Captain Cook. With these seeds of a new country, the *Bounty* returned to Tubuai in hope. But the pigs destroyed the Tubuians' gardens, and soon there was open hostility between the mutineers and their neighbors. Within three months, conditions were so intolerable that the *Bounty* returned to Tahiti.

Seduced by the comforts offered on the island and wary of an uncertain future under Fletcher Christian's command, sixteen of the mutineers—two thirds of the total remaining crew—opted to remain on Tahiti, including Seaman Burkett. Just nine men remained loyal to their new master. Within a day, the *Bounty* sailed again, with twelve Tahitian women, six Polynesian men and one child, willingly or unwillingly, joining her.*

Boatswain's Mate James Morrison wrote in his journal that Christian chose to "Cruize for some Uninhabited Island where he would land his Stock . . . and set fire to the Ship, and where he hoped to live the remainder of His days without seeing the face of a European but those who were already with him." Christian must have said a small prayer for his former commander's devotion to navigation when he unearthed a description of Carteret's 1767 discovery of Pitcairn Island in Bligh's cabin copy of *An Account of the Voyages undertaken by the order of His Present Majesty for making Discoveries in the Southern Hemisphere.* From the deck of the *Swallow,* Captain Carteret had noted an island "scarce better than a large rock in the ocean." Tiny Pitcairn could have been, like so many other islands dotting eighteenth-century charts, nothing more than an apparition. Encarnation, Michel and San Pablo were all islands within two hundred miles of Pitcairn that were plotted on the Admiralty's charts until the mid-nineteenth century. Not one of them was real.

Captain Carteret had noted the island's inhospitable coastline and heavy vegetation—suggesting fertile land—and spotted a running stream. With a supply of fresh water, uninhabited, fertile and harborless, the tiny island was a haven. But Carteret had also, crucially for the mutineers, miscalculated Pitcairn's latitude; when Christian sighted the shores, the island was more than three degrees out from the position that Carteret had charted. Even with all the information available, no British frigate could reliably find them. On January 21, 1790, the rebel leader and his crew landed on Pitcairn. By making the island their home, the mutineers would, for all intents and purposes, disappear from the face of the earth.

---

* The identities of the women are difficult to confirm as most were renamed by the mutineers. Mauatua became Isabella, Teio became Mary, Teraura became Susannah, Toofaiti became Nancy, Vahineatua became Prudence, and three of the thirteen women including the child are said to have been renamed Sarah.

. . .

In the same month, Bligh was sailing from Cape Town to England, eager to recount his story. After being forced overboard into the launch, he had headed for Tofua, just thirty miles away, hoping to reprovision. But, defenseless, the men were attacked by the inhabitants and, in fleeing from the island, Quartermaster John Norton was killed—the first man to die as a direct result of the mutiny. Although the launch was provisioned for only five days, Bligh made the bold, some say reckless decision to sail 3,618 nautical miles from Tofua to the Dutch settlement of Timor, from where he hoped to take a ship homeward via Batavia (Djakarta), the main port for the Dutch United East India Company, and more quickly report the events that had occurred on board HMAV *Bounty.*

The schooner *Resource* took Bligh and his men from Timor to Batavia. Weak from the open boat voyage, four crew succumbed to fever in Batavia and died, but Bligh took the first packet boat to Cape Town, from where he immediately posted news of the mutiny. On March 14, 1790, Bligh arrived in England, greeted as a national hero for his outstanding feat of navigating the *Bounty*'s launch from Tofua to Timor. To avenge his wrongdoers, the Admiralty appointed Captain Edward Edwards as commander of HMS *Pandora,* with orders to hunt down the *Bounty* mutineers and bring them back to England for trial. Captain Edwards sailed in November 1790, bound for Tahiti.*

Within a year, when the fate of Christian and his followers was still unknown, Bligh's detailed log, *A Narrative of the Mutiny on Board His Majesty's Ship the Bounty,* was published. It was a runaway bestseller, translated into French and German, and musicals were performed on the London stage celebrating the captain's courage. Later, in an attempt to

---

* Captain Edwards captured fourteen mutineers on Tahiti; on the return voyage, the *Pandora* was shipwrecked on the Great Barrier Reef and Edwards—a far crueler captain than Bligh—refused to free the shackled, caged prisoners. Four died; ten survived to face trial in England.

defend Christian's actions, John Fryer, the *Bounty*'s master, who had followed Bligh into the launch, published his version of events. All testimonies by eyewitnesses conflicted; no one who told the story of the mutiny did so without an overbearing need for self-justification and even self-preservation. For while Bligh was in danger of losing his hard-fought-for reputation, others were under sentence of death.

Since these early accounts, the tale of the mutiny on the *Bounty* has been told and retold in more than two hundred books. Titles vie for authenticity—*What Happened on the Bounty?* has been answered with *What Really Happened on the Bounty. The Bounty,* with Mel Gibson's portrayal of Fletcher Christian and Anthony Hopkins's Bligh, was only the most recent of five movies, which have added yet more layers to the legend.

It was Captain James Cook who introduced the South Seas to the Western imagination. The explorer had returned from his voyages with information, drawings, specimens, a South Sea islander known as Omai and fantastical tales. Although renowned for his staunch, unpoetic manner, Cook spoke of being "imparadised" by what he had seen.

In 1776, twenty-two-year-old William Bligh had been taken on as the *Resolution*'s sailing master for Cook's third and final voyage. Sailing with him was David Nelson, later to be botanist with the *Bounty*. (William Peckover, whom Bligh was to employ as gunner, had accompanied Cook on all three voyages.) When, eleven years later, Bligh set about gathering together a crew, the South Seas suggested such a wealth of possibilities and enrichments that finding the men had been simple; Bligh's ship may well have been the first Royal Navy vessel to sail without any pressed men on board. The *Bounty* was following in Cook's imaginative wake.

But missing from the tales of untold promise conjured up by Cook's discoveries was a blank spot; Cook's Pacific had been populated, and often with people less than welcoming. An island, to be perfect, to be paradise, ought to be empty; "uninhabited" is a word attached only to islands, never to land. Land suggests borders, which can be crossed, violated, invaded; but an island, being empty, can be all ours.

Everything about an island suggests a complete and private world, upon which you can make your mark. You can plant your footprints in a circle around the shore. Even the geology of an island is itself an act of creation. I read in Rachel Carson's *The Sea Around Us:*

> Isolated islands in the sea are fundamentally different from the continents . . . islands are ephemeral, created today, destroyed tomorrow. With few exceptions, they are the result of the violent, explosive, earth-shaking eruptions of submarine volcanoes, working perhaps for millions of years to achieve their end. It is one of the paradoxes in the ways of the earth and sea that a process seemingly so destructive, so catastrophic in Nature, can result in an act of creation.

Carson could have been talking about the events of April 28, 1789.

The fantastical tale of the mutiny on the *Bounty* and the discovery of Pitcairn fulfilled our longing for perfection like no other before it. Pitcairn soon became our island, everyone's island, anyone's island.

Mr. Walter Brodie, stranded on Pitcairn when the ship on which he was a passenger broke free from its anchor and was lost over the horizon, wrote in 1850 that it was "the realisation of Arcadia, or what we had been accustomed to suppose had existence only in poetic imagination . . . there is neither wealth nor want, a primitive simplicity of life and manner, perfect equality in rank and station, and perfect content." In *The Romance of Pitcairn Island*, W. Y. Fullerton, who had stopped offshore for two hours in 1921, insisted that the island was "a living example of the transformation that can be wrought in human life . . . It shows the way from the Worst to the Best." In whichever century the title I chose had been written, it told me the same appealing story: Pitcairn was "an isle of peace" and the Pitcairners were "the friendliest people in the world." There was a court house and jail, but neither had ever been used; crime was unheard of, and personal safety guaranteed. While the rest of the world suffered revolutions, Pitcairn was unchanging. It was comforting to know that, however uncertain our own futures seemed, there was always the constant rock of Pitcairn, harboring our hopes. Somewhere, far away, the garden of Eden flourished.

As the days grew shorter and shorter outside, inside I began to construct from these fragments my own paradise isle. From sources in the British Library, I jotted down that Pitcairn was one of a group of four islands scattered over three hundred miles—Henderson, Oeno, Ducie and Pitcairn. All except Pitcairn itself were uninhabited. The 1990 census said there were forty islanders, aged five months to ninety-one years—eighteen males and twenty-two females—who lived in Adamstown, the capital of Pitcairn and the only settlement on the mile-by-mile-and-a-half-square island. Pitcairn Island School had a register of nine.

Much of Pitcairn was steep, black volcanic rock and dense valleys, and only eight percent of the land was flat and therefore able to be cultivated, but on this the islanders could grow sufficient vegetables and fruit to feed themselves. The coastline was inhospitable and often inaccessible, more than one quarter of the land being sheer cliff, and a primitive map of the island showed place names recording past accidents—Where Dick Fall, Tom Drop Off, Oh Dear and the Hill of Difficulties winding up from the Landing at Bounty Bay. Nevertheless, there were isolated points from which to fish in relative safety, so the islanders could rely upon a plentiful supply of protein.

The Pitcairners were reported as a "hybrid race," looking part European, part Polynesian. Even their language, Pitcairnese, was a blend of Polynesian and the mutineers' eighteenth-century English. Words that had long since been lost in Anglo-American conversation were still in everyday use on Pitcairn—such as *tardy* (for "late"), *musket* (for "gun") and *yonder* (for "faraway").

In 1886, nominal adherence to the Church of England, roughly modeled on the islanders' reading of the *Bounty's* Bible, had been abandoned when an American missionary called John Tay arrived, clutching some Seventh-day Adventist literature. I asked the General Conference of the Seventh-day Adventist Church Trans-European Division, whose head-quarters are at St. Albans, Hertfordshire, for some information, from which I distilled the main tenets of their faith:

- Second Coming of Christ
- Sabbath on Saturday
- Baptism by immersion only
- Resurrection of just and unjust—just will resurrect at Second Coming of Christ; resurrection of the unjust 1,000 years later
- No dancing, no drinking, no smoking, no card playing
- No Hell

It didn't seem such an objectionable creed.

As far as the government of the island was concerned, Pitcairn was Britain's last colony in the South Pacific, administered by a governor resi-dent more than three thousand miles away in New Zealand. Because the island was so remote, Mr. David Moss had unfortunately been unable to visit his dominion. He did, however, appoint a New Zealander as his representative on the island, whose official title was Government Adviser and Education Officer and who acted as schoolteacher.

The island published its own monthly newspaper, *The Pitcairn Mis-cellany*, four foolscap sides long, edited by the schoolteacher. I had found an old copy tucked in the back of a book in the British Library, and searched for clues in the fishing report, weather report, shipping news and pastor's piece. Despite its unremarkable contents, the *Miscellany* had the highest per capita readership population of any newspaper in the world: five thousand copies were produced, more than one hundred for every Pitcairner, and distributed worldwide to *Bounty* followers. I put a five-dollar bill in an envelope, addressed it to "The Editor, *Pitcairn Miscellany*, Pitcairn Island, South Pacific Ocean," and waited for my first copy; it took six months to arrive. By the time the *Miscellany* reached its overseas sub-scribers, it was always hopelessly out of date. The October issue might arrive in the spring; the June edition in the new year. And often the mail arrived in a different order to that in which it was posted; the length of time an issue took to reach its destination depended upon which ship picked up the mail bag, and where she was heading.

I was impatient to discover more about the island now, and wrote to the Expedition Advisory Centre at the Royal Geographical Society asking if they could recommend an expert on present-day Pitcairn; they put me in touch with Tim, who was writing a book about his experiences on the island. He suggested we meet in the bar at the Tower Hotel, a concrete building constructed like a messy pile of books to maximize the number of river views. The bar was busy with tourists taking a quick drink before a show, rings of businessmen swinging large scotches and babysitting mobile phones, and strangers who were using the landmark hotel as a convenient place to meet for the first time.

Tim stood up when he saw me and patted the seat opposite. He was dressed in beige casual wear—a beige cotton fitted jacket, an off-white shirt, beige cotton trousers, and soft beige leather shoes with white laces that stretched over his neat feet like skin. His compact body and smooth, putty-colored face made him appear like a mannequin in a seventies shop window. But there was a tiny bloody nick on his chin; he must have shaved just before coming out.

Tim pronounced every word very clearly and softly, leaning across the low, tinted glass table and assuming an air of great intimacy, as if we were plotting our plan of escape from the hollow world that surrounded us. We weren't really central London early evening cocktail drinkers, but lotus eaters on our way to Paradise.

Over a limp Greek salad in the hotel coffee shop, Tim told me about the storms and whales he had encountered during his single-handed, eight-month passage to Pitcairn on his yacht. While he was on the island, a cliff fell into the sea at Down Rope, Polynesian artifacts were unearthed, underground caves discovered, human skeletons sent to the Smithsonian Institute for examination, and two lives lost in a landslide. Tim had strapped a microlight to his yacht's deck and, one windy day, carried it to a high cliff and jumped off. I was enthralled. Tim's Pitcairn was full of unsolved, ancient mysteries and alarming physical challenges. We huddled together in the coffee shop, locked in our shared fantasy.

Tim was heading for his home in the suburbs, and I to my boyfriend's flat on the other side of the river. Tim squeezed my arm, leaned toward me and whispered, "Let's go together. On my yacht." And then, coconspirators in the night, we parted.

I strolled over Tower Bridge. The Gothic towers were floodlit like a film set, and the tide was high and running fast. I began to skip; I had found someone who understood and, most important of all, *knew* Pitcairn. What if Tim would sail to Pitcairn again? What if I could sail there with him?

In a sense, however, I was already there, just as Tim was, and that is why, despite his contrived casual wear and eagerness to impress me, I felt close to him. I had a map of the world pinned above my desk. If I put my finger in the middle of the blue blanket of the South Pacific, stretching from New Zealand to the arc of Panama, it would land near Pitcairn. Soon the smudge marks from my fingertip had obliterated the island altogether. If you are lost in a strange city and come across a map in the street helpfully erected by the local tourist office, the spot where all the road markings have been rubbed out and there's nothing but a dirty mark is where you are standing. And, in the same way, it was as if I were already on the island I had created. I could look at the smudge on the map above my desk and know where I was. I spent the watery English summer on this Pitcairn.

At my home in a seaside town, there is an amusement park. Between the carousel and the waterslide is a ride called The Bounty, a thirty-foot-long replica of the mutineers' ship, which swings like a crazed pendulum while the riders are hurled backward and forward as Bligh must have been when he attempted the Horn. I was always too frightened to clamber on board. I would wander down to the seafront on a fine Sunday and watch the excited riders shrieking with dreadful delight before a painted backdrop of palm trees, crashing surf and maidens in grass skirts and garlands. Then, tempted by the heavy scent of fried food from a nearby cafe, I'd go and buy a bag of chips and eat it on the shore. When the summer weather came to an end, the ride was shut down.

As the nights closed in, the real world around me began to shut Pitcairn out. It grew cold and there were storms along the coast. Two teenagers were drowned, and a whale was washed up from the Channel and onto the beach below my house.

I contacted the Foreign and Commonwealth Office in London to find out if I needed permission to go to the island. Did I realize, they said, that they were inundated with applications from people who wanted to go and live on paradise isle, but no one could set foot on the island without a license to land? I would have to apply to the governor's office. If the governor approved the application, he would forward it to the Pitcairn Island Council, which would then hold a meeting and vote on whether to grant the license.

The conditions an applicant had to meet, the Foreign Office warned, were very strict and it was rare for an application to be successful. First the applicant had to prove he or she was "in good health and free from all infections and contagious diseases and shall produce a certificate to that effect." I went to see my doctor, who scribbled that I was "fit to travel worldwide" and suggested I buy some antihistamine tablets in case I was allergic to some local flora or fauna.

"And they may help you to fall asleep," he added. "Which might be useful if you're in acute pain."

Next, all applicants had to complete a questionnaire set by the Island Council. This was worrying. I imagined that I would be examined on my capability of living on a Pacific island, and I would inevitably fail. Have you ever lived on a small island? (I had lived only in big cities.) Can you

cook sweet potatoes? Do you know the difference between a barracuda
and a shark? Surely these were the sorts of things the islanders would want
to know before they cast their votes.

When a copy of the questionnaire arrived, I opened it nervously.
Perhaps I could beef up on island skills before I left, and refer to child-
hood holidays on the Isle of Wight. The questions ran, "Marital status,"
"Amount of money you will bring with you," "Are you in possession of a
valid passport?," "State your religion and denomination of it," and "Reason for visiting Pitcairn Island."

Only the last question troubled me. I needed a practical purpose that
appealed to both me and the islanders. I couldn't answer that I had been
inspired by a movie one rainy afternoon at the Elephant.

Friends had already come forward with suggestions as to how I
might amuse myself if and when I reached Pitcairn. I could study the
women's baskets, making intricate drawings of the different patterns into
which the pandanus leaves were woven. I might write a cookery book of
coconut recipes. I could learn to fish. An academic acquaintance suggested
I compile an oral history of the island; this might be the sort of thing the
Pitcairners would appreciate, he said. I needed to convince them that I was
not a paradise seeker. But none of these seemed substantial enough answers to swing the Island Council in my favor.

Following a further recommendation from the Royal Geographical
Society, I approached the Pitcairn Islands Study Group (PISG), expecting
to be told that my lack of knowledge in the field of the geomorphology of
South Pacific atolls would exclude me from membership. But the PISG
turned out to be a collection of vicars, air-conditioning salesmen and
retired bank managers. One member lived in a cottage called "Pitcairn";
another had named his first son Fletcher. Their interest was philately, and
for the seventy PISG members, Pitcairn's postmark and postage stamps
were the subject of intense scrutiny and lively biannual meetings in London or Bath. They approached their subject with the joy of a being allowed a boyhood hobby in middle age, swapping stamps and auctioning

envelopes among themselves, and publishing a Pitcairn postage fanzine called the *Pitcairn Log,* whose articles discussed such items as "A History of Pitcairn Postal Rates, 1940" and "Postmarks and Pioneers."

The Pitcairn postal service seemed to offer the solid purpose I sought. The Pitcairners themselves were dedicated to it. It might be erratic and subject to six-month-long delays, but it was their only contact beyond their rocky shores, and the sale of their sought-after stamps was the island's main source of income, raising almost half a million New Zealand dollars a year.

I approached British Royal Mail International, pointing out how important the postal service was to Pitcairn, and suggested that they sponsor me. Pitcairn was, I pleaded, the most remote place to which a letter could be delivered. It was a miracle of the mail that you could post a letter at the Elephant and it would arrive (if up to a year later) on Pitcairn. The Royal Mail obliged with a modest grant, and with gratitude and relief, I wrote under "Reason for visiting Pitcairn Island": "To research a book on the delivery, sorting and importance of mail to the Pitcairn Islanders."

Accommodations on Pitcairn also posed a problem. There were no hotels or guesthouses, and private arrangements had to be made with a family, who, for a standard charge of one hundred New Zealand dollars a week, would provide board and lodging. But how could I arrange somewhere to stay before I arrived when it was so very difficult to contact the island? And how would I know when I was arriving or when I would leave? I would have to write an open letter to the islanders saying that, at some time, for an unspecified period, I would be requiring a bed on Pitcairn, and could someone kindly let me know if they could provide one.

The PISG president had given me the name of Ron Thomas, a radio ham who was in contact with Pitcairn Island and had visited twice, one of the few people in Britain to have done so. Ron suggested that I go to see him on a Sunday morning. Sunday morning was Saturday night on Pitcairn, and a good time to try and make radio contact. He had mentioned my visit to Irma Christian, his contact on the island, and she had offered to put me up. Irma lived with her husband, Ben, and adult son, Dennis. It would be a good idea if we tried to talk to her.

"You'll have no trouble finding me," he said on the phone. "You'll see the antennae as soon as you leave the station."

Coming out of Buxley Green station, I ambled past the square front gardens looking for a metal structure that, I imagined, would resemble those washing lines shaped like giant spiders' webs. I saw several washing lines—some spiders' webs, others even more elaborate, held up with collapsible plastic and metal sticks—but could not find Ron's house. After having crossed the pavement and walked up and down the same street several times, I eventually lifted my eyes to the rooftops and saw, sticking up behind a bungalow, the most enormous pole, taller than any of the neat houses. I had spotted it from the station platform, but presumed it to be part of an industrial complex. It was Ron's antennae for talking with Pitcairn.

Ron was perched uncomfortably on the edge of a hard-backed chair, as if he were in a doctor's waiting room rather than his own home. He was a big, shy, shaggy man who managed to wear clothes that were too big even for him, topped by a tight woolen bobble hat. Down each side of his soft face ran furry gray whiskers. He was over seventy, but apart from a slight limp and cautious walk, appeared much younger.

Running out of things to talk about, he put on a video he had made of the island. With the color and contrast turned right up, it conveyed a shaky vision of fluorescent green valleys and lurid scarlet mud paths. It looked more like a badly executed painting by numbers than a place I could ever imagine walking through.

When the time scheduled for us to talk to Irma came, we went through to Ron's radio shack, a shed at the back piled high with radio equipment. In the winter, the temperature could fall below freezing and snow floated through the hole in the roof. He could be out there at five in the morning; that was often the best time to talk. He switched on the power, and some dials began to register bleeps, burps and the occasional scream. Ron spoke into the crackle.

"G30KQ, G30KQ. VR6ID, VR6ID. Victor Romeo Six India Delta."

On the airways, all Ron's reticence vanished and he spoke confidently and loudly.

"That's America," he said. I heard nothing but more burps and bleeps.

"How do you know that's America?"

"I can hear the accent."

"Accent of what?"

"The handle's accent. The bloke who's speaking!"

I couldn't even make out a voice.

Ron played with the black knobs, raising a series of sounds like Morse code messages. At last he sat back.

"There's Irma. VR6ID, VR6ID, G30KQ, G30KQ. Over."

*Bleep, bloosh, crackle.*

"VR6ID, G30KQ. You're coming through at five seven. Over."

*Eeeeeeee.*

"I've Dea here. Over."

*Eeeeeeee.*

"I have Dea here. Delta. Echo. America. VR6ID, G30KQ."

*Burp.*

"What's your full name?" Ron asked me.

"Deborah. Dea's my nickname."

"Deb-or-rah. I've got Deborah here. Over."

*Bleep. Bleep. Bleep.*

"VR6ID, G30KQ. Yes, *Debbie.* I'll put her on. Over," and he handed me the microphone.

"Hello," I said. "Thank you very much for offering to put me up. It's very kind of you."

I had noticed that Ron repeated everything he said.

"Very kind of you. Very kind of you. Over."

*Eeeeeeee.*

"Answer her!" said Ron.

"But what did she say?"

"She said you're very welcome. 'You are very welcome to our island.'"

I turned back to the mike. "Thank you. That's very kind of you. Very kind of you."

*Eeeeeee. Burp.*

I knew by Ron's smiles and nods toward the dials that Irma was saying something to me. But only a veteran radio hand like Ron could tease out words from all the crackles and pops that came out of his machine. I felt as if I were trying to hold a conversation through a glass wall. I knew there was someone on the other side, but the wall blocked out everything they said.

"It's been snowing here," I said, trying again to strike up conversation with Irma. "It's snowing. Snowing. It's very cold. A very bad winter. Very bad."

*Blurp*, then a sound like heavy rain falling.

"She says they've had bad winds, but it's been calm for the last few days," said Ron.

I felt defeated by the huge wall that separated me from Irma. But I had also run out of things to talk about. We had exchanged courtesies—or I presumed we had—and I had thanked her for the offer of accommodations. We had talked about the weather. I could think of no questions to ask her which could be answered in the staccato language of the airwaves, and could not see how I could translate my life into brief, repetitive phrases. I could think of no point at which we might meet and share common experiences. I couldn't chat about my vegetable plot, or my latest fishing expedition, or the carving I was working on, or any of the activities I imagined filled a Pitcairner's day. I couldn't talk to her about the new features editor at the woman's magazine I was working for, or my new fax machine. Even world news was not shared. What would the disintegration of the former Yugoslavia mean on Pitcairn? I handed the mike back to Ron.

"Seventy threes, seventy threes. Good contact, Irma. Eighty eight. VR6ID, this is G30KQ. Signing off."

*Eeeeeee. Burp.* And Irma was gone.

The next day I wrote to Dennis Christian, Irma's thirty-six-year-old son. Dennis was Pitcairn Island postmaster.

I told Dennis that I was hoping to visit Pitcairn early next year, and my application for a license to land was being considered. I was sponsored by Royal Mail International, and was especially interested in discussing with Dennis the importance of the mail delivery to the people of Pitcairn. I sent him a copy of a book I had written about my voyage on a West African cargo vessel. I wrote a couple of sentences about myself—the other books I had written, my work, and that I lived by the sea. After that, I felt the same sense of floundering for something to say that I had in Ron's radio shack. What more could I tell Dennis about myself that would mean anything to him? Then I added one final sentence, "I am thirty years old and unmarried." I did not know it then, but seventeen thousand miles away on Pitcairn this last line would read like a proposition.

Winter was melting away, the days were getting longer again, and I seemed no closer to reaching Pitcairn. People would call and ask if I could give a lecture in the spring, teach a course on travel writing at Easter, write an article on transsexuals for next week, and I would say I could not, because I would be on Pitcairn Island in the South Pacific. Yet after more than a year of research in the British Library, odd rendezvous with Pitcairn aficionados and securing a sponsor, I still had no idea of how I was going to get there. The commissioner in Auckland, who handled the day-to-day administration of the island, had been unable to help. There was a supply ship that called at Pitcairn approximately every four months, but any spare berths for passengers were booked at least a year in advance by Pitcairners who had to go to New Zealand for an education or to see a doctor. There were already twenty-seven on the waiting list, more than two thirds of the island's population. "I regret no place is available for you," the commissioner wrote.

I found comfort in reading a pile of typewritten pages that Ron had sent me. They were a manuscript of an autobiography by Kari Boye Young, a Norwegian woman who had been living on Pitcairn for twenty years. Much of the book was about growing up in Norway, skiing to school and drinking buttermilk. But the girl herself was dreaming of somewhere else. "I saw the movie *Mutiny on the Bounty* with Clark Gable and I fell in love with him. I was thirteen years old, and I decided I had to come to Pitcairn. It represented all my ambitions and dreams."

Kari trained as a ship's radio officer, all the time thinking that this would be the best way to realize her plans. She mailed off her first application for a license to land when she was twenty-five. "I couldn't give serious and scientific reasons. They thought I was a dreamer and would be a burden to the community." Her application was refused.

But Kari was persistent. She petitioned the commissioner, who wrote back bluntly that Pitcairn was not what she thought it was, and informed the consulate in her home country of their correspondence. The British Consul in Oslo called her parents: "Do you realize that your daughter is trying to get to Pitcairn Island?"

Undeterred, Kari continued sailing around the world, working the ship's radio and writing letters to the commissioner. "I just kept bothering him. And he eventually gave in." She was twenty-seven when she arrived as a guest at Tom and Betty Christian's. After seven glorious months on Pitcairn, she was obliged to return to her work with the shipping line.

On her second visit, Kari fell in love. Brian Young, descendant of mutineer Midshipman Edward Young, was of grand stature, dark and ten years younger than Kari. Their wedding twenty years ago was the last marriage to take place on Pitcairn.

Kari's story reminded me of my own days at sea, and I contacted the seafaring chums I had made when sailing back from Africa, now lounging in early retirement in the Wirral. Some of them said, "Oh yes, Pitcairn!"

They had vague memories of drifting offshore while basketloads of fresh fruit were hoisted up on deck from a longboat, with a dozen dusky islanders working the ropes. A couple of the seamen had wooden replicas of the *Bounty* or a flying fish hanging above their tiled mantelpiece that they had purchased from the islanders. But within an hour the engines would be restarted and they would sail on to Panama or New Zealand. And that was decades ago. None of them had any idea how I might reach Pitcairn today.

I called Tim to tell him I'd made contact with the island and would be staying with Irma Christian. He was excited; he had sailed his yacht down to Ramsgate marina on the South Coast of England and was going to cross the Channel to France tomorrow. He would come to see me as soon as he was back at the beginning of next week.

I spent a weekend buried in my books; on Sunday evening, the phone rang and I thought it might be Tim.

"This is the coast guard at Dover. Tim asked us to call you," a man said. "Don't panic."

I confirmed that I wouldn't.

"He's stuck in Calais because of the weather and won't make it back to Ramsgate. He'll be leaving on the six-fifteen tide on Wednesday for St. Katherine's Dock."

The following morning a single red rose arrived from Tim. The message read: "To Dea, I sailed toward a rainbow rising through the mist. Today I send a flower for it made me think of you." It was as if we were already making love beneath the Southern Cross in our private paradise.

When Tim hadn't phoned by the end of the week, I called him. I asked when he was planning on next leaving for Pitcairn. He became vague, mentioned problems with his chandler's business, and said his yacht would need to be refitted for the voyage. He suggested we meet again at the Tower Hotel, perhaps go on to a more upmarket restaurant, talk about Pitcairn. But I had been planning and plotting for so long now, I wanted more concrete assistance. I wanted to be there. If Tim could not help me, I would have to try and work my passage to Pitcairn on a cargo vessel.

Pitcairn lies in the center of the South Pacific Ocean, and a ship, having worked Europe, the Eastern Seaboard of the United States or the Caribbean, and transiting the Panama Canal heading for Australia or New Zealand, may pass close to the island. The Admiralty's *Ocean Passages for the World* states: "The recommended power vessel routes between the Panama Canal and some Australian ports pass about 30 miles off Henderson Island and about 35 miles south of Pitcairn Island." Since the opening of the Canal in 1914, this accident of geography has been Pitcairn's lifeline. Passing ships sometimes drift offshore, trading tinned food, flour and oil for Pitcairn's fresh fruit, vegetables and fish. A few ships will also, in the case of emergency, pick up passengers from Pitcairn who need to go to New Zealand for medical attention. One or two have even been known to let someone join the vessel in Liverpool, Rotterdam or Houston and drop them over the side off Bounty Bay.

There was always one copy of the daily shipping paper *Lloyd's List* at the newspaper stand at my local train station. Sometimes I would get there in time to buy it; at others, whoever was the other *Lloyd's List* reader in town would have been there first and grabbed the only copy. At the back of the paper, ships' movements were updated daily, and from these I could work out which lines served the Panama-New Zealand route.

I approached the shipping lines. "We have recently sold our fleet which used to frequent the South Pacific area, and are therefore regrettably unable to offer you any assistance with respect to passage to Pitcairn Island" was a typical reply. The shipping industry is in decline; once several ships might pass Pitcairn every month, now the islanders are lucky if a single ship stops. And those that still serve the route were reluctant to incur the extra expense of drifting for just a few hours off the island to offload a nonpaying passenger.

I had been racing for *Lloyd's List,* writing off letters and receiving nothing but rejections for more than three months, when Ron once again came to my rescue with the practical arrangements. It was already spring, and his radio shack was beginning to warm up. The sun spot activity was high, so conditions for talking to Irma had improved and Ron rang me up after each contact to let me know the local news. During one conversation, he told me he had once arranged a passage from Pitcairn for Dennis on a Norwegian chemical carrier, and gave me the name of the company.

I wrote off to Norway and a reply came—a tanker, NCC *Najran*, was scheduled to transit Panama and cross the South Pacific in May, bound for New Zealand. I could join her at Bayport Chemical Terminal, Houston. It never occurred to me to ask when, or if, I would be able to get a passage back.

I raced up to the railway station and handed a note to the man behind the newspaper stand.

"Could you please give this to the person who buys *Lloyd's List?*"

The note read: "Your *Lloyd's List* is safe. I'm off to Pitcairn Island!"

It was almost two years since I had seen *The Bounty* and first dreamed of leaving for Pitcairn. Now I had little more than a week to prepare for the voyage, and Pitcairn was not a place to travel light to. I had no idea how long I might be away, and everything I might need during my stay had to be taken with me. I was determined to be as self-sufficient as possible and not become a drain on Irma's resources. I would need a trunk to take on the ship.

I went to Terry's, which advertised itself as "England's Largest Trunk Store with Large Selection of Steamer Trunks" and turned out to be a well-stocked stall in Shepherd's Bush market, and bought a reinforced tin trunk solid under the trademark Afrique-Trunk. Designed for the West African Muslim market, it was spray-painted with scarlet crescent moons.

Predicting lazy writer's days at my desk overlooking the lapping surf, my Afrique-Trunk was packed with writing paper, a portable typewriter, two dozen ribbons, and four bottles of correction fluid. Ron had assured me that the mosquitoes, although not malarial, were vicious, so I bought twenty bottles of Jungle Formula Insect Repellent and wrapped six bottles of calamine lotion among my underwear. Ron also advised me to take a rubberized, waterproof flashlight, for use in the longboats at night, and plenty of batteries. Knowing the islanders were Seventh-day Adventists and would have no stimulants, instead drinking a powdered drink called Milo, I packed a large tin of instant coffee. I took enough tampons to last until my menopause. On top of all this I laid my copy of Elenore Smith Bowen's *Return to Laughter*. Smith Bowen was a distinguished American anthropologist who, concerned that an involved, partial account of her time among the Tiv people in West Africa would damage her academic reputation, wrote *Return to Laughter* under a pseudonym and called it fiction. I had found a secondhand copy—it had long been out of print— and took it on every journey, using it as a guidebook for my moods.

A friend bought me *Bugs Bunny in Mutiny on the Bunny*, a children's book she had found in her local department store. Another brought me a lot of little gift-wrapped packages, with a different future date written on each of them.

"I can't phone and I can't write," she said. "But I can keep in some sort of touch if you have a different thing to open from me each fortnight. It will be like having a conversation with me; you can react to each thing. Otherwise you won't realize that there's another world back here, which is carrying on and changing, just like where you are."

Ron phoned to say that Irma had asked me to take a couple of paintbrushes; her son, Dennis, was decorating his new home.

Friends were full of ideas as to what I might miss. Importing alcohol onto the island was illegal, so they plied me with booze and I spent my last week at home in a drunken haze. More adventurous acquaintances donated bottles of whiskey, which they suggested I smuggle ashore. Someone gave me a box of meat pâté tins, knowing that the Seventh-day Adventists were vegetarians. Others wondered how I would survive without regular electricity, a proper bathroom, TV . . . But I knew it was none of these things that I would miss. If I missed anything, it would be easy-flowing conversation, and the comforting, familiar touch of another human body.

I gave out my address to friends and family, just in case a ship reached the island with bags of mail.

D. Birkett
Pitcairn Island
South Pacific

"That's it?" they'd ask.

"That's it," I said.

Bon voyage cards began to arrive in the post, full of uplifting senti-
ments. "It'll be an amazing adventure, adieu," "Hope it's fascinating, fun
and trouble free, God speed," "Have a wonderful trip." A few friends sent
me birthday cards, marked "Not to be opened until August 21." It was
only May.

My boyfriend wrote me a poem.

> *The joy, the rush into another life,*
> *Detach all your baggage from your heart*
> *And just begin.*
> *Just travel in the ocean wind . . .*

Only one note was anything but overwhelmingly optimistic. "An island is
a very small place," it said simply. "I shouldn't like to go there much."

The day before I was due to leave, Ron phoned to ask if I could
collect some specimens of fungi and mushrooms for the Royal Botanic
Gardens at Kew; a botanist would like to identify them and they could be
used for a fungi series of Pitcairn postage stamps. Could I photograph
them in situ, then pick them and keep them in empty film canisters? I
packed a dozen more rolls of film.

But the weighty contents of my Afrique-Trunk were meager com-
pared to my mental luggage. During almost two years of research in the
British Library, I had constructed a concrete portrait of Pitcairn. On my
final night at home, I sat and watched my video of Mel Gibson in *The
Bounty*. The next morning, I said farewell to England and headed for
Paradise.

# 3 · N C C    n a j r a n

Houston rippled in the heat like a lake on a calm day. The cab driver, sent by the shipping company, met me at the airport with a huge handwritten sign, MISS BIRKETT. NCC *NAJRAN*. PITCAIRN ISLAND, and the greeting, "Well, ma'am, I sure didn't know they made seamen as pretty as you are, nope."

Houston appeared to have been abandoned. There was no one on the streets, and nowhere for them to walk if there had been. There were no sidewalks or curbs, just dusty, undefined edges to wide, flat, seemingly endless roads. Every ten minutes or so we would catch a glimpse of human life in the shape of an obese man, emerging from one of the small porched houses. He would be wearing enormous checkered shorts and a baseball cap that was far too small for him, and would lumber down the wooden steps into a parched yard with a garden hose in his hand, as if holding a gun against the desert heat. Even the cab responded to the stifling temperature and we drove slowly enough for a wild dog to overtake us.

As we crept through this wasteland, the steely silhouette of downtown and the Exxon building stalked us like a giant predator, rearing up in the back window.

The cab driver asked if I had ever visited this neck of the woods before. *Nope!* Then he'd take me on a tour of the sights.

We passed petrochemical plants and oil storage tanks, and always downtown reared up sharp-edged in the haze. It was hard to imagine life among its skyscrapers, where I imagined people wore business suits and strode about with great purpose, or stopped for lunch and a determined chat, sipping regular coffee on air-conditioned indoor terraces. From the cab, it was like looking out at a spaceship docked in the desert, buzzing with activities undertaken by forms of life that fed from an atmosphere different from our own.

"That's Solomon's Bar. Burned down," slurred the cabby. Over a parking lot with brown grass spiking up between the cracks was a cross between a barn and a house, badly charred, as if the scorching sun had set it on fire.

"Insurance, yep," said the cab driver.

We crawled past more arsoned bars in derelict parking lots. These, together with the nods toward distant downtown—"Exxon out the rear . . . ," "Exxon out the left now . . ."—the cabby considered the highlights of Houston.

"Not much going on in Houston, nope," he said. "Part from driving around."

As we drew closer to Bayport Chemical Terminal, tangled pipes lined each side of the highway where sidewalks should have been, behind which rose an ominous, twenty-foot-tall wire fence. The dry air stung my nostrils. At a break in the fence, a uniformed man let us through with a languid wave, and we crawled toward the ship. The heat rising from the pipes and the stench from the chemicals made the air shimmer, and it felt as if we were traveling through a time tunnel. At the end lay a long, low orange vessel, tied to the earth by ropes. This vessel was also covered with pipes, and shimmering. I could make out the huge letters painted under a Norwegian flag—NO SMOKING. NCC *NAJRAN*—and a low-slung gangway hooked to her side.

As we sloped alongside, four small men appeared on deck and scurried down the gangway toward us. They nodded and smiled at the cab driver, nodded and smiled at me, and the smallest hoisted my Afrique-Trunk onto his shoulder, and I followed them back up the gangway and into the ship.

"We are a floating bo-oomb," said the Captain. He spoke with the overly correct English of a nonnative speaker and lingered on the last syllable of each sentence, giving everything he said the appearance of great weight.

He was sitting behind the desk in his office, leaning back in his swivel chair, obviously amused. His office looked as I imagined a Scandinavian suburban drawing room would if it had been furnished with office equipment rather than a sofa, chairs and occasional table. The entire room was paneled in wood vinyl, with wood vinyl cupboards and shelves. The Captain, dressed in a T-shirt and jeans, rested his forearms on his desk. There was the tattoo of an anchor on his left arm. He detailed the twenty thousand tons of corrosive acids, methanol and oils—all classified as "difficult" cargoes—that the *Najran* carried in her stainless steel tanks.

"That is what we are carrying. Chemicals," he said. "We are informing you that we generally do not carry passen-gers."

I explained that I had served on a cargo ship before, although not a chemical carrier, and was quite accustomed to life at sea.

"Captain Skjo . . ." I struggled with the pronunciation.

"Call me John," he said, but I never did.

He slipped a form over his desk, headed "Free Pass Agreement." It warned that there was no guarantee that the ship would pass Pitcairn and I would reach my destination. Poor weather, or the possibility of being delayed in transiting the Panama Canal and having to race for New Zealand, might prevent a Pitcairn call. I signed on the dotted line. It was still the best chance I had.

Captain Skjoelsekth gave me a brief rundown of his vessel. There was a crew of twenty-eight, "Twenty-nine, now we have observed that you have come aboard"—five Norwegian officers, the rest Filipinos. I was in the cabin next to his own. There was a small pantry at the end of the alleyway for snacks and hot drinks and the mess was three decks below. Soon we would be sailing out from the port and anchoring offshore for the night. We would be back into the same dock by first light tomorrow; it was a way of saving on harbor fees.

"We ask you do not worry," the Captain reassured me. "I am gathering the men together, all of them, Filipinos and officers, and I am telling them that young woman is joining us. I am telling them, 'I know she is British and we are Norwegian officers. But let me tell you, men, it is an open competi-tion.' " And the Captain beamed at me, boastful of not pulling rank when it came to courting female company. So, as best I could, I beamed back.

"When we are settled," he added, meaning when we were at sea, "I will be putting you to work."

My cabin was compact and comfortable, but when I turned on the shower, it looked as if it were serving coffee, the water was so brown. I washed in it and emerged with a blotchy tan. The bathroom cabinet contained enough bars of Lux toilet soap to keep all the seamen shipshape for several ocean crossings, so I climbed back into the shower and rubbed myself down, falling into bed in a scented cloud.

By the time I rose in the morning, we were already hooked back up to Bayport. At breakfast, I played with the triangular knife that cut paper-thin slices from a large dung-colored square of sweetened goat's cheese, and sipped at my buttermilk. The Norwegian officers ate together on a table at one end of the narrow mess; on the other side of a low counter, several tables of Filipinos chatted noisily and scoffed rice. I struggled silently with my goat's cheese, while the Norwegians downed pints of buttermilk and swapped hearty stories, or seemed to do so, as I could not understand a single word they said.

"I will try to obtain for you shore pass," said the Captain. "But very easy it is not. Since Gulf War, they do not like people who are wandering around their chemical plants." And he turned back to speaking in Norwegian, miming explosions and missiles and donning a gas mask.

There was a gas mask hanging in my cabin next to the life jacket. The *Najran* had crossed the Strait of Hormuz and entered the Persian Gulf during the war, while missiles plopped into the water about her. Her crew had spent several nights camped in the alleyways, wearing their masks and fireproof suits, and unable to sleep.

"One spark and *woof!*" said the Captain. "From which you may observe, we are a floating bo-oomb."

When I got my shore pass, the shipping company's agent, who had come on board to check our cargo manifests, said he would give me a lift to wherever I wanted to go. Houston didn't seem to be overrun with tourist attractions, so I asked the agent's advice. He suggested I visit NASA.

The Lyndon B. Johnson Space Center is where America's astronauts train on mock-ups of moon missions, and where America's spaceships are built. It is also the home of Mission Control, nerve center of space flights, from where all launches are monitored. "Five, four, three, two, one . . . We have liftoff!" is announced by the public affairs officer at Mission Control.

I wandered in and out of the buildings, estimating that the whole site covered up to two thousand acres, almost twice the size of Pitcairn. Building 9A housed the mock-up and training facilities—an orbiter crew computer trainer, manipulator development facility and space station mock-up. These "high fidelity representations" could imitate weightlessness. This would enable astronauts to learn how to "ingress" and "egress," which I took to mean get in and out of the spaceship; "camera utilization," which must mean how to take photos; and "general house-keeping," which should cover how to hold on to your supper in zero gravity.

In the Lunar Sample Building, I stared through a screen at a labora-tory of sealed glass cases. In each case, like a newborn baby in an incuba-tor, was a lump of rock. Some were gray and mottled like granite, others pink and pockmarked like coral. These were chunks of the moon. More than eight hundred pounds of moon rock now live in the Lunar Sample Building in Houston.

I sat in the cafeteria and wondered what it would be like to live on the moon. At least a moon dweller would be in constant communication with Mission Control. You could have conversations with your controller; your family could come into the space center and talk to you, and you could even see them on a screen. You could keep in touch with the news around the world, and follow the matches of the Houston Astros. And within weeks, you could be shot down to Earth again. Maybe more Ameri-cans had walked on the moon than in Adamstown. The place I was head-ing for was more remote than a planet.

I hitched back to the port. It must have been twenty miles, but it took me three hours and several lifts to reach the gate to our dock. I was in a gloomy mood, terrified not of the voyage, but of arriving on a distant planet called Pitcairn.

The boatswain and assistant cook had thrown a line over the side of the ship into the leaden water. I would have thought it impossible for anything to survive in this industrial desert, but the assistant cook had felt a bite and pulled in a respectable fish. He displayed his catch by the tail, then hurried down to the galley. By the time it appeared as sweet-and-sour on the menu that night, we were already heading out to sea.

.  .  .

It was a five-day passage to Panama, through the Gulf of Mexico and out into the Caribbean, passing between Yucatán and the western tip of Cuba. As I hung over the deck rail, a seaman would come and ask me my name, and I'd say Dea. Then I'd asked him his, and he'd say "Boatswain" or "Deckhand" or "Third Engineer."

The second officer, a short, soft-bodied man who flapped around in a pair of pink fluffy mule slippers, spotted me on deck one afternoon and brought some books he had in English: a five-year-old *Reader's Digest* with some pages missing; *Who's Afraid of Virginia Woolf,* which Second dismissed as "trash"; and a thin book of doctor jokes titled *Laughter Is Good Medicine,* which Second insisted had been made into a film. Then he whispered to me how, in Birkenhead, they'd had fifteen ladies on board for a party.

The next time Birkenhead was mentioned I was reading a sign on the noticeboard outside the mess.

> TO ALL OVERSEXED PEOPLE
> VD can be cured by a shot
> And herpes lasts until you drop
> But this AIDS stuff really sucks
> 'Cause you can die from just one fuck.

Captain's Steward, looking very natty in a pair of rainbow-striped suspenders, saw me reading and asked, "Where you from? Birkenhead?"

"No, London."

"Is London in Birkenhead?"

"No, Birkenhead is in the northwest of England, and London is in the southeast. London is the capital of England." I sounded like a tetchy schoolmistress.

"So it's the same!" he said.

"Well—"

"Just I want to know about AIDS in Birkenhead."

"AIDS?"

"Is it bad? Does the government give medicine?"

I answered yes to both questions, lost as to where the conversation might lead. But the steward seemed satisfied, thanked me, and went off to the galley.

I wanted our voyage to roll on forever. I felt safe on the ship, among her burly Norwegian officers and diminutive Filipino crew. The closer we drew toward Pitcairn, the more I clung to the deck rail of the *Najran*. On board, only Boatswain made me anxious, a wiry man with a stub of a ponytail and a concave chest. He never smiled. Packages of English reading material arrived from him, too, but always sent through Assistant Cook.

"Boatswain gives you this," Assistant Cook would say, handing me a pile of dog-eared magazines.

As I was looking toward Cuba one balmy afternoon, Boatswain came and leaned on the deck rail beside me.

"Are you married?" he said. I felt there was only one answer to this question on a chemical tanker in the Caribbean.

"Yes."

"How many years?"

"Two." Two seemed a safe number, less glassy-eyed than a newlywed but not yet suffering the seven-year itch.

"Do you have children?"

"No." Children are much more difficult to invent than husbands.

"Why?" This was harder to answer.

"Because I have to go to Pitcairn," I said, sounding ridiculously pompous. "We will try when I get back."

I thought this would close the conversation, but, "Do you love your husband?"

I was shocked by the intimacy of his question. Boatswain didn't have a pleasant face; it was concave like his stomach, and tense with muscle like the rest of his body.

"Of course, of course I do," I stuttered.

"Does your husband love you?"

"Yes."

There was a pause before he answered, "Then why do you go this island?"

There were at least a dozen ships flashing on our radar. It was two in the morning, and we had been at anchor in Limon Bay for more than an hour, waiting for instructions to proceed. As the *Najran* was a chemical tanker and a "floating bo-oomb," she had to transit the Panama Canal during daylight, accompanied through the three locks by a bright yellow fire engine.

The Captain passed the time by telling me a tale about cutting off a crewman's crushed fingers.

"We gave him too much whiskey. We were using a knife. It was these fingers here," and he held up a V. "I had to cut right through. I was observing there was blood everywhere. Every-wheeere."

"Cristobal signal, NCC *Najran*. Cristobal signal, NCC *Najran*." The Canal controller interrupted the Captain's flow, giving us the names of other ships anchored off the breakwater so we could make contact. We chatted over the radio as if meeting people at a dinner party. "You been here long?" "Have you come far?" "Do you know anyone else?"

"Cristobal signal, NCC *Najran*. Cristobal signal, NCC *Najran*. Proceed to breakwater as quickly as possible. How long do you think it will take you to reach breakwater? Repeat. How long do you think it will take you to reach breakwater?"

"Fifteen minutes," said the Captain. "We will proceed. Roger and out."

As we sailed toward the breakwater, the ship was gradually wrested from her master. First the pilots clambered on board, two white Americans wearing stretchy checkered shorts and caps just like the men I had seen from the cab in Houston. Then, as we approached the first giant lock, two dozen laborers in hard hats and khaki boiler suits climbed up a

Jacob's ladder with bulging plastic carrier bags clutched in their free hand. It was as if we were being boarded by pirates. The *Najran*'s population doubled within minutes, and the Captain surrendered control and stood at the back of the bridge watching the invasion and drinking coffee. He had put on a white shirt and his master's gold epaulettes for the transit, although this was the only part of the voyage in which he was not in command of the ship.

The laborers were called headhunters by the seamen, and were all black Panamanians. Their job was to hitch the *Najran* to the six powerful locomotives that would pull her through the locks, while her wiry Filipino crew looked on and smoked cigarettes.

I joined the first pilot on the bridge wing, where he stood with a handheld radio into which he shouted his instructions to the helmsman. The headhunters blew kisses up to me from the deck below.

"We call them headhunters 'cause they're right out the jungle," said the pilot.

The pilot was a bright pink Tweedledee who suffered from the heat. Although the sun was hiding behind a veil of gray, the thermometer still registered ninety-eight degrees. Trickles of sweat ran down his round face as if he were taking a shower and the shower head was hidden inside his pilot's cap.

"Only one problem with Panama," he said. "Cancer. You get cancer real easy from this sun.

"Cancer. And the sand flies," he continued. "Used to be the mosquitoes. They killed off the canal workers. Now they've been killed!" The pilot was delighted with the justice of it.

He asked for the awnings to be put up over the bridge wings to protect him from the rays.

"There's rain coming over from Balboa," he said, although I could see no evidence of it. Twenty minutes later we were in a downpour.

"Slow astern," he shouted into his radio. "Dead slow astern . . . Stop engines."

Between giving instructions to the helmsman, the pilot adroitly chatted me up. "Hard to starboard . . . Midships . . . Port twenty. Come ashore with me for a couple of days. I'll show you around. Great place, Panama. You'd have a great time . . . Port ten."

"I'm going to the South Pacific," I said feebly. "I need to stay with the ship."

"I'll get you on another one. No problem!" he boasted. "You can stay with me a couple of days, I'll show you around, have a ball, then get another ship."

"I'm going to *Pitcairn*," I said.

"No problem!" he said. "Where's that?"

We were making a slalom around the buoys that marked the channel. When I declined the pilot's kind offer a third time, he shrugged it off.

"I only meant you could join my harem. I've got so many girls I don't know what to do with them. Do you know that there are seven girls to every one man in Panama? Seven to one! You'd just be one of them."

I climbed down to the deck to watch the headhunters attach the cables to the locomotives.

"Exchange, exchange." I was surrounded by the hard-hatted men, waving their plastic carrier bags full of ripe mangoes. I asked how much they were.

"Exchange, exchange."

"What should I exchange?" I asked a deckhand.

"Your soap!" he said, astonished that I didn't know. My bathroom cabinet was intended to be used as my bank, not my beauty box. I brought a dozen bars of Lux from my cabin. They got me four bags bulging with mangoes.

"Used to be drugs. Now it's mangoes," said the deckhand, sadly resigned to the change in trade.

A tug guided us into the lock. With only a few feet to the chamber doors, the pilot was still ordering, "Hard to port . . . Half speed ahead . . . Hard to starboard," then, "Stop the engines!"

"Engines stopped, sir," responded the helmsman, and we floated in between the lock sides, the gates closed behind us, and the waters began to rise.

From the viewing gallery, a gaggle of nuns peered across at the ship. The bright yellow fire engine drove slowly up and down while the waters rose about us. As we left the last lock, our side screeched against the rubber lining. Sometimes, the pilot said, the flare of a large container ship knocks a locomotive right off her tracks and crushes her.

Gatun Lake, eighty-five feet above sea level, was dotted with islands for us to dodge. Pelicans lifted lazily from the fresh water and fish jumped around the thick green edge of the land. One island, the pilot told me, was owned by the Smithsonian Institute and inhabited by scientists.

United States military bases sprawled along each side of the Canal, concealed by the dense vegetation. The jungle was kept that way on purpose, said the pilot, to hide them. Occasionally, helicopters shivered above us or a wide-bellied fighter jet rumbled low along the Canal's course like a giant bird about to drop her eggs into the calm water.

"The fish, you should see the fish they get here. Beautiful. Freshwater fish. There's the yacht club over there." The pilot pointed at the jungle. Even the yacht club was camouflaged. "Water sports. Panama's a wonderful place."

The second pilot came up to take over. The two pilots worked the bridge like a comedy duo. Pilot Two was as tall and thin as Pilot One was short and round, and his hair and complexion were a matching gray. And he hated Panama.

"Glad I've only got eighteen months to go. 'Cause these damn Panamanians are taking over. I'm sorry," said the second pilot with no hint of regret, "but if you'd seen what a mess they're making of things . . . Port ten . . . Port twenty . . . Hard to starboard . . . Slow astern . . . Never used to have bribes or anything. But if it's a Panamanian pilot, they expect two hundred cigarettes." Pilot Two lit another Marlboro.

We wiggled through the final lock and out toward the Bridge of the Americas.

"Panamanian fishing vessel," tutted the second pilot, as if the tiny boat had no right to be there at all.

The pilots were lowered back over the side and their boat buzzed off toward Panama City. At 14:15 hours the Captain, now a captain again in T-shirt and jeans, turned toward the navigational officer.

"Commence sea passage at fourteen-thirty," he ordered, and we steamed toward the Pacific Ocean.


Now we were at sea and everything was settled, I could be put to work. The Captain wanted me to decorate his cabin. He had bought some tinted glass wall lamps at Bayport shopping mall and ordered some new wood vinyl from the agent. The orange net curtains had been dry-cleaned in Houston. There was plenty of spare paint on board.

"I am wanting to make it look like home. As we observe, this *is* my home," he said.

At first I was glad I had been given the job of painting. I was down on the crew list as secretary, and had worried that I might be asked to type up menus and maneuvers in Norwegian, causing chaos in the galley and disasters at sea. But the movement of the ship and the strong smell from the industrial paint made a day's decorating unpleasant work. I was on deck taking a break from the fumes when Second flapped over to me. He was wearing new K-Mart Wranglers, his pink slippers and the same rain-bow-striped suspenders as Steward. He leaned against an inflatable life raft and told me he had also bought a baby stroller in K-Mart. His wife was pregnant. They had a thirteen-year-old daughter, and had been trying since then for another child. Finally they went to the doctor. He had said one of his wife's fallopian tubes was blocked with a clot, which would have to be sucked out.

If I had been a hard-nosed anthropologist interested in the sexual mores of foreign peoples, the men of NCC *Najran* would have been ideal informants, for since my joining the ship they had talked about nothing but sex. Even on the bridge, where I spent the early evenings with Third Mate, conversation would center on copulation. As we were steering a straight course to Pitcairn, the helm was set on automatic pilot. The radar was turned down to standby and the lookout just lounged about the bridge, so there was little to do except chat.

"We have two different sorts of married," Third Mate explained. "Totally married. And not totally married."

Running his finger down the crew list, he indicated which marital status applied to which seaman. Third Mate himself was "not totally married."

"I have a girl. She lives in my house," and he continued to explain how personal relationships were properly conducted in Quezon.

I began to wonder if this sort of information was being offered because I was destined for the South Pacific, a region that had long aroused seamen's passions. Comte Louis-Antoine de Bougainville, who claimed Tahiti for the French in 1767, named the island La Nouvelle-Cythère, the "New Isle of Venus." The surgeon on board HMS *Pandora* had found "fair ones ever willing to fill your arms with love." The Captain and his crew echoed these centuries-old images. I could hardly blame them; I was steeped in them, too. It was a passionate portrayal of the South Pacific that had, after all, first drawn me to Pitcairn.

We rattled along, the half-empty tanks roaring and slapping as the ship keeled with the waves. The hot water from the shower had turned an even deeper brown, and a new problem had developed: the cold water tap was piping hot, as if a cauldron were boiling below in the engine room.

"We will be getting to bottom of it. I am promising you that!" assured the Captain. "This I very well can do without."

It was the first day of June and we were sailing between the islands in the Galápagos group. The gray pimple on our port side was Isla Santa Maria, which the *South America Pilot* said was a volcanic island, like Pitcairn, with large numbers of wild cattle, pigs and goats, but only fifty people. A gull swooped across our stern and headed for Santa Maria. "We could drop you off there instead," the Captain offered.

There were more than 25,000 islands scattered like dust across the Pacific, yet a ship could sail for five thousand miles and never make landfall. The ocean covered 63,838,000 square miles, a third of the globe. There were less than two square miles of Pitcairn, too little to appear as a pinprick on the map.

Isla Santa Maria was the last land we would see for more than a week, and each day the emptiness engulfing Pitcairn became more apparent. Since the gull we had seen no more birds, being too far from land. Even the Captain couldn't remember a time when he had spotted another vessel when following this route. The horizon ran uninterrupted wherever and whenever you searched for it, a thin gray line cutting all that was our world into two—the sea and the sky.

For the past two days we had been trying to make contact with Pitcairn over the radio. Then, thirty-seven hours before our ETA, the Captain called me up to the radio room.

"I am informing you that it is Pitcairn," he announced.

"ZBP. ZBP, Zulu Bravo, Papa, Pitcairn Island Radio. Any ships in the area? Do you have anything for us? Over." It was a woman's voice.

"LAFLX, LAFLX, Lima Alpha Foxtrot Lima X-ray. Zulu Bravo Papa. To whom am I speaking?" asked the Captain.

"Betty. Betty Christian. Over."

The Captain offered the microphone to me, so I could talk. But I shook my head. What would I say?

But Betty and the Captain chatted away easily through the crackle. They talked about ships, about carriers from the same line that had called at Pitcairn before, but mostly about the weather. Betty and the Captain shared a knowledge of and reliance upon the conditions of the sea. Their days, though very different, were both determined by the strength of the wind and the height of the surf.

Betty said they had been suffering heavy seas, so they wouldn't have any fresh fish for the ship as it had been too rough to go out in the canoes. The weather did seem to be breaking and, God willing, by the time of our arrival it should be calm enough to launch the longboat.

"So perhaps you will not be going to Pitcairn!" The Captain was delighted at the idea. "Perhaps you are coming with us to Auckland."

I retreated to my cabin. Half an hour later the phone rang.

"There's a message for you," said the radio officer. It read:

> DEBRIE KIRKETT
> WELCOME TO PITCAIRN ISLAND LOOKING FORWARD TO
> MEETING YOU AND HOPE FOR GOOD LANDING.
> BENIRG DENNIS CHRISTIAN

I had finished painting the Captain's cabin and spent most of the day pacing up and down the bridge, hovering over the chart and studying the anchorages off Bounty Bay. The *Pilot* recommended berthing three and a half cables off, taking a bearing from the rocks at St. Paul's Point, but, it warned, it was affected by severe swell and "the wind is liable to change suddenly and if it blows from the E with any strength this anchorage becomes uncomfortable."

The chart was divided into five squares; in each of four of them, one of the islands that made up the Pitcairn group was depicted. Ducie was shaped like a wedding ring, nothing more than a fine circle of coral surrounding a large lagoon. Oeno, where the Pitcairners went on holiday, had the same basic design as Ducie, except it was larger, and the land and the lagoon it encircled were both heart shaped. Henderson was the shape of a teardrop, with a coastline that seemed to have been sanded, it was so smooth. Pitcairn Island was a rhombus of gray with dark, serrated edges, indicating vertical cliffs. The fifth and largest square was empty, as if the island that had once occupied it had been obliterated, after being found not to exist; or perhaps the empty square was in anticipation of another discovery. The chart, the most recently available, was compiled by Captain Beechey of HMS *Blossom* and dated 1825.

We first sighted Pitcairn in the few moments of dusk. The sea was calm, the sky fluffed with gray clouds, and the island sat on the horizon. Second Mate took a photograph of me with Pitcairn in the background. I am clinging to the deck rail as if it were a lifebuoy.

By the time we reached the anchorage, it was dark. I peered through the binoculars for any sign of the islanders. Then Third spotted a light on the water. It looked like a firefly bouncing over the waves, but it was the Pitcairn longboat coming out to trade and to fetch me to the island.

I hurried down to the open deck. As the longboat drew closer, it seemed no larger, and when its aluminum hull knocked against ours, it was as if a limpet had stuck itself to the side of the ship.

Boatswain threw down a rope ladder, and the first to climb up was a young man whose long, matchstick legs stretched up to a perfectly spherical body. He introduced himself to me—"You Debbie? I'm Dennis"—and scuttled off.

Third Mate came to join me, peering down at the longboat, while one by one the Pitcairners grabbed the ladder and scrambled up the side of the ship.

"That's dangerous. That's *really* dangerous," he said. He was talking about the thought, in abstract, of boarding a chemical carrier in the open ocean by means of a flimsy rope ladder, though the Pitcairners were embarking with such nonchalance and grace, they made it *seem* easy.

The Pitcairners seemed to have the distinctive Polynesian physical characteristics—a high forehead, a broad nose, black hair, a portly frame and dark skin—dealt out between them at random, with some sporting a single Polynesian feature and others several. One man had a high forehead but was white-skinned and spindly nosed, while another looked entirely

Polynesian apart from his light brown hair. At the tiller stood a swarthy man with an Italian mustache, the only one among them who could have appeared in the film *The Bounty.*

They were wearing printed Pitcairn Island sweatshirts and baseball caps, like supporters from a visiting team, except the sweatshirts were worn into holes. The women carried plastic woven baskets that seemed to be stuffed with newspapers, while the men's contained bananas, oranges and fish, which they either slung over their shoulders or hoisted up the side of the ship on a rope. On each man's right buttock was a stubby knife in a sheath, hanging from a leather belt.

The Pitcairners occupied the *Najran* as if on military maneuvers. She would drift offshore for an hour and a half at most, and they had to make the best of this brief contact. As I wafted about aimlessly, feeling as if I were a waifish ghost among solid human beings, the ship was transformed into a floating market. The women and children had seized the open deck, where they were unwrapping the newspaper packaging from wooden shark carvings, painted leaves, small woven baskets, Pitcairn T-shirts printed in Miami, and Pitcairn stamps, and fanning them out on pieces of cloth. "You got any waterproof trousers?" a stout woman with a round face but thin nose and mouth, and a child's baseball cap balanced on the top of her head, asked Assistant Cook. "I've some nice carvings here for you, if you like to do exchange."

"Where is the trading?" The young man had blond hair, blue eyes, a perfectly equal tan like a model from a magazine, and a coconut-frond basket of bananas slung over his shoulder. I pointed in the direction of the open deck.

"I do not mean souvenirs," he said. It sounded like a German accent. "I mean the fish and vegetables."

I led him down to the galley. Another blond stranger was already there, taller, older and less lean than the first, introducing himself to Chief Steward as Rick Ferret, Pitcairn Island pastor. He sounded Australian.

"Keep this cool. But *not* in the freezer. Just in the fridge. Do you understand?" He handed Chief Steward a vial of blood. "Someone will collect it from the ship in New Zealand."

I sauntered up to the bridge, where Dennis was asking the Captain if he would take the island's mail on to Auckland in return for a basket of bananas. In the galley, half a dozen children were being fed frankfurters, ice cream and bars of chocolate. I watched as they scooped up several bars and stuffed them into their pockets.

I wandered through these scenes, watching the people with whom I would leave the ship. Then as quickly as they had come on board, unpacked their goods and begun to barter, they were wrapping up their unsold carvings in newspaper, rolling up their cloths and heaving their baskets over the side. Boxes of frozen chicken pieces had been brought up from the galley, along with four fifty-can packs of 7-Up and Coca-Cola, which I had bought from Steward as presents for the Pitcairn children. Someone had acquired an old fridge, which swung wildly in a rope basket, dangerously close to the ship's side. Then one by one the people began to descend, climbing down to the bottom rung, where, swaying over the water, they waited for the longboat to rise on the swell.

"Jump!" shouted someone already on board, and they leaped backward into the longboat as it fell back into a trough, and the ladder shot away from them like a whip.

Then it was my turn. I clambered over the side of the ship. The ladder no longer seemed a substantial link, but a flimsy thing waving in the wind. I climbed down to the final rung, but still the boat seemed a good ten feet below. Then the swell rose and the boat surged toward me. If I could just let go at the right moment, before the boat fell again.

"Jump! *Jump!*" someone cried. I felt a pair of hands around my waist, and Dennis tore me from the ladder.

I sat in the longboat among the islanders, saying nothing. Nobody spoke to me or to each other as the longboat rose and fell with the sea and the last few people jumped on board. I looked up at the Captain far away on the bridge wing, and Boatswain and Assistant Cook hanging over the deck rail at the top of the ladder. Boatswain took the ropes that tied us to the ship and threw them down, and the longboat slowly moved away from the side.

Out of the darkness rose one man's voice, leading the song.

> *Now one last song we'll sing*
> *Goodbye, Goodbye*
> *Time moves on rapid wings*
> *Goodbye, Goodbye, Goodbye*
>
> *And this short year will soon be past*
> *And soon be numbered with the last*
> *We part, but hope to meet again*
> *Goodbye, Goodbye, Goodbye . . .*

As the islanders sang, they raised one hand and waved up to the men of NCC *Najran*. I looked up and waved, too. I could swear, even at that distance, that the Captain was winking at me. Then the *Najran*'s whistle blew two long blasts and she was away.

# part two

·······································

≈   ≈

# 4 · *p i t c a i r n*

The island had hardened to a granite gray, set against a jet-black sky. When the singing died, the islanders lowered their waving hands and turned away from the ship. The longboat slapped the waves and the heavy spray drummed on the sheets of plywood covering the cargo.

I tried to put names to the sea of faces. After all my reading, I ought to have been able to identify the mustached, swarthy man at the tiller, distinguished from the others by wearing, not a Pitcairn Island sweatshirt, but a T-shirt advertising an Australian beer, "I'd Like a Toohey's . . . or Two"; the young woman with tight black curls and a cylindrical body, the shape of a large roll of carpet; and the tallest, thinnest man, with a high, medieval forehead and the broad nose of a boxer, who had led the song.

The longboat's hold was stacked with the women's bags of curios, the boxes of tinned and frozen foodstuffs the men had bartered for, and my Afrique-Trunk. Over the top, balanced from gunwale to gunwale, lay sheets of plywood on which the old men, women and children sat cross-legged, their eyes narrowed against the sea and salt. The young men stood stiffly at the prow, one arm raised in salute to protect their eyes from the spray. Under the lowering sky, with the mighty swells, a rubicund figure at the helm, the women and children huddled together in the heart of the boat, and one white man—the pastor—among them, I was reminded of a primitive holy picture showing a people lost in a storm. But the pastor wore a habit of fluorescent pink shorts that barely covered the bulb of flesh at the tops of his thighs and showed clearly the outline of his underpants, and he was barefoot, as if about to mount a surfboard on Bondi Beach. The moss of hair on his thick, tanned legs was bleached blond.

"What brings you all the way out here?" he asked, as casually as if inquiring from a member of a neighboring congregation why she was visiting his parish for tea.

"Royal Mail International. It's the most remote place in the world their mail reaches. Post a letter at the Elephant, it ends up in Pitcairn!" I sounded absurdly chirpy. "But it's a bit of an excuse, really. I've always wanted to come here."

"Lots of people do," said the pastor, and turned back toward the island.

Pitcairn was the color of a magnet, and the longboat a shiny metal shaving plowing homeward. The islanders fixed their gaze in the direction of the island, not once looking back toward the ship. It was as if NCC *Najran* no longer existed, and when—it seemed like only minutes after she had blown her whistle—I turned to look for her, she was indeed gone.

I heard yelping, and soon saw the silhouettes of dogs. The man at the tiller let the engine die. We were a few hundred yards out from Bounty Bay, which was little more than a dent in an ironclad coastline bound on one side by a short stub of a jetty and the other by sheer cliff. The swell heaved up into the bay, washing over the jetty and scattering the dogs. We hovered outside, the sentries at the prow keeping watch on the rushing water, and the helmsman standing at the ready with one hand resting on the throttle, as we waited for a wave that would wash us in. Even the dogs were quiet.

*"Go ahead!"* shouted a sentry, the engine was kicked back to life, and we rode up on a swell and surfed alongside the jetty.

The women called out news of the trading to those waiting ashore, and instructions and cheers of encouragement were given to the men as the sheets of plywood were raised and the bags and boxes passed out from the hold. A pair of hands grasped my waist from behind and hoisted me up onto the quayside like another piece of cargo. The dogs sniffed at the boxes and at me, while the islanders searched among the woven baskets for their own bounty. I stood awkwardly among the trade goods, waiting to be claimed.

A woman with a broad brown face, tiny sea-blue eyes and a body built like an armchair lolled over and smothered me in a hug.

"Welcome to our island." She was wearing a pair of pink nylon leggings and a T-shirt that fitted her like stretched upholstery covers. "Welcome to our island."

She held me out at arm's length, looked me up and down, and pulled me toward her again. It felt as if I were being bounced off a wall of cushions.

"Welcome. Welcome," she said, smiling broadly. I sank back into her arms, pleased that I had, at last, arrived safely on Pitcairn.

Behind buzzed an elfin woman with cropped gray hair, hopping up and down as if trying to overtake the welcoming woman's ample bulk, either by dodging around her side or leaping over her shoulder. The bolster arms opened slowly, like a lock on the Panama Canal, and released me to the insectile woman.

"Wha side Dennis put ha bike?" the tiny woman blurted out, look-

---

*wha side?*—where?
*ha*—the

ing about nervously. She turned to me and said, in considered English, "Do not worry. Do not worry. Dennis brings your things. I take you up to the house," and hurried me along as if we were already late for an important appointment.

I glanced back at the elephantine woman as she strolled off to claim her trade goods, with the feeling of having been snatched from my rightful host.

At the end of the jetty was a large wooden boat shed to house the two longboats *Tin* and *Tub,* as well as the no-longer-seaworthy wooden longboat, *Stick.* Above the shed hung a painted sign, WELCOME TO PITCAIRN, and alongside the open walls were parked half a dozen red motorbikes, each with three wheels as big as those of a tractor and long, broad saddles. The tiny woman threw one of her narrow legs over a saddle, checked that the wire basket at the front was securely fastened by rattling it violently, and flicked the headlight switch on and off.

"Piss. Real piss," she spat, as the light faded out. She played with the switch until it flashed back on again, and patted the seat behind her.

"Jump on!" She revved up and we were off.

We were ascending the legendary Hill of Difficulties, whose route I had traced on the map in the British Library, when my driver introduced herself as Irma and again told me not to worry, her son, Dennis, would bring up my things. Ben, her husband, was down at the Landing, helping offload the trade goods. She was sorry neither she nor Ben had come out to the ship to greet me, but they were a bit old now, and we'd be home soon.

Irma continued to trot out calming phrases in a tone of near panic as we ascended the hill, a steep path, about five feet wide, scarred with deep ruts from the bikes' heavy tractor tires. I was thrown around behind my driver, whose whip-crack body rodeoed around on the saddle. With the violent jerking up and down and the broken beam from the faulty headlight, I saw Pitcairn as a series of brief, bright flashes. It was as if I were taking a ride on a ghost train: the shape of a man-size fern hung with wiry vegetation would flare up, brush against me menacingly, then be snatched away as we swooped around a bend, or as the light bounced off again as we bounded over a particularly deep ditch. Between the tangle of creepers I caught the shapes of houses, like abandoned shacks on a cheap fairground set, half-concealed behind verandas hung with bunches of bananas. When my head was thrown back going over a bump, I could see the sky, a stream of stars no wider than the road running between the tops of the trees.

We rattled to a halt in front of one of the verandas. Irma flung herself from the bike and jostled me through a curtain of banana chandeliers. Satisfied that we had reached our destination in good time, she smiled, announced with twiglike arms outstretched, "Stay with us. This is your home," and switched on the light. I was dazzled by the brightness. The bare bulb was faint, but it shone upon surfaces of gleaming white and stainless steel. I counted three industrial-size deep-freezers, three cookers, two video machines, two TV screens, a heavy-duty microwave, a food processor, an electric frying pan, a deep-fat fryer, and two kettles. Irma's home in paradise resembled a secondhand electrical appliance shop.

Irma began immediately to demonstrate her appliances to me, as if she were a salesman for the electricity board and I a potential customer. She opened a fridge door, peered inside with her whole body as if to smother herself in eggs and ice cream cartons, then threw it shut. She lifted the doors of the freezers to show that they were all full; she would have trouble fitting in the frozen chicken portions. She could rustle me up something in the microwave, which she communicated with an elaborate mime act of choosing an item from the freezer, unwrapping it, putting it on a plate, and popping it into the microwave. It would take only a few— she held up three fingers—minutes.

When I declined her offer of food, Irma tried to tempt me elsewhere. "Would you like to go *out-side?*" she whispered, as if making an improper suggestion.

Outside? I'd traveled seventeen thousand miles to reach this point, and had only just arrived, I wanted to settle in, not move on.

"No, thank you. But I'd like to use the toilet."

Irma was busy wiping the top of a clean table.

"Yes. *Out-side,*" she mouthed, "through here," and took me through the kitchen, past an open cooking fire and out the back of her house. Irma pointed to a small corrugated-iron wardrobe teetering on the edge of a precipice before a valley thick with banana trees. "The duncan," she proclaimed.

Inside there was a wooden box with two holes cut into it, one larger than the other. I looked down the holes into a deep, rancid well. I tried the holes for size, settling on the larger one. A giant spider, as big as my fist, pattered across the wavy wall, stopped to look at me, then ran on.

The storms that had threatened my landing on the island had cleared the air, and the weightless night was heady. I could hear palm fronds rustling like grass skirts and the sound of the surf washing the rocks. They were familiar sounds. I had heard them many times before in England, staring at the smudge on my wall map, which for so long had been my imaginary Pitcairn. Then, the knowledge that the island was too small to appear on any map, lost in the blanket of the ocean, was daunting; now the same thought was comforting. It would make getting to know the island and the islanders relatively simple, and meant it would be easy to become one of them, a member of the Pitcairn family. And with little more than a square mile to explore, within a week I should have a clear understanding of the island's geography. I was pleased at the neatness of the idea. I reckoned that, within a month, I could conquer Pitcairn.

I negotiated the path back to the house with caution, unable to see anything in the dark except the threatening outline of the valley below. Entering the house again was like walking under the lights of a stage set, as the approach from the duncan, past the open grate with the embers of a fire, was a passage from the subtropical night into a brilliant, sharp-edged world. The stage-set impression was made stronger by the fact that Irma's home was constructed from sheets of weatherboard tacked together clumsily with nails. There was no decoration apart from a couple of lopsided, out-of-date calendars advertising industrial and construction companies.

Although Irma boasted all the latest electrical appliances, she did not have much furniture. In the main room, which was also the kitchen, there was a large, vinyl-topped table surrounded by hard-backed chairs. Off to one side of the main room was a short hallway, with doors to the bedrooms. Next to the hallway, partitioned from the kitchen by a waist-high wall, was the parlor, known as the big room, the smallest room in the house, apart from a walk-in cupboard to one side of the veranda where all Irma's radio equipment was stored.

In the big room, there were two large televisions standing flush against each other on a sideboard, and pointing toward them four armchairs into which the shiny shapes of backs and bottoms were worn. I couldn't imagine Irma making any of those marks. She was on her feet continually, taking the ice cream cartons out of the fridges, checking their contents, then carefully putting them back in the same order, tutting or whistling throughout.

I indicated that I was tired and would like to go to bed. Irma showed me to my room, which was as spartan as the kitchen was packed. There was a bed and a set of rough-hewn wooden shelves opposite one small window, from which there was a steep drop to the valley below. Across the ceiling, scores of tiny, soft-footed lizards pattered on suctioned feet. Netting was stretched across the window, with a tear in it, and the walls were dotted with tiny black mosquitoes.

I searched for any sign of an earlier, human occupant, and found, at the back of one of the shelves, a letter addressed to Dennis, postmarked 1987, Kansas City, USA. I opened it; it was a love letter, signed, "Love you, miss you . . ." Between the freezers and the food processor, I was glad to know that there was passion to be found on Pitcairn.


When I emerged from my bedroom the next morning, Irma was hidden inside a walk-in larder, where her food stocks and a fourth freezer I had not spotted the night before were stored. The larder contained more cans than an English corner store; tins of something called glutton hid the walls and were stacked up on the floor. My fifty-can packs of 7-Up and Coca-

Cola had been brought up from the Landing by Dennis, along with my Afrique-Trunk, and Irma was trying to find space to stack them. Satisfied that the cans were in their correct positions, Irma set about talking me through a map of Pitcairn, galloping about the island at great mental speed. Adamstown was the main town—the only town—on Pitcairn, where everyone lived. Irma's house sat in a hollow "out of town," being fifty yards from the Square and considered too far to walk. If Irma was going "into town," she'd take her bike. Down a narrow path in front of the house was the shortest route to the Square, past the home of Mavis Warren, the woman who had met me on the jetty, her husband, Jacob, and their grown daughter, Meralda. The wider path running behind the house went up to Flatlands and the west of the island, called Tedside. If I took that same path in the opposite direction, I would pass the home of Carol and Jay Warren, the island magistrate, and reach the Landing, where I had arrived the previous night. The path leading straight up the hill behind us would take me to the center of the island and Taro Ground, where the commercial radio station was, and where Irma worked as assistant radio operator number two. Irma's home was built on a major junction, sitting in the center of a web of red, rutted paths. Within minutes, Irma's bike could get us everywhere.

As Irma drew the island for me, the freezers snarled like cross dogs in the corners. Then the sound died. Irma apologized, as if she had caused them to pack up herself. The electricity, she explained, was intermittent; as fuel was in short supply, having to be transported by the barrel from New Zealand, the island generator was turned off at eleven o'clock in the morning and turned back on again at six. It was an extremely inefficient system: the freezers had just enough time to defrost during the long afternoon before they were switched on again in the early evening, requiring a fresh surge of power to cool them. Often the electricity needed to serve the island's eight households, with an average of two and a half cookers and three freezers each, caused the system to blow. If Irma wanted to use one of her cookers, she tutted, she had to turn off the freezers so as not to overload the circuit and plunge her home, as well as Mavis's below, into darkness.

Ben came in from the duncan and greeted me with a smile and firm handshake as if he was genuinely pleased to meet me, then started about his day. While Irma's natural habitat was the steely, hard appliances, Ben belonged to the well-worn chairs. He pottered about, humming some slow, dreamy tune, while Irma hopped and clattered around the room. I watched the strange show of Irma fiddling with her appliances while Ben rhythmically podded peas and peeled some sweet potatoes. After half an hour, Ben had two pots of vegetables boiling on the stove, had flaked enough coconut meat for tomorrow's sweet rice and had settled on the bench along one side of the veranda to smooth his carving—a tall, tulip-shaped wooden vase with a hand wrapped around it—with a sliver of glass. Irma was still bouncing about, muttering that she had so much to do and so little time to do it in. It was as if the parable of the tortoise and the hare were being performed before my eyes by slothful Ben and electrically charged Irma.

I saw little of Dennis during the morning. He would idle in, help himself to something to eat with an I-don't-care look, toss me a lazy smile, pick up a tool from the shed at the back, get back on his bike and roar off. Dennis was, said Irma with regret, building his own house. He was moving a few hundred yards away, to a patch next to the pastor's at the Edge, just below the Square.

"The trouble is, you're really out of town up here," he whispered, not wanting Irma to hear, as he dropped in to find something to sharpen his saw. "The Edge is right next to things. It's much more convenient. And you have to break away from your parents sometime."

I made myself a cup of coffee from the tin I had brought with me, struggling with the mechanics of the futuristic, plastic electric kettle, while Ben moved slowly around the kitchen. He said very little, but as he went about his work he often erupted into a fit of giggles, as if telling himself a private joke. He would take a break from whatever he was engaged upon—put down his knife, stop wiping the saucepan, leave sanding a carving—shake his head, laugh a little, then take up his task again. When he smiled, his old, brown face was as creased as a piece of corrugated cardboard, but he looked as mischievous as a boy.

I sat and made a mental plan of my Pitcairn sojourn. I'd have a stress-free time among these South Pacific people, observing, listening, joining in and then recording my impressions in my journal each night. I'd live as they did, and I saw waves of lazy days stretching out before me as I dabbled in the island's craft—making bundles of putty-colored paste known as pilhi,* weaving baskets, painting hattie leaves and engaging in the other gentle arts I'd read about in books. If the weather was fine, I could go for a swim or fish from the rocks, take a walk to the other side of the island, and settle under a pandanus tree to read or write in my journal.

Paradise was cheap; I counted out a month's rent in advance—four hundred New Zealand dollars—and handed the envelope to Irma.

"No. No. No. I would like you," said Irma, "to work for me."

Irma outlined my duties: I would type up the accounts from the commercial radio station, which was part of her job as typist in addition to assistant radio operator number two; I would address the envelopes to her *Pitcairn Miscellany* subscribers; I would help with the cooking; I would weed the garden; and I would trade on ships. Ben, she explained, had damaged his vertebrae when a rock fell on him as he worked down at the Landing and had lost most of the sensation in his right foot and some up his leg. Irma was frail and frightened, although she did not spell this out, expressing why she, too, could not climb the ladder only with a flutter of her hands. As I was young, I could trade for them. Then she added, as if it followed on perfectly naturally, "Ben and I do not allow hard liquor into the house, dear."

---

* Pilhi is made from a paste of bananas, sweet potatoes, pumpkin or breadfruit, usually with coconut milk added, baked in a banana leaf. *Pilhi* is Pitcarnese for "mixture."

I considered the conditions under which I was accepted as a guest very reasonable, and I felt good that I had been given a role in this pocket-size community so early on; it was my first step toward acceptance. I had expected far more wide-ranging restrictions on what I could eat and imbibe, and on how I should behave in an Adventist home on an Adventist island. I was relieved that I had only to do odd tasks for Irma and keep teetotal. I only hoped one of the surprise presents in my Afrique-Trunk didn't turn out to be a miniature of whiskey.

*Dong, dong, dong, dong, dong.* I heard the paced striking of a bell, as if sealing our contract. The ringing was quickly followed by the burr of bike engines being started, and Dennis roaring up the path. He dismounted and began to hack away at the banana chandeliers, loading them onto the back of his bike.

"Coming?" said Dennis, who was pulling a Pitcairn Island sweatshirt over his head. "There's a ship."

Then I knew what the bells were. I should have realized that I had heard the public bell in the Square, which was rung to call the community together. Two strikes for church; three for calling the men to public work; four for the share-out of food from a ship; and five for announcing the arrival of a ship offshore. I had the list in my notebook, and ought to have remembered. It was the same as with the sea of faces in the longboat, which I had been hopelessly unable to match with the family trees I had sketched out in England. My myriad of notes on Pitcairn were proving useless when confronted by the real thing.

"Love to," I said to Dennis, and climbed up beside the bananas.

"We don't have any ice cream," called out Irma, banging a freezer door. She could have been making a casual observation to no one in particular, but she was speaking in English, so must have been addressing me.

"Would you like me to try and get some?" I offered.

"It's just we don't have any ice cream, dear," and she handed me some postcards of Pitcairn depicting "Jetty and Landing at Bounty Bay with St. Paul's Rock in the distance," "Surf at the Landing," "Boiling juice from sugarcane to make molasses" and "Polynesian petroglyphs Down Rope." She pulled out a sketchy map of Pitcairn from a pile of photocopies and wrote in blue Biro at the bottom, just under a spot identified as Break Im Hip, "Ben Christian, 5th Generation, Fletcher Christian," as if Ben had signed it himself. "You might like to take these out with you."

As we tumbled down to the Landing, only the severe jolting reminded me that this was the same route we had driven just the night before. The air was skin temperature, as cozy as a cotton vest, and so clear that everything looked unnaturally crisp and sharp. The fierce red of the path and the intense green which it hacked its way through were, after all, as vibrant as Ron's video. In some of the houses, which had appeared abandoned, people were hacking down the curtains of bananas and loading up bikes. The sound of their engines almost drowned out the surf.

We shouted across to other bikes carrying men, women and children fitted out in Pitcairn Island sweatshirts and baseball caps, as if off to a friendly match with the sailors on the visiting ship.

"Bout ha ship comen from?" The driver was a young woman, as brown as a coconut husk and built like a bull; there was an older woman sitting behind her, and two children—one on the woman's lap, the other balanced in the front basket.

"Auckland," said Dennis.

"Who se spot her?" someone called out from the veranda at Carol and Jay's.

"I ka wa," cried Dennis.

"Bound Panama?" asked a small child.

"Filipinos!" called an immense woman from a veranda.

"I gwen marry me one Filipino wife. Good fer trade," joked Dennis.

"You gwen out ha ship?" he asked a rakish middle-aged man in a pair of baggy khaki shorts encrusted with dirt.

---

*ka wa*—don't know.
*gwen*—going to/going

"I count I gwen," the man replied, lifting his baseball cap and wiping his brow.

"Surf's up!" Dennis turned back to me. We could see the whitecaps on the water as we rode down the Hill of Difficulties.

"What one you got there, Dennis?" A young man, alone on his bike, sped up behind us, swerved suddenly and braked.

"Shi Debbie," said Dennis. "Shi long fer me."

Down at the Landing, half a dozen men were playing tug-of-war with the longboat, hauling it from the shed down the short slipway and into the bay. Her silver hull slid into the water like a giant fish. I trotted behind Dennis, shouldering a basket of bananas and clutching my souvenirs, and jumped on board exhilarated. Only last night I was looking out from the deck of the *Najran*, searching the swell for the shape of a longboat. This afternoon, I was tracing the horizon for the silhouette of a cargo ship clasping a handful of goods to trade.

Soon she rose over the horizon, so small and indistinct at first that I wondered if there had been a mistake; perhaps she wasn't a cargo ship at all but a Scandinavian fishing vessel on her way to eastern waters. I knew that would disappoint the islanders, as she would carry a crew of less than half a dozen, so have limited spare supplies to trade and few potential customers for their curios.

We reached the meeting point, where the ship could drift at a safe distance from the rocks, long before the ship herself did. For half an hour, we lolloped about on the open sea, responding to the rhythm of the waves as a paper boat to the ripples on a river. The pastor videoed our movements, although as he rocked too, I imagined that the film would show a static longboat sitting on a flat sea.

The motion wasn't pleasant, yet I was astonished when, within a few minutes of stopping our engines, Betty was sick. Then Terry, a burly

---

*count*—believe/think
*long fer*—belongs to/with

young man with the appearance of great resilience, leaned over the gunwale, and Timmy, a teenager, soon joined him. Before long, most on
board had thrown up.

The few who weren't sick ate ravenously, gorging the bananas, oranges and molasses candy they had brought out to trade. If the ship didn't
reach us soon, we would have nothing left to barter for the oil, flour, eggs
and ice cream that we needed.

As the ship drew closer, she grew larger and larger, and the longboat
shrank.

"Here come binoculars!" said Tom Christian, Betty's husband, the
tall, tawny man who had led the "Goodbye Song." "They think we have
swords through our noses."

The side of the ship rose up before us like a rampart, against which
hung a rope ladder, whipping in the wind. From forty feet below, it was
the sailors staring down on us over the deck rail who seemed savage. Each
held an instrument before his eyes—a camera, a video, a pair of binoculars—giving him the appearance of a strange Cyclop.

I watched the women hoisting their bags of curios over their shoulders and stumbling over to the ladder. Only when we rose to the tip of the
swell did the rungs come within grasp from the longboat. A young woman
hesitated. *"Go!"* shouted a man standing at the bottom of the ladder, as it
began to rush out of reach and we sank again into the valley of a swell.

I felt confident that I could crack the method of ascent. Waiting until
the boat reached the summit of a swell, I had to reach out and grasp hold
of the rope ladder very hard. I must not look down at the heaving water. I
stood up and staggered toward the ladder like a drunkard, waiting until we
seemed to have reached the crest of a swell, and leaped. But I had jumped
too soon and the longboat continued to rise up behind me until I was
sandwiched between the aluminum hull and the steel side of the ship,
clinging to the rope ladder. I was in a hard, dark crevice, with a crack of
light high above, and I could hear shouts as if from a great distance. As the
splinter of light continued to soar away from me, I had the sensation that I
was falling downward and wondered when I would reach the bottom, and

whether it would be wet. Then, as if I were being jerked up on an invisible rope, I felt the side of the longboat scrape down the back of my legs as she fell, and I emerged, still grasping the ladder, back into the light. The shouts died down as I hauled myself up and was helped over the deck rail by a Filipino seaman while his colleague focused a video camera on my face. Only yesterday I was one of the crew; now the crew thought I was one of the islanders. I was delighted that they hadn't seemed to notice the difference between my ascent and a native Pitcairner's.

The Monrovian-registered *Tundra Queen* was a working ship, and I wandered about the familiar territory and struck up a conversation with the Polish electrician, who invited me into his cabin, trailing smoke signals behind him along the alleyways.

There were twenty of them altogether, he told me, sucking on a Marlboro, all Filipinos except himself and the Norwegian captain and chief engineer. They carried nothing but Kiwi fruit, bound for some European port, he didn't know where. It would be another four weeks at least before he set foot ashore, he said, looking toward the porthole. Then he raised himself from the bed and began to mimic a hula dance, pumping his hips and nodding excitedly toward Pitcairn.

"They're Seventh-day Adventists," I tutted. "No dancing permitted."

"You are saying?" he said, continuing his dance, with a cigarette in one hand and twirling a shirt picked up off the bed in the other.

I mentioned that it was also illegal to smoke on Pitcairn. It did not perturb him.

"I would like very much to visit," he said, wagging his cigarette in the direction of the island before, exhausted by his performance, he slumped back onto the bed.

"As you can't go ashore, you can have this," I said, and handed him the signed map of Pitcairn. He nodded energetically at the map and pinned it above his desk, between the photos of two children wearing blouses buttoned to the very top and an out-of-date calendar for a Swedish refrigeration company, showing two pouting women in G-strings, their arms resting lightly on each other's shoulders. Pitcairn Island and pornography were fitting neighbors, both being the electrician's, and many others', fantasy.

He showed me to the galley, shook my hand, wished me good luck and handed me over to the chief steward.

"Do you have any spare ice cream, please?" I asked, as a child might request seconds. "For these," and I fanned out some of Irma's postcards. The steward seemed pleased at my offer, returning with a gallon container marked "Raspberry Ripple," and asked politely if he might take my photograph. He wanted to show his wife what a Pitcairner looked like.

Other exchanges had been more vigorous. Cardboard boxes and large orange plastic bags, in which hazardous waste was usually stored, were being lowered over the side into the longboat, and the islanders' curio baskets were near empty. The choreography of our departure began, as one by one we descended the ladder; the younger men arranged themselves at the prow, the women around the gunwale, and the boatswain threw the ropes down from the *Tundra Queen*.

I hummed along to the "Goodbye Song," waved and turned toward Pitcairn. The peaks and jagged rocks all pointed skyward, as if the island were poised to spring up out of the ocean, like a lion about to pounce on its prey. Meralda was sitting next to me. Someone called out "Daughter!" and she turned around, acknowledging the name that first her father, Jacob, and now everyone called her. It conjured up someone small, delicate and obliging. But a more appropriate nickname might have been Womanbulk; her huge, dark, cylindrical body had stood out from the others when I first stepped into the longboat. The only thing small about her were her eyes, which were sharp, like those of her mother, Mavis.

"Been lots of beautiful places," she said. "Been Auckland. Been Hawaii. But not to live there. Only living to be done on Pitcairn. This place where I belong."

I had to remind myself that, for the foreseeable future, this short, strange voyage was the journey home.

.   .   .

By the time I reached Irma's, the Raspberry Ripple was sloshing about in the bottom of the tub. But I felt triumphant, and held the container out like a smuggler parading his loot. Irma was on the veranda with her sister-in-law, Royal, whom I recognized as the Pitcairner who'd come aboard the *Najran* wearing the child's baseball cap. She had a don't-mess-with-me look about her, and smiled with only one side of her mouth, so it was more like a smirk.

When Irma opened the tub and found a couple of melted inches in the bottom, she feigned gratitude, rubbing her hands together and congratulating me, saying how useful the carton would be for storing things in the freezer, but I could tell by Royal's expression that it was a poor catch. I determined to do better next time.

"Lucky not break em legs," said Royal. "You must go on top of surf—when boat's high—or she rise up behind you and—" and she broke a strip of dried leaf in two. "You *mus* listen to wha time people larn you go."

I was sure I hadn't heard anyone shout *Go!* at me, but I apologized: "I should have watched more closely what other people were doing. I was stupid. It was my fault."

Later, I overheard Royal say to Irma, "Clarice push ha boat from ha side. She se save em legs."

Of course they had told me when to go, I just hadn't been listening. I felt that I was already in enormous debt to the islanders.

This island was running at a far faster pace than I had anticipated; I felt as if I were on a crash course called "Living on Pitcairn." By the time I arrived back from the *Tundra Queen,* less than twenty-four hours after my arrival, I received my first party invitation, delivered by the hostess herself.

> To Debbie
> Please come to my birthday party
> Sunday June 9th

Time 6:00 P.M.
Place Carol and Jay's
Thank you, Charlene

Charlene was going to be twelve.

The island magistrate's house was laid out just like Irma's, except it was much bigger. The veranda was large enough to house an off-the-road three-wheeled motorbike, a partly dismantled outboard engine, a settee and several redundant industrial freezers. If Irma's was the showroom, Carol and Jay's was the repair shop.

In the big room, a twenty-foot-long table was smothered with food—bowls of oily crimson stew; bundles of pilhi wrapped in banana leaves; whole deep-fried fish glistening with fat, golden plantain chips; piles of breadfruit fritters and green banana pancakes; sweet potatoes baked in their red jackets and cut into chips; pumpkin pie; and roasted chicken legs from the *Najran*.

I had been flattered by Charlene's invitation, but as the guests filed in, each bearing an overflowing plate that he or she placed like an offering on the long table, I realized that the whole island was here and this must be what was known as a Pitcairn general party—a bacchanalian banquet without any wine, held to celebrate a birthday, to which every islander, without question, was invited.

The pastor's wife, in a nod to the edicts of her faith, brought a vegetarian dish.

"It's made with glutton, dear," said Irma, as if glutton were the Sacrament itself. Irma had brought a bowl of lettuce.

The Pitcairners came in two by two: Tom arrived with Betty, who was as fair skinned as I, with light brown ringlets. Their two teenage daughters had long auburn hair waving down their straight backs and moved about like mermaids, as languidly as swimming, with faces as smooth as a lake.

The Magistrate Jay Warren, father to Charlene and Darrylene, had the high forehead and wide eyes of a Polynesian, but his face tapered in from under his nostrils and ended in a neat dimple at the tip of his tiny chin, as if the top of a Polynesian face had been joined to the bottom of a perky European one. His wife, Carol—the hostess—was solid rather than fat, with the bonhomie of a British barmaid. She didn't talk, she boomed.

I went and sat in a spare seat against the wall, next to Mavis. More couples came in, followed by the odd person who seemed to have no partner: the Germanic boy who had asked me where the trading was on the *Najran* and a blond woman with two brown children.

Watching the line of my eyes with her smaller, sharper ones, "That's Kari, Brian's wife," said Mavis. Brian had left the island to get computer training, although I knew of no computers on Pitcairn. I smiled toward Kari, but she appeared not to notice me. I was astonished that a stranger on the island elicited such little attention.

After Kari came an impossibly handsome young man, as large framed as the other islanders, but lean and loose limbed, with an easy smile that, although he was only another guest, made him appear the host.

"And that's Nigger," said Mavis. "His wife and baby visiting their people in New Zealand."

The table seemed full, but Carol was still bringing dishes from the kitchen at the back when there was a large crash.

"You se arsehole," Charlene called out to her mother, who smiled. Charlene was a pea from her mother's pod—stout, firm and with the impression of great physical strength. She swore like an adult too, and answered back to her elders.

"You are from the post office," said Mavis.

I nodded.

"You know Jennifer Toombs."

I pursed my lips and shook my head.

"Jennifer Toombs is a lovely lady. She designs our stamps. She come here one time."

I widened my eyes, hoping to look interested. I remembered ordering *The Pitcairn Islands Stamp Catalogue*, which had been prefaced by a stylized black-and-white photograph of "Miss Jennifer Toombs, English

Graphic Design artist, who gained a National Diploma in graphic design at the Watford School of Art in 1961," sporting hair so hard and so black it looked like a hat.

"She's a lovely person, Jennifer Toombs," said Mavis, and smiled. She tilted her head to one side and gazed at me. I tilted my head in the opposite direction and smiled back foolishly. I was no philatelist, and couldn't design anything. Among such no-nonsense people, I felt a fraud.

"*Quiet*," the pastor bellowed. "Bless this food, kind Father, and make us thankful."

"Amen," the children muttered, and surged toward the table, dodging the bowls of salad and piling their plates high with anything chunky and fried. The food came in a variety of shapes, but with one thing in common—everything was huge. The sweet potato chips were not dainty slivers like pinkies, but as thick as a Pitcairner's toes. The green banana pancakes were like little blankets, and could smother a baby. If anything came in unnaturally small parcels, like the chicken legs, the guests would compensate by helping themselves to three or four at the same time. The container for the lime juice at the end of the table was not a jug, or an urn, but a small water tank.

Many dishes were already empty by the time it was the adults' turn. The pastor's pallid wife helped herself to several thick slices of tinned corned beef. I scooped up a teaspoonful of flesh-colored glutton, just to try, but as there was plenty left it was obviously not a popular dish.

I sat back down next to a mammoth woman with a gray ponytail, classic Polynesian. The room was full of chatter, and mouths worked hard talking and downing vast quantities of food, but from the neck down the plump bodies were static, sinking farther and farther into the seats. Only Irma skittled along the row of chairs, pretending to pick at a leaf of lettuce.

I made my food last as long as possible, circling the last few pieces of deep-fried breadfruit around my plate several times before putting them slowly between my lips. I found it difficult to contribute to a conversation being conducted in Pitcairnese.

The Germanic boy strolled up and, in midstep, whispered in my ear, "They will not come to you. You must talk to them," without interrupting his fluid pacing around the big room.

A short, stout, cappuccino-colored teenager with the look of forlorn youth sank down in the seat next to me.

"That's Perry. He's from Switzerland looking for the simple life," he said. "What are *you* doing here?"

Not waiting for my answer, he continued, "What are *any of us* doing here?" And he stood up and walked off.

My contact with other guests at Charlene's general party resembled two billiard balls bouncing off each other rather than attempts at conversation. I decided to take the initiative; I put down my plate and said, "Hi, I'm Debbie," to a man with an islander's elephantine build but bright red hair, translucent skin and freckles, making him look as if he were a Polynesian in war paint. I hadn't introduced myself as Debbie since I was a child.

"I'm the Education Officer and Government Adviser, Tony," he beamed. "What brought you here?"

I held out a hand. "The Royal Mail. I'm interested in the Pitcairn postal system."

"What you going to do? Write about it?"

"I hope so. I write for newspapers, magazines. Books . . ."

"People don't like writers much here," Tony said. "I wouldn't mention it if I were you."

Full of food, I had a bumpy ride to Irma's, never considering that I might have more comfortably walked the couple of hundred yards. I went outside to the duncan. The spider was still there. He cocked his head at me and pattered from one side to the other, his eight padded feet sounding like soft drizzle on the corrugated iron. It was as if the spider knew he lived on an island the dimensions of Pitcairn, and had accepted his lifestyle accordingly. If people on Pitcairn were restricted to moving no more than a mile in any one direction, on arachnoid scale, the inside of a duncan would be appropriate for a Pitcairnese spider.

By the beam of my waterproof flashlight, in my spartan bedroom, with the dry tickle of the tiny lizards across the ceiling and the whine of the mosquitoes, I recorded the first entry in my Pitcairn journal. It was my strongest impression of Irma's household: *Lovely Ben.*

Outside the wind was coming up, the bamboo was creaking like arthritic bones, and louder than my own breath was the hiss of the surf.

## 5 · h e n d e r s o n

Dennis sauntered into the house, swinging his arms and smug with the news: there was going to be a trip to Henderson. Nothing definite had been said yet, but Dennis reported that Charles Christian had mentioned to Jay, his son-in-law, that he was running out of *miro* wood for his carvings. Jay had mentioned it to Steve Christian, the swarthy skipper of *Tub*. Several other carvers had let Steve know that their piles of wood were getting low. Winter was approaching, and if they were going to collect any more logs before the gales set in, they had better make a trip soon. Dennis and Ben still had plenty of wood drying out the back, but you could never have too much. If news came through that a cruise ship was going to call, then they would be up all night working on carvings to sell to the passengers, and the pile would soon shrink.

Pitcairn had been severely deforested by the islanders' thirst for fuel and carving material, but on Henderson, an uninhabited island 110 nautical miles to the east–northeast, there was still a plentiful supply of tau and the fiery-red miro, which the carvers preferred to the gray-grained miro, all that was left on Pitcairn. Reaching Henderson used to be relatively easy; when ships had called frequently and their schedules were less tight, friendly captains would offer to hoist the longboat up on deck and carry her and her crew to Henderson, where she would be lowered outside the reef circling the island. That way, the islanders only had to make a one-way voyage on the open ocean. It was considered improper for the women to spend so much time in the company of seafarers on board a cargo vessel and, as the work of sawing and collecting the wood was also hard labor, only the men made the trip. But the last time a ship had offered them a lift to Henderson was almost twenty years ago, and now the longboats had to sail both ways under their own steam. Women went too, now, as there were not enough men to chop, collect and load the logs.

"Are we really going?" I pestered Dennis.

"Might be," he shrugged, and sat down at the table with a bowl of sweet rice.

"Should I pack?"

"Semiswe," said Dennis, who had only minutes earlier walked in and announced the news of our imminent departure with a great show of having the certain knowledge of an insider.

"When will we know for definite?" I was anxious to plan out my next few days, and the prospect of a trip away from the island threatened to disrupt the schedule I had set myself.

"When they decide."

"*Who* decides?"

"The people."

---

*semiswe*—seems + this + way

"But we—you *are* the people," I said. Dennis couldn't see what I was getting so worked up about.

"We know soon enough," he said.

It soon became obvious that plans were being laid, as the phone in the corner of our veranda tinkled throughout the morning, although seldom for us. Irma provided me with a running commentary so that I would know the meaning of whatever I saw and heard, much as a parent would talk to her baby, never expecting a reply: "I just put the bread in the oven, dear," "There goes Meralda on her bike," "Ben is back early from the garden. That's lab-lab—that's wild beans, dear—he has in his basket . . ." And when she wasn't talking, she whistled, as if even her mouth had to be in constant use.

When the phone rang, Irma said, "That phone ringing for Up Pulau, dear," and began to explain the Pitcairn Island phone system.

The island shared one internal party line, and each family had their own call sign. Irma and Ben's was *long-short-long-short-long.* To make a call, you cranked out a call sign by turning the handle on the side of the phone, and the person you were calling would pick up the phone, whomever's house they were in.

"That's fer Tom," said Irma, when the phone went *short-long-short-short,* and she would tell me what the caller must be talking to him about. In this way, I was kept in touch with everything that was happening on the island. Soon, the accuracy of Irma's reports didn't matter to me any more than it mattered to her.

A single unbroken ring, called a long ring, meant everyone should answer, and was used to spread news that should be shared—a ship would be calling, there had been an accident such as someone falling from the cliffs, or a trip was planned. It appeared an inexact telecommunications system, as it required a finely tuned Pitcairner's ear to distinguish the cranking out of a *long-long-short* from a *long-long-long,* and any cranking might possibly be a long ring. Irma was particularly keen to ensure that she didn't miss out on any important news, and at any call that seemed to include an extended ring she would mutter, "Is that a long ring, dear?"

and scurry over to the phone. Several minutes of silent listening were necessary before she was satisfied that the conversation was not intended for her. In any case, there was no privacy in any conversation; anyone could listen in undetected to anyone else's calls.

Dennis strolled back in at midmorning with calculated sloth, ignoring Irma's pleas that he stay for "breakfast," which was Pitcairnese for lunch. I was busy smothering my legs in Jungle Formula; the mosquitoes had been as Ron predicted—voracious—and from my knees down, my legs were ablaze. So far, the Jungle Formula had seemed to make no difference; sometimes I would even catch one sitting on my shin, licking it up like soup. But I had twenty bottles in my Afrique-Trunk, and perhaps I just needed to build up a layer of repellent, like a second skin, which the proboscis couldn't pierce.

"We going?" I called out to Dennis, and he raised the palms of his hands skyward, as if to say how should he know.

"I meet Charles, and he larn Steve larn we gwen." Then, as Irma left for her shift at the commercial radio station, he whispered, "Do you drink?"

When the long ring came through late in the afternoon, Ben shooed away a red cat that was rubbing up against his legs and hobbled over to the phone. The message was repeated several times: "Yourley there? Yourley, Henderson this night. Henderson this night. Henderson this night." Ben immediately phoned Irma at the commercial radio station— *long-short-long*—even though she would have already listened in to the message herself.

"Shi se comen hoo-um," he reported back to me. "Fer prepare em wickle." Ben fetched his ax, sat down on the veranda and began to sharpen the blade with a stone. Dennis would need it for chopping the wood.

---

*yourley*—you all/everyone
*wickle*—food, from *victuals*

The evolution of a decision on Pitcairn baffled me. The trip to Henderson seemed to have begun as an unattributed rumor, then to be repeated so often, by so many, that the notion that we might go grew slowly into fact. All that was necessary was for Council to be called to a meeting in the courthouse, formally to approve the trip. This would be little more than a rubber stamp, as the decision had already been reached by common consensus, but it was nevertheless important to gain Council's official sanction. Although only twenty people wanted to make the journey to Henderson, they couldn't just launch the longboats and set out to sea. The Council, consisting of the Island Magistrate Jay Warren, the Island Secretary Olive Christian, the Government Adviser Tony, the four councillors— Meralda Warren, Kari Young, Carol Warren and Dave Brown—and the pastor in an advisory capacity, had to agree to such a mass exodus. And with so few people left on Pitcairn, Dennis explained, many tasks would have to be put to one side, the school would be closed, and, with the longboats gone, the islanders left behind would be stranded ashore.

Within half an hour of the long ring, Pitcairn had been transported from a soporific Pacific afternoon to a frenetic production line, as the clanging of stone against metal echoed through Adamstown. Then, as the sound faded, I imagined all the men, as Ben, were carefully wrapping their ax heads in pieces of old cardboard tied about with string to prevent an accident if the freshly sharpened edge broke loose in a storm, testing and oiling their chainsaws, and wrapping these blades, too.

While the islanders busied about the practical arrangements, I delved into the few books I had brought with me for any references to Henderson. I learned that Henderson was constructed entirely from coral, a reef that, about one million years ago, was thrust through the surface of the sea by the same movements in the Earth's crust which had thrown up the volcano of Pitcairn. It stood thirty meters at its highest point, and just four and a half miles long. The trees and plants that grew on the plateau wind their roots between the cracks in the coral, and fallen leaves made the soil in which they grew. Despite the intensive studies of the Sir Peter Scott Royal Commemorative Expedition, a group of Cambridge-led scientists working in five-month stints on the ancient atoll's unique flora and fauna, how the first trees were established remains a mystery, as there is no indigenous soil anywhere on the island.

The scientists had a solar-powered radio on which they talked to Pitcairn daily, usually to Irma. Irma relayed news to England for them, and it was through Ron, Irma's contact, that I had first learned of the scientific expedition.

The scientists had fought a prolonged battle to gain control of Henderson, Ron had explained, as they had been in competition with a Texan oil billionaire called Smiley Ratliffe who wanted to buy the island outright. Every few weeks, Irma would attribute a different motive to Smiley Ratliffe. One week she said he wanted to turn Henderson into a cattle ranch, but as Henderson has no soil, what would the cattle have fed on and how would they have roamed on top of the razor-sharp coral? Then, it was claimed, realizing Henderson's commercial prospects, he wanted to build an airstrip and turn the island into an exclusive resort. Next, Irma reported, Smiley Ratliffe wasn't a Texan oil billionaire at all, but a retired and much-decorated U.S. Army General, who simply wanted a private island to call his own. Where Irma heard all these conflicting accounts was unclear, but she relayed them to Ron as gospel truth, who then used to phone me early every Sunday morning with the latest news. The asking price for Henderson, he had said, was one million dollars.

When the scientific community got to hear about Ratliffe's interest in the world's only intact raised coral atoll, the battle for the beaches of Henderson began. The scientists petitioned Her Majesty's Government, who had probably never heard of Henderson before Smiley Ratliffe had reminded them that it was one of the few remaining territories under their imperial control. The conservationists pointed out that Henderson's evolution and isolation had produced a unique ecosystem, and made the island home to a very few but distinct species. Of particular concern was the preservation of the giant hawk moth, one of Henderson's 220 insects, and the Henderson rail, which the Pitcairn Islanders disdainfully called the chicken bird, and which was black as a moorhen, as big as a rooster and incapable of flight.

The war for Henderson raged in governmental offices, academic institutions and the international headquarters of conservation pressure groups until finally, in 1988, Ratliffe was beaten, and a treaty was signed designating Henderson a World Heritage Site, alongside the Taj Mahal and Sistine Chapel. The following year, the scientists made a bid to invade the island and, after three years of planning, arrived on Henderson's north beach on July 28, 1991, offloaded four tons of food and equipment and set up their camp.

It struck me as strange that the Pitcairners, who were closest to the land under dispute, who used it and whose country officially included this outlying, uninhabited island, watched the struggle for its shores as bystanders to a battle being fought tens of thousands of miles away. Most of them, if pushed, Ron had said, would have sided with the American billionaire; it was rumored that the scientists' true mission was to record carefully the culling of the tau and miro trees, and then make recommendations to some distant authority that the chopping of wood on Henderson ought to be curtailed. In addition, the scientists offered no financial inducements to the Pitcairners, and the islanders knew that Smiley Ratliffe must be very, very rich.

I asked Dennis, "What's Henderson like?"

He shook his head, unable to find the words, then said, "Se big. Se *wery* big."

Irma returned and set about preparing food as if we were embarking upon an Antarctic expedition, not a trip of two days to a neighboring island. She cooked a couple of dozen lamb chops and potatoes, removing the meat from the bone as Dennis liked, and packed them alongside a five-pound bag of sugar, four packets of spaghetti, tins of crackers, bags of chocolate buttons, loaves of bread, ten packets of sweet biscuits and several of crisps, a great sack of rice, a box of two dozen soft drinks, four dozen tins of corned beef and another two of glutton. Everything was wrapped, then double wrapped to keep out the rain and spray. Sometimes, Irma said, the boat gets quite wet. She folded enough blankets to equip a Salvation Army hostel, and filled two flagons with fresh water. I was fitted out for a pair of rubber-soled sandals, for walking on the coral.

"Do you want to come to the shop, dear?" Irma asked. "We need to get some food."

The Pitcairn Island Co-Operative Society Store's regular opening hours were Monday at two and Thursday at seven, for as long as there were customers, which usually meant about ten minutes at the most. Trade was slow; a few tins of glutton would be a good taking. But the store, on Main Road, which ran from the top of the Hill of Difficulties all the way to the school at Up Pulau, was opened especially so people could get supplies for Henderson. By the time we arrived, the small room with its creaking wooden floors and wooden shelves, mostly bare, was seething with shoppers, each taking items one by one and making their own little pile on the counter by the door. There were even more people outside, and a bench had been constructed along the entire front of the shop, where people who weren't going to Henderson sat and watched the shoppers going in and out. Tom and Betty's teenage daughters were sitting astride a very shiny red bike, flirting with the forlorn youth Glen.

"Going to Henderson, Debbie?" asked the pastor, who was serving behind the counter. I nodded, and tracked Irma like a dog following its mistress.

I soon found myself in a race with Irma to buy up the store's remaining stock. I was determined to prove I was the perfect houseguest; Irma wanted it made known that she was the ideal host. We raided the jars of peanut butter and raspberry jelly stripes, and took the last talcum powder, by mutual agreement giving the pairs of outsize pastel-pink 100 percent nylon knickers a miss. Irma picked two cans of Irish stew with potatoes from a shelf at the back; I took down three. Irma put down four packets of toilet tissue by the cash desk; I matched them with a further four. Irma chose glutton scallops; I dived for the last can of tinned lamb tongues. I opened a huge black bin full of floury brown powder—Milo— but regrettably had brought no container to put it in. We were weighed down with ready-made meals, sweet spreads and toiletries, but the store had no flour, oil, fat or eggs. The supply ship was overdue by more than a month.

We left at night, when the Pitcairners said the sea was becalmed. Those not joining us still came down to the Landing, laying out flattened corrugated cardboard boxes to sit on and watch the parade of watertight plastic barrels containing the food file past. Both longboats, *Tin* and *Tub*, were hauled down from the sheds and the rubber dinghy tied to *Tub*'s stern. I was again impressed by the orderliness of the procedure; everyone had a place and an allotted task, except me. I tried to make myself look busy, offering to lift some of the containers, but the crocodile of carriers was already organized and I only got in the way. I went and sat on the sheets of cardboard with the children until the loading was completed, and then went and joined Dennis on *Tin*. A tarpaulin had been erected like a tent on top of the plywood to the fore of the longboat, under which we could sleep protected from the spray. I laid out one of the blankets Irma had given me and folded my sweater against a food container as a back rest, feeling like a child setting up camp. Carol, Charles Christian, Tony the schoolteacher and Reynold Warren were with me under the tarpaulin. Charles was night blind, so would not be taking the helm in the dark. Reynold, in his sixties, no longer took a watch. The crew consisted of Jay the skipper, Dennis his first mate, with glum Glen and, during daylight, Charles making up the watches.

The pastor said a prayer for our safe passage, the dogs barked, the ropes were loosened, and the sounds on the jetty were sucked away from us as we set out to sea, arranging our belongings and staking out a patch of plywood on which we could sleep. Dennis had warned me that the boat would roll once we left the lee of the island, and soon *Tin* was rocking almost up onto her side and back again. There was only one sound, as deafening and relentless as white noise, of the water slurping and thumping against our hull.

The tarpaulin blocked the view ahead from the tiller, and the helmsman had to steer blind with only the compass as his guide. As Pitcairn was on the New Zealand-Panama route, I was worried that a ship could plow straight over us in the night and we would have no forewarning. I remembered that on NCC *Najran*, once we had cleared Panama, the radar was switched to standby. Only the lookout would have spotted us, if we had showed lights, which we did not.

I asked Jay what would stop us from being run over by a 28,000-ton chemical tanker. "We go a different route," he said.

He explained that *Tin* and *Tub* would sail side by side through the night, the two helmsmen keeping in contact by using their flashlights: one flash every five minutes to let the other boat know all was fine, two flashes to tell them to turn on the handheld VHF radios. If the radios were left on, the batteries would run flat.

"And we won't run into anything!" He considered it the most ridiculous idea, and my only anxiety was buried at the bottom of the ocean.

I had a vision of what we would look like from on high—two toy boats, with the tarpaulins seeming like a wrapping of badly tied brown paper, tossed about on a black sea, with no sails and no lights. But while the ocean battered against itself outside, under our tent we were dry and warm, breathing in each other's breath.

It was impossible to talk to one another because of the noise, and Carol, Charles and Reynold had already hidden themselves under their blankets. Tony was popping pills and trying to look cheery. He pulled a small plastic bag out from his provisions and, as if we were taking tea in an English seaside town, said "Would you like a scone?" then lay down next to me and went to sleep, too. I sat up for a while, wondering how I had ended up here, in an open boat with near strangers, in the blackest night, on the ocean. I looked at Jay standing at the helm, picking up his flashlight to beam at whoever was at *Tub*'s helm, then glancing down at the compass. He must have made this voyage scores of times, since he was a boy, and the wind and the waves washed about him unnoticed. If he was anxious, if he thought there was any possibility of danger, his face didn't show it; his face showed nothing at all, as if he was engaged on a task so familiar that he no longer needed to think about it.

Dennis was checking the engine. "Aw-right?" he shouted over to me. Neither Dennis nor Jay bore any resemblance to the image of a man you might trust with your life. They had cartoon faces with smiles like a child might draw, and soft bodies on spindly legs. But the sight of them aft was comforting, and soon I lay down in the cocoon of our tent.

We arrived off Henderson with the dawn, dropping anchor outside the reef and tucking into breakfast. Reynold remained horizontal, lying at the back nibbling breadsticks, while I had another of Tony's scones with a lump of corned beef Carol had scooped out of the tin with her finger for me. Jay was busy with the engine, and Dennis was talking to *Tub* on the VHF.

A few hundred yards away, the island sat like an iced cake on a sea of silver foil. I could see along its entire length, almost three times as long as Pitcairn. By the time we had idled over our breakfast, *Tub*'s crew and passengers had already gone ashore and Charles disappeared with them. The rubber dinghy came over to pick us up, with young Trent Christian's boy's body at the tiller, his wide-eyed, childish expression crossed by a thick, dark mustache. Trent must have been about eighteen years old, teetering between teenagerdom and manhood, and the two ages were battling within the confines of his skimpy body. He was very, very excited about taking the launch over the reef—he had never done it before, but, wanting to present the attitude of an adult, he assumed an "I-can-handle-it" expression that was so contrived it was almost comic.

Trent was the son of Steve, the swarthy man at the tiller of *Tub*, and Trent obviously modeled his manhood on his parent, from the thick mustache to the way he stood solemnly at the helm of the rubber dinghy, as if he were at the wheel of a four-masted sailing schooner. Steve was already ashore, and waded out from the beach to help guide his son through the reef with hand signals. He seemed to be dragging one of his legs behind him like a log.

The coral reef was impassable at low tide, but at high tide the Pitcairners could negotiate a passage through to the east beach. The essence was timing. You had to hover outside the reef until a roller approached, throw on the engine, and ride through the passage on the crest of the wave. The passage itself was only a foot wider than the rubber dinghy. Dennis pointed out the line of coconut palms they had planted behind the beach as a marker.

Carol, Tony, Glen and I climbed into the launch, while Trent stood at the helm, making the shell-shaped, overloaded boat wobble. We had lingered over breakfast too long, and already the tide was on the turn. Steve—out of earshot—waved his arms to indicate that we should not attempt to cross the reef. Trent turned the tiller and we cruised up and down outside the reef, searching for another opening, but the turbulent surface from the turning tide made it impossible to see through the water, and an increasingly distant Steve was still waving his arms furiously toward the launch in place of shouting, *"Noooooooooo!"*

Trent continued to buzz up and down, studying the surface of the water seriously, before announcing that he was going to wait for a big surf and ride the launch clear over the reef. No one, he said proudly, had ever attempted this maneuver before.

I had an uneasy feeling that this was some sort of initiation ceremony for Trent's journey into manhood, and Carol, Glen, Tony and I were the sacrificial chickens.

Trent shouted, "Read-dee!" and we all shouted, *"No!"*

Uncertain whether this was customary banter before an attempt at crossing the reef, I looked at Carol; if Carol seemed calm, then everything must be under control. Carol looked terrified, and was gripping the ropes lacing the side of the boat.

Tony said, mustering up his authority as governor's adviser, "Don't do anything stupid, Trent," and Trent shouted, "Read-dee!" and then we were balancing on the crest of a wave, tumbling forward at incredible speed.

It was only seconds until there was a horrible crunch. The boat was embedded on the top of the reef like a fakir on a bed of nails.

*"Out!"* screamed Glen. *"Swim!"* And we all threw ourselves into the water.

It was like landing on cut glass; the coral tore at my feet and shins. Behind, the surf was rolling toward us like a moving snow-capped mountain, yet standing on the reef the water barely covered my knees. It was too shallow to swim, too difficult to walk, so, following Glen, I thrashed my way ashore, clambering onto the beach.

The cuts on my legs bled perfect red spots onto the white sand.

"It scars, you know, coral," said Tony, as Glen removed a black anemone's spike from his hand with the point of a knife.

I watched my legs bleed, the spots soon becoming little streams, as if they belonged to someone else. The way the blood ran down the skin and found its way between the crevice of two toes was extraordinary. Following the direction of the trickle, I saw the virgin beach was littered with flotsam and jetsam—a shoe that had lost its heel, pieces of frayed orange rope, coat hangers, a tea strainer, an asthma inhaler and a large number of tiny plastic soldiers. The soldiers lay on their stomachs, their half-inch-long rifles pointing toward the palm trees, as if a Lilliputian army were advancing on Henderson's east beach.

"They're Japanese," said Charles, emerging from the coconut palms, his dirt-encrusted shorts in the style of a shipwrecked sailor who has only one set of clothes.

"The Japanese are very funny people," he said. "They throw plastic soldiers over the side of the ship, huge numbers of them, to bring good luck with fishing."

I asked him how he had heard of this strange custom, and he tapped his temple with his forefinger. "It's in here."

Charles Christian was Pitcairn's expert on international affairs, due to the fact that he had been born in San Francisco. His mother had been a Pitcairner, his father an American. His mother had brought her young son back to the island when he was five years old.

Although he had never returned to his birthplace, Charles still cultivated a faint American accent—or he seemed to, but perhaps it was only suggested by his manner and look, which was rather like that of a retired baseball coach. Perhaps, over the phone, Charles would sound completely Pitcairn.

Tony suggested we go for a walk along the beach to collect shells for the Pitcairn Island School shell project. We walked along slowly, the sun bouncing off the sand. Every few yards, Tony would bend down, pick up a delicately stippled shell—a whipped cone of pinks, browns and grays— say, "Oh, it's only a up'e," or "hi'i" or "potala," and throw it back down on the beach again. Tony said he liked organizing projects; Pitcairn was a great place for them. The shell project was one of his ideas, as was the Pitcairn Island Museum.

The Pitcairn Island School stamp project had been particularly successful. Mail came from all over the world, he said; I'd be surprised, hundreds of letters at a time, and collecting the stamps was a good geography lesson for the kids. He'd had a letter from Burma in the last mail, as well as stamp hinges from the Pitcairn Islands Study Group in England, who had heard about the stamp project, but unfortunately the termites had nibbled pinpricks in the paper hinges, and turned them into dust.

Tony was picking up shells and throwing them down without even looking at them now; he missed, he said, New Zealand. He'd been teaching in a two-room school on the South Island, with not that many more pupils than on Pitcairn. His wife, Christine, missed New Zealand, too, but the kids loved it here, it was like a big adventure for them.

It was an extraordinary place, Tony had to admit, and of particular interest to him was how the island worked. If he had the time, he'd set himself the project of writing a book entitled something like *Politics and Power on Pitcairn: the Government Perspective.* It was wrong to think that the political leader held any real power; Jay Warren might be island magistrate, and therefore chairman of the Island Council, but he did not hold court. The most important person on the island was the supervising engineer, because he was the one who could fix things, and that was Steve Christian. Steve also had three teenage sons—Trent, Randy and Shaun— all hard workers. And sons were far less likely to leave the island for good than daughters. There was even, Tony thought, a hangover from the days of the mutiny, and an islander with the surname Christian was accorded more status than a Warren, Young or Brown, who were not considered natural leaders.

But the most obvious display of this division of power, Tony continued, was in the crewing of the two longboats. *Tin* was the older, smaller and less powerful vessel, and her crew were considered junior to *Tub*'s skipper Steve and his men. *Tub*, the more sturdy and prestigious boat, had been purchased to replace the old wooden longboat *Stick*. In Auckland, *Tub* had been officially christened *O'Leary* in honor of the then Governor Terence Daniel O'Leary, Companion of St. Michael and St. George, who had rubber-stamped the expense. But on her arrival at Pitcairn the islanders, unimpressed, had renamed her *Tub*.

"And you're not a man," Tony added, filling me in on the symbols of male authority, "if you don't carry a knife." Tony was weaponless.

Tony continued to pick up shells, now holding their small frilled shapes up as if tiny crystal balls, and talking into them.

"If you want to say 'I don't want to conform' in the big wide world, you can find other people, join a club, be seen as a radical. But here, if you're out of line, everyone looks at you very strangely," he said to a hi'i, then threw it down. "This island fosters the sense of belonging, of belonging to Pitcairn."

Tony wore as many hats as any other islander. In addition to being education officer, government adviser ("the man-on-the-spot," said Tony) and government auditor, he was editor of *The Pitcairn Miscellany*. Last mail, he received 137 letters, and, proud of his efficiency, he had written eighty-four replies to requests for information about Pitcairn.

"People think that Pitcairn is a romantic place where there's still much evidence of the *Bounty*. People keep telling us they have a desire to come to Pitcairn—*many* people—but know that it's so isolated that they'll never get here. Other people name their yachts *Pitcairn*. Perhaps they think that it's a sort of omen, that the yacht will then come here," and Tony sort of laughed. "Some write poems about Pitcairn in all sorts of languages, and about the *Bounty*. One told us how excited he was to fly over Pitcairn from Tahiti to Easter Island, although he couldn't possibly have done. It's not on the route. Many people have a wish to get to Pitcairn, but never will."

Mary from Kansas City had been one of the few. She was a painter, and had designed the new masthead for the *Miscellany*.

"Good, isn't it? She was a great artist." Tony spoke of Mary as if she were dead.

As we walked and talked, the sawing began. At first there was just the faint warbling of a few blades, but soon more chainsaws were pulled, and the brittle island vibrated. We padded back toward the sound, coming from a small forest of trees immediately behind the strip of sand. I went searching for Dennis, finding him deep in a copse, in a felling frenzy. He was surrounded by trunks that had suffered severe amputations, and branches of all sizes were thrown about him. I gathered up one of the smaller ones and dragged it backward out onto the beach. Clarice was emerging like a tank pushing through another part of the wood, balancing what seemed to be a whole tree trunk on each shoulder, which she dropped in a pile next to mine. Behind her she left just the track of her footprints; behind me was the evidence of my feebleness—the scar of a slender log being dragged through the sand. And by the time I reemerged from the copse for the second time, I noticed that Clarice's pile had already been added to by two more thick logs, and Clarice was pounding back into the trees.

I came out from the copse struggling with a particularly heavy log, wishing I had left it for Dennis to bring out later, when Clarice came up and offered to help, not by speaking, but by nodding toward the log. I nodded back, and hugged one end, waiting for Clarice to hoist up the other. She grabbed it and, with the same muscle that had saved my legs on the rope ladder two days before, threw it over her shoulder and marched down to the water's edge. I watched, empty-handed and humbled, and wondered how Pitcairn women had ever been thought too weak to make the Henderson trip.

Royal threw a log down next to me, and scoffed at my puny pile. I tried to distract her.

"Are you going to visit the scientists?" I asked, and she scoffed again, returning to the wood.

Every so often, one of the scientists would appear from the path that led to the camp, stand and watch the Pitcairners as each family built their own pile of wood on the beach, and disappear back up the path. It was like being observed by a wild animal who shied from human contact, as these creatures looked so different from the islanders. Each scientist seemed emaciated, with a bare chest and a bony body covered by a pair of brief shorts. The only part of the Pitcairners' bodies that was always naked— their feet—the scientists had clad with thick, ankle-high mountain boots. Once, a female scientist crept out of the wood to observe us, wearing nothing more than a skimpy bikini and these heavy boots.

I suggested to Charles, who was sitting on the beach looking out toward *Tin*, that we go and look at their camp.

"They're mad," he said, shaking his head. "You should see the things they do back there."

At last admitting to myself that I was of little use to Dennis, who had many more willing helpers far more capable than I of stacking his wood, I ventured alone up the path leading to the camp. It emerged in an opening in the wood, about which were scattered several tiny canvas, khaki-colored tents. In the center of the clearing was a massive homemade wooden table, with one leg sprouting leaves. A large tarpaulin had been hung over the table as a primitive roof. Walking about the camp, like toy trains running on predetermined tracks, were the scientists, each on a different path. I interrupted one of them who was younger and taller than the others, with a mop of sunset hair. Dr. Alexander Chepstow-Lusty was responsible for microfaunal studies. This involved collecting, washing and sieving minute particles of seaweed on which could be found ostracods and foraminifera, which were then sent for analysis to an expert in Aberystwyth, Wales. The other scientists were engaged in similar specialist research. Two millimeter-long snails were being preserved in alcohol, preserved rats were to be posted to Wellington, live ticks had been collected for the Institute of Virology in Oxford, fruit dove feces were gathered for laboratory analysis in Canada, petrel-feather lice were being obtained for New Zealand's National Museum, and the Henderson warbler was being DNA fingerprinted.

"Some species," Chepstow-Lusty informed me, "may be new to science."

He offered to take me on an expedition into the interior by way of one of the paths the scientists had hacked through the coral. As he strode out in front, I followed the soles of his huge boots, the only substantial part of his long and lanky body. The coral earth crunched under our feet and ripped away at my rubber soles as if we were walking over broken china plates. The doctor advised me to watch out for coral crevasses; if you fell into one it would rip your leg open. I had the strong impression that Henderson was not designed for human beings, either in coming ashore or getting about, and perhaps that was another reason why the scientists had such an alien look about them.

"Have you brought anything to sustain you?" asked Chepstow-Lusty.

I hadn't realized he was planning a daylong trek, and thought longingly of the watertight containers of cooked lamb chops and potatoes.

"Mentally, I mean," he continued.

I mentioned that I had packed my copy of *Return to Laughter,* as I did on every journey, and each time I found in it comforting thoughts and fresh guidelines for my own experience. By the light of my torch on the night of Charlene's party, I had discovered another succinct reflection of my barely formed fears:

> It was hot when I awoke, and clear. The yard was full of women's voices punctuated with laughter . . . I peered around the mat. About a dozen women were sitting under my tree, knee deep in calabashes and children. I stood behind my mat, silent, immobile, wrestling with a sensation I came to know all too well in the months that followed: *I wanted to talk to people; I couldn't bear to meet them.*

I paraphrased this for Chepstow-Lusty's benefit. Pitcairn was, he said, an awkward place if you didn't belong, like being a gate-crasher at a family funeral.

"Perry isn't liked very much," he added. "He doesn't fit in."

I found this perplexing. I had seen Perry helping unload trading goods from the *Tundra Queen,* and, from the back of Dennis's bike, I had spotted him up on a roof, hammering nails into someone's new home. Irma had said that he fished and worked the garden for Betty and Tom, in whose house he stayed, in the same way she hoped I would work for her. On the passage to Henderson, Dennis had pointed to Perry, as he took a watch at *Tub*'s helm. I was lost as to what more he could do.

The day's sawing drew slowly to a close, the noise died down, and most of the Pitcairners were being ferried back out to the longboats, where they would sleep for the night. Not wanting to make an unnecessary journey over the reef, I opted to spend the night ashore with three of the Pitcairners—Charles, Nigger and Trent—and the pastor and Tony. We sought the protection of the scientists' camp, laying out our blankets under the tarpaulin. Nigger asked me, "Do you drink?" which I answered with a quizzical look. I knew Nigger was the police officer, and responsible for preventing the importation of alcohol onto the island. He shrugged, and went off to see Henderson's lone female scientist.

I slept on the ground between Tony and the pastor, the long-nosed rats that had escaped being preserved using our three pairs of ankles as a hurdling course.

The sea brewed up overnight, but the sky was clear, which meant another day of felling ahead, and shortly after dawn the island resounded with the sound of chainsaws. Over breakfast one of the scientists asked what I hoped to find on Pitcairn: I answered that I was looking for a place free from the petty stresses of London life, somewhere gentler, a little piece of Paradise, perhaps.

By the afternoon, most of the wood had been dragged down to the beach. The logs were lined up like railway sleepers, and each had to be tied to the one in front until they formed a giant track across the sand, as if a train running lemminglike out to sea. I helped to tie them together, noticing that Clarice checked each of my knots; if one slipped, the whole web would untangle, and all the wood would be lost. The end of the rope-and-log railway was tied to the back of the boat, and one by one the logs bounced over the sand and were pulled into the water and out over the reef, where Steve and his helpers loaded them onto *Tin* and *Tub*.

"Amazing, isn't it?" said Tony, as we watched the last ladder of logs float out. It was such a simple, purposeful system and I was full of admiration for the Pitcairners' ingenuity.

The sea was noticeably more choppy than in the morning, and the wind had turned and was blowing briskly from the direction of Pitcairn, which meant we would be battling against the swell. The female scientist, whose belly was so flat that from the side you could hardly see her at all, informed me that the choppy weather was due to El Niño, a southeast current in the Pacific that, every few years, becomes so warm that it kills the coral, plankton and fish, and the seabirds and seals which feed on them abandon their nests and lose their young. The decaying fish accumulate on beaches, producing clouds of sulfurous gas. The climatic changes bring torrential rain and floods to usually dry regions, and produce drought. Freak waves sweep across the ocean. Our skipper, Jay, wary of the changing weather, suggested that we stay an extra night to see how it developed, but Steve, master of *Tub*, was eager to set sail now the job had been done.

Reboarding *Tin* was like crawling back into a tent that, for a while, you've come to regard as home. It smelled of our bedclothes and two-day-old breakfast, which wasn't unpleasant at all, but reassuring. Henderson was so very plain compared with Pitcairn, with nothing to break the plank of gray coral except for a few stunted trees, like the difference between the flat tarmac of a schoolyard and the richness of a park. And there were strangers on Henderson, people who weren't Pitcairners, who could have come from anywhere, who weren't related to anyone else. The sea might be brewing up and the wind not in our favor, but I was snug among the Pitcairners, and in capable hands.

The return voyage would be far less comfortable than the outward leg as *Tin*'s hold was stacked with wood, so all our belongings had to be kept above deck and there was even less room to lie under the tarpaulin. Tony settled himself in, took the film canister in which he secreted his travel sickness tablets from the depths of his bedding and popped it open. His eyes and mouth fell, as if all the muscles had suddenly gone. Very, very slowly he tilted the film canister and let the seawater trickle out onto the deck, staring down at the little powdery puddle. The waves washed it like a miniature river toward one gunwale, leaving a white trail behind it.

Tony looked up at me. "You feeling all right?" he asked, hoping that I shared his horror.

"Fine," I said perkily and, snuggling under my blanket between him and Carol, fell asleep, dreaming I was in a battle for Henderson's east beach, commanding a battalion of Pitcairners each armed with a chain-saw, which they brandished before them.

*Whaaaaaaaaaaaaaaack!*

For a waking moment, I thought a thunderbolt had hit the boat. But I was wet, and water was surging in. Below me, where before I had seen logs, was a whirl of water. A freak wave had come up over the bow, smashed through the plywood on which the tent rested, and flooded the overloaded boat. The engine sputtered, coughed once, then stopped, as it disappeared beneath a wave. We began to sink.

I turned to Carol; she was screaming, but no sound came out, as if I were deaf. We sank not as they do in films, slowly, but very fast, falling down into the ocean like a pebble. The water, which had been yards below me, had soon risen so high up the side of the boat that I could trail my finger in it. It was the temperature of a stiff bath—not *so* cold, I thought, calculating how long I might survive in it. But as black as a bottomless pit.

The rollers heaved about us. There was no point in screaming out loud, because no one could hear us. We were thousands of miles away from any form of rescue, with no means of communication. The ocean had invaded, the spell of being safe on *Tin* had been broken, and now our smallness, which had made me feel so snug, was terrifying. No one could ever find our tiny unlit longboat on these seas.

We searched the water for *Tub*, but we couldn't see her. We must have been separated in the heavy seas, and *Tub*'s VHF radio had been turned off to save the batteries. Jay was standing by the helm, furiously flashing his light.

We all scrambled for our own flashlights and began flashing, too. We flashed and flashed as the water teased us, washing over the deck and lapping at our ankles. Still nothing.

"One more wave like that, and we sink," said Jay, and sent up a flare. The red light exploded in the sky. Our faces turned up, and we fell down again as we watched it fizzle out and drop into the ocean.

"You feel all right?" asked Tony.

My fingers sank into his fleshy arm. "Afraid," I breathed. It was the only word I spoke.

It was Dennis who first spotted *Tub*'s light. "Put on ha radio. *Put on ha radio!*" he screamed at the ocean.

But *Tub* just flashed back as if winking at us, innocent of the fact that her sister ship was sinking.

Jay screeched into the dead VHF, "We take in water. We going down. Engine gone . . ."

*Tub* seemed to be coming closer, ambling over the ocean as if spurred by curiosity rather than on a rescue mission. At first the faces on board were indistinct, just a huddle of humans, but it was buoying to know that there was someone else out on the black ocean, who might save us. Then I could make out Royal and Clarice, and saw Terry Young at the helm. I whispered their names over and over to myself, because their names, other people's names, killed my fear. Steve Christian took charge and tied a rope to our prow, and *Tub* towed us ignobly back to Henderson, where we anchored off the reef, sleeping through what was left of the night.

. . .

The scientists treated us to breakfast ashore. Their canvas larder was well stocked, and we feasted on pâté on Scandinavian-style whole-wheat crispbread. Charles was in good form, and regaled us with morbid tales. On one trip to Henderson, human skeletons had been found in the mouth of a cave on the northern tip of the island. The scientists said they were from shipwrecked sailors, and had sent them back to an expert in Ohio for carbon dating. But Charles knew better. Once, centuries ago, before the mutineers found Pitcairn, Polynesians had inhabited the Pitcairn group and made excursions to Henderson to have feasts, much like a general party, except that they ate each other.

The near sinking and near loss of *Tin* was another gory tale for Charles's repertoire.

"Should've been a mutiny, if you ask me," he said. "Never should have gone out in that headwind. I remember when . . ." and he repeated a story that was all too familiar to the Pitcairners, of a trip to Oeno, another uninhabited island in the Pitcairn group. Once two boats, with twenty-nine men, had made an expedition to Oeno to collect bêche-de-mer. It was the winter season, and the seas were heavy, but the weather had been fair for a good week and a period of calm was promised. They sailed from Pitcairn on December 6, planning to gather their sea cucumbers and be home for Christmas; one week later, the men and boys who had remained on Pitcairn decided they, too, wanted to share in the crop, and went to join them in a third boat. Christmas came and went, and there was no sign of the men. December 25 was celebrated only by the women and girls. By New Year's, the men had still not come home, and there were no celebrations; instead, prayers were said.

Five weeks after they had set out for Oeno, the boats were spotted off Pitcairn, the faint crew near starvation and smothered in boils. They had been battling to set sail from Oeno for five weeks, and had been continually thrown back by the headwinds. They had packed provisions to last until Christmas, and, for as long as they could remember, had been rationed to two biscuits a day. Now all Irma's tins and parcels of cooked chops seemed like a sensible precaution. We had planned only a two-day trip, but we could have been stranded on Henderson for weeks.

We arrived back on Pitcairn at three o'clock in the morning, with the dogs and the islanders there to greet us with hot drinks and warm blankets as if it were the middle of the afternoon. It was, incredibly, only my second day on the island. Already my hopes for a lazy South Pacific sojourn were seriously shaken. On one of the postcards that Irma had given me for the steward of the *Tundra Queen*, I wrote my first letter home: "Arrived safely. Since then, life threatened several times."

# 6 · *s a b b a t h*

"So you're having an affair with my husband?"

Christine was kneading, and her thickened arms, her crisp dress smothered in small flowers, and her short, neat, dark hair all drew the portrait: here was a capable schoolteacher's wife baking bread for her family.

Her clenched fist thumped the dough.

"I've had a visitor," she said. "Who told me all about it."

She pounded the dough into a loaf pan, opened the oven door, threw the pan inside, watched until it clattered to a standstill and slammed the door shut. I felt all queasy.

"Uaach," a strange whelp emerged from my mouth, as if I were drowning.

Chris cleaned the flour from the table in one wide, efficient swipe, and burst out laughing. Her solid chest moved up and down in time to each slow, deep chuckle—*ha, ha, ha, ha, ha.*

"You don't think I *believe* it, do you? You should never believe what people tell you round here."

Chris explained how, two days after we had arrived back from Henderson, one of the older women who had remained behind had come to pay her a call. The schoolteacher's house, Up Pulau, as it was called, was on the far west side of town, at least five hundred yards from the Square. Some of the women used to visit in the long afternoons, to take a break from the bustle of the town center, have a chat and sample some of Chris's excellent baking. Her meringues were particularly popular; competent Chris kept hens in a wire coop at the back of the house, so the schoolteacher's family had a constant supply of eggs. She also had a dehydrator, which had been delivered on the last supply ship, an appliance that was as yet unknown to the islanders. The dehydrator could dry vegetables and fruit, in particular bananas, in fourteen hours, a great saving on having to spread them outside on a table in the sun for weeks, turning them each day, with the threat of a sudden downpour ruining them.

The islanders coveted Chris's appliance, and were soon writing letters to relations in New Zealand asking them to put a dehydrator on the next supply ship. But while they waited on the response to their requests, Chris remained the proud sole owner of a dehydrator on Pitcairn. It sat on top of a cabinet in the corner of the sitting room, letting off wind as the lid rattled with each labored puff like an elderly relative who had come for tea and never gone home.

When the woman had paid Chris a visit two days ago, she had brought some bananas to be dried, a small, thick variety, like chubby children's fingers, which the islanders called China. They had sat together with the burping dehydrator, weaving baskets, while the older woman told Chris the tale of Chris's husband's passionate affair with that new girl, Debbie.

The evidence was irrefutable. Tony and I had snuggled up to each other in *Tin;* we had gone for a long walk, alone, on Henderson's east beach; we had even had the audacity to lie out next to each other at night in the scientists' camp, with the pastor only a few feet away. By the return voyage, we were openly flaunting our attachment; when *Tin* was struck, we sat close, holding hands and whispering to each other. The woman felt obliged to inform Chris, as they were such good friends.

"But she wasn't even *there,*" I pleaded. "How *could* she know all that?"

"Someone must have told her."

"Then why would she come and tell *you?* Why would she hurt you?"

"Perhaps she knew I would never believe it of Tony."

"Does *she* believe it?"

"God knows."

The weather had brewed up, even since our return. The sky would darken and burst with a screech of rain, the sun break through with unnatural vigor, then the rain would strike again. It was as if a giant strobe light were being shone on the island, and we were all dancers at the disco. One minute the windometer up at Taro Ground would be recording a gentle blow at twenty knots, the next gusting to fifty. The whipping of wet palm fronds and banging of the duncan door alternated with still moments, when the surf reasserted itself as the beat of Pitcairn.

"You coming to church?" Ben said at breakfast. "You don't have to wear anything special. Just something nice and clean."

Ben was dressed in his Sabbath best, a pair of nylon trousers, a checked Viyella shirt, and knitted tie. The nylon trousers had a polished patch on the top of Ben's right thigh, where his Bible hung. Irma was wearing a dress that one of her radio contacts had sent her as a present. The contact's vision of Pitcairn was obviously of a Sunbury-on-Thames in the South Seas, as the dress was nylon, too, with a fitted waist, and patterned with minuscule pink flowers.

Irma would be playing the organ, and it was Ben's turn to read the lesson. He sat at the table mouthing the verses to himself. Ben, who executed every task at a snail's pace, nevertheless spent a great deal of time patiently waiting for Irma, who always found the contents of another freezer to rearrange or cupboard to tidy before she could leave the house.

I sat down next to Ben, and repeated the conversation I had had with Jay on the way to Henderson about my fear of the longboat being run over by a chemical tanker. How silly I had been. Of course I knew now that the big ships took a different route from the tiny longboat!

"Tip out one time," said Ben.

"What do you mean?"

"A ship jus keep comen. Tip us right out ha boat."

"You mean it hit you?"

"Ye-es. Tip us right out."

"All of you?"

"Ye-es. Tip ha boat right over."

"How were you rescued?"

He was chuckling away quietly to himself, remembering. "Ha other boat come and fish us all out."

"Do have a cup of coffee, dear," Irma fussed.

I shook my head. "No thanks."

"No dear, do," and she pressed an empty cup into my hand as a grown-up might squeeze a five-pound note into the palm of a child.

"Please make it yourself," and she rushed off to check the sweet coconut rice baking in the oven.

The Seventh-day Adventist Sabbath commences at sunset on Friday night, and no one is allowed to cook again until sunset on Saturday. But the Adventist faith had had to adapt to the gargantuan Pitcairn appetite, and it was agreed that turning on a cooker did not count as cooking, so you could boil, fry and bake on Sabbath—as Saturday was always known—but you could not peel, pod or slice. So Fridays—known as Preparation—were spent chopping peppers, mixing sweet rice and kneading dough, which was left to rise and bake on Sabbath.

Dennis was slumped in front of the television set, watching a

*National Geographic* video "The Great Barrier Reef." His whole body oozed defiance—his tightly crossed arms, his feet slung up on a stool and spiraling around from the ankles, his unswerving stare at the screen only a few feet away from him. His father was an elder of the church and his mother one of the church's most vigorous supporters, and Ben and Irma must have longed for their only son to join them in the pews. Dennis intended to hurt them, and did so with the defiance of a teenager, although he was thirty-six. Perhaps he also wanted to demonstrate to me that he, Dennis Christian, was his own man.

Dennis's stand for independence had its limits; although the video cabinet was stacked high with made-for-TV miniseries and Dennis's favorite Charles Bronson movies, on Sabbath the only material it was permissible to read or watch was that which glorified God—the Bible, *National Geographic* (in magazine or video form) and the *Reader's Digest,* which Irma informed me was a religious publication.

The fossil fish swam about the opal sea as music tinkled in time to its graceful movements. The narrator's voice was slow and soothing, making the underwater world on screen seem as welcoming as a warm bath. Dennis's toes began to wiggle, as if swimming themselves, and he seemed oblivious to the shaking of the weatherboard walls and tin roof as a sudden gust of wind whipped over the house.

The wind seemed to be subsiding when Ben called out, "See you in church! Dunner capsize!" and he and Irma, who had at last put all the freezer contents to rest, ventured out from the veranda. I thought it a typically overcautious warning from Ben; I had had almost a full week's practice at negotiating Pitcairn's steep paths, and it was only a five-minute stroll to the Square and the church.

I had put on a pink-and-white-striped cotton seersucker skirt and blouse, the most appropriate churchgoing outfit I had with me, and a

---

*dunner*—don't
*capsize*—fall over, from the old nautical term

proper pair of shoes. I covered myself up in my waterproof, borrowed Dennis's Bible so I could follow the lesson and stepped outside. My waterproof tore against me like a sail. I spotted frothy whitecaps on the waves, before the rain came down like a sheet of smoky glass, pounding at my waterproof, and the wind tore down my hood. Within seconds, I was as wet inside as out.

The most direct path to the Square was curved and steep, down past Mavis's, where I would have to ward off her dogs, which would jump all over me with their wet paws and dirty my seersucker outfit. I decided to take the longer but less steep route via Carol and Jay's.

The red mud paths managed to be slippery and sticky at the same time. Within a few paces, my shoes had been sucked off so many times that I had to abandon them under some Indian Shot, to be collected later. It was like wading through a sea of quicksand, and great effort was needed to extract my feet. My toes began to ache, as they had to work in a way in which they never had done before, clawing into the earth like an eagle's talons clinging to a rock. I now understood why the Pitcairners' toes spread out like fingers, as the mud forced itself up between them, splaying them, so the ends of their feet were far broader than their heels.

I put my next foot down more gingerly, and gripped some overhanging palm fronds, hoping that if I skipped nimbly over the mud's surface I wouldn't sink in. Instead I slipped up, landing heavily on my bottom with my waterproof ruffled up around my waist. My skirt was streaked with red slime. I pushed myself up, as my hands and cuffs sank into the earth. The rain was unrelenting, although I was more likely to get wet from rivulets running along the ground, for in many places the leaves above the road were knitted so thickly that only a few drops stung through. The rain and the leaves also blocked out the light, and it was dusk under the vegetation.

By the time I turned the corner at Carol and Jay's for the final descent down to the Square, I had been on the road for twenty minutes and had traveled less than two hundred yards. The service was already underway, and I could hear singing rising from the Square and Irma pounding away at the organ.

> *There'll be no dark valley when Jesus comes.*
> *There'll be no dark valley when Jesus comes.*
> *There'll be no dark valley when Jesus comes*
> *To gather His loved ones home.*

It sounded like a mighty chorus, and the church beckoned as a haven from the elements outside.

I disrobed at the church door. Apart from a waistcoat of clean blouse, my clothes were red with mud and clung to me like a winding sheet, revealing every bump and crevice of my body. I wasn't only barefoot and dirty, I was also indecent. The singing had just stopped, and I opened the door softly so I could creep unnoticed into a pew at the back.

"*Welcome, Debbie.*" The pastor's greeting boomed from the stage at the front of the church. "Good you could join us."

If he had not been standing where the pastor ought to, I would hardly have recognized him. Instead of his undershirt and see-through fluorescent shorts, he was wearing a white shirt and dark trousers, and had put on a pair of heavy black-rimmed glasses, the sort usually attached to a plastic nose. To his left stood Ben, and to his right Tom Christian, a pillar in shirt and tie. Behind the elders was a crude painting, reaching to the roof, of Pitcairn Island, with an unnaturally calm sea lapping against the rocks. Written on the painting in flowery script were the words "The Lord Is My Rock and My Fortress." In a glass case below the stage was displayed the Bible from the *Bounty*.

Tom's family—his wife, Betty, and their two teenage daughters— lined one wooden pew, decorated in fussy dresses with puffy sleeves trimmed with lace, in the style of Southern Baptists. The pastor's wife, Jenny, and their three children sat nearby. Just in front of me was Kari with her two children. She seemed absorbed in her Bible. Mavis and Jacob, the only man not on the stage, were on the opposite side of the aisle, alongside Carol and Charlene, with Royal in a pew to herself a couple of rows behind. Irma had mentioned that Royal had not spoken to Mavis, her sister, for more than ten years. When I had asked why, Irma said, "You know how it is, dear," and had changed the subject.

The church was well wired. The pastor spoke into a microphone, and there was an overhead projector to display the words to the hymns. But the wooden pews, designed to hold about two hundred, were home to only fifteen.

The congregation had followed the pastor's gaze and turned to rest their eyes upon me.

"Maybe your safe return from the boat trip made you think you had something to thank God for," he said.

I sank into the pew, wishing a hole would open up into hell. Then Ben beamed at me, so delighted that I had come, and caring so little about my disheveled appearance, that I beamed back, knowing that I had done the right thing.

The pastor launched into his sermon. The subject was secularism.

"Of all those things," he jabbed at the air, "which question our religion—atheism, evolution, secularism—sec-u-lar-ism is by far the worst."

Secularism was the most pernicious way in which our faith was being attacked, he continued, and the most difficult to pin down. Secularism was the stealthy enemy, pervading our lives without us even realizing it.

"How many times have you seen a religious program on TV?" The pastor quizzed the congregation. "You may see a late, midnight show, or a brief prayer in the morning, but how many times have you seen a whole program devoted to Christianity?"

He repeated the question over and over again, getting louder each time.

"How many times? *How many times have you seen a religious program on TV?*"

I wondered if he was genuinely asking a question and, if so, whether I should respond as if to a litany, citing all the Christian TV channels, satellited throughout the world—*The Old Time Gospel Hour,* the *700 Club,* the Jimmy Baker and Jimmy Swaggart shows. But more, I felt like shouting out, "How the hell should we know? *We don't have TV on Pitcairn.*"

But it was dispiriting enough for the pastor, as the congregation talked throughout his sermon, the younger children ran up and down the aisle while the older ones sat and read nature books, and nobody seemed to be paying much attention except Irma, and Tom Christian's family, who sat with their hands resting on their laps and a fixed smile, as if a royal family having their portrait painted.

I had seen this portrait of Tom's family before, as they were the most photographed of all the Pitcairners, being the most handsome. They had, a couple of years earlier, been invited by the church to the United States, soon after the centenary celebrations for Pitcairn's embrace of the Adventist faith in 1886, and been toured as an exhibit from the South Seas from an island billed as the perfect Adventist community, free from earthly sin and waiting for the Second Coming.

The story of the islanders' conversion was another fantastic chapter in Pitcairn's history. In 1856, the island's population had grown rapidly to 187, and there were fears that the land would no longer be able to sustain them, especially after the fish had deserted coastal waters since the landslides caused by the great storm a decade earlier. A total evacuation was organized to Norfolk Island, a former penal colony equidistant between New Zealand and Australia. But many of those who left quickly became dissatisfied with their larger, more accommodating new home, and, after two years in exile, sailed back to Pitcairn.

When the returning families walked into Adamstown, rather than finding their homes had become disheveled and overgrown, they saw that they had been lived in while they had been away, and a few had been carefully dismantled plank by plank. A message was scratched on a slate in the school explaining these strange circumstances, signed Captain J. N. Knowles.

Captain Knowles had been on a voyage from San Francisco when his ship was wrecked seventy miles southwest of Pitcairn. Abandoning his crew on a deserted island (perhaps Henderson), he had taken six men off in the ship's boat to look for help. But, after only a few days at sea, this boat, too, was wrecked, thrown against the cliffs in Bounty Bay. Discovering Adamstown abandoned, Captain Knowles and his men set about disassembling some of the homes and using the timber to construct a boat, which, knowing the story of the mutiny on board HMAV *Bounty,* they named the *John Adams,* and in which they sailed away.

Twenty-two years after his ordeal, the Captain returned to the island, bringing with him letters from the leaders of a rapidly growing religious movement in the United States, the Seventh-day Adventist Church. In 1886, John Tay, an Adventist from Oakland, California, became the first missionary ever to visit Pitcairn, and within five weeks all the islanders were converted. It was inconceivable that anyone would dissent. Tay returned to California with the good news, and the Church immediately commissioned the building of a mission ship for the South Seas, calling her *Pitcairn.* Pitcairn Island was the new ship's first port of call, where she arrived in 1890. The pigs were thrown over the edge of the cliffs to remove the temptation of consuming pork, and the entire community was baptized by immersion.

The pastor called out more questions concerning the secularism threatening our small community, but nobody offered any answers.

"What do you think is a really good sign about a society? What tells you what a society is like?" The pastor pecked like a hen as he spoke.

The children went on banging their toys against the wooden pews, the pastor's eldest son more vigorously than the rest, and the adults gossiped in a whisper.

"Go on—guess," the pastor challenged. *"Guess."*

There was no response.

"The buildings." The pastor answered his own question, his whole body sighing. "The buildings give a very good idea of a society. The tallest buildings show what is most important. Look at the Parthenon in Athens, on the top of a hill. You can still see it today. Look at the cathedral that used to be the tallest building in the city. Now what is it? *Now what is it?* Financial institutions dominate nearly every skyline."

It was still raining heavily outside, bouncing off the concreted Square, the tin roofs of the one-room dispensary, one-room library and the one-room post office. It could be heard pounding against the timber of the island magistrate's office and the courthouse opposite, where the Council sat and in front of which the anchor of HMAV *Bounty* was displayed on a plinth.* The church was partly stone built, the only building on Pitcairn to be so. There was no two-storied construction on Pitcairn; the public buildings were single-story concrete or timber boxes topped with tin, the private houses weatherboard. There was no bank.

"Finance dominates our lives. People's main concern the world over is money." And the pastor read Matthew 6:24: " 'No one can serve two masters. Either he will hate the one and love the other, or he will be devoted to the one and despise the other. You cannot serve both God and Money.' "

He was quoting from the New International Version, published by the New York Bible Society, copies of which we all held in front of us. His sermon might have been meaningful in Manhattan, but in a storm on Pitcairn his dire warnings rang hollow.

We sang number 470 from the Seventh-day Adventist Hymnal—"There's Sunshine in My Soul Today"—and Tom put on his glasses and read out the Pitcairn news in English: Pathfinders this afternoon had been canceled because of the bad weather; sunset tonight would be at 5:29, and at 5:29 again next Sabbath. There would be a prayer meeting on Tuesday night. A list showing the family to be prayed for each week was pinned up on the board. Every family on the island had a week of prayer dedicated to

---

* The *Bounty* would have carried at least five anchors—two bowers, a sheet, a stream and a kedge.

them, whether they were churchgoing or not. This Tuesday, Nigger Brown's family would be in our thoughts.

Ben came around with the collection bag. Some put in coins, others notes of American or New Zealand dollars. Our lesson book, which was distributed to every Adventist community, showed the weekly target worldwide, and on what the combined collections would be spent. This week the collections would raise money for twenty-five bicycles for pastors in Burma, at U.S. $175 each, making, I quickly calculated, less than five thousand dollars needed in all.

On an easel in the corner, a pin placed in a map of the world showed us where this week's money went—Burma—and a chart recorded how much had been collected on Pitcairn each week. Last week, $47.50 had been put into the collection bag. If Adventist congregations throughout the South Pacific, numbering in tens of thousands, raised as much, Burma would be awash with pedal power. The surplus must be accruing at a furious pace.

As the pastor shook our hands when we filed out of the church, I could hear the *chink-chink* of Royal counting out the collection on the pew.

The fierce weather continued through Sunday, and we were trapped inside with only Royal brave enough to visit us. On Monday, the wind tore a branch off the big mango tree at the back of the house. Irma's corn crop was destroyed. El Niño was causing havoc, slashing away at tiny Pitcairn. But with no reliable way of making contact beyond our shores, at least the awesome power of El Niño connected Pitcairn to the rest of the world. I liked to imagine that the gust now shaking the door to our duncan had once rattled a roof on Rarotonga.

Dennis spent the morning in front of the video. When the island generator was shut down halfway through *The Fourth Protocol,* he sat staring as the screen fizzled away into a red dot and did not move, so I wondered if he had been asleep all the time. Then, a few moments later, he cocked his head, heard that the rain had ceased and asked if I would like to go to St. Paul's Point.* It was at the eastern tip of the island, so a major outing, especially in this weather.

We drove through a scene of destruction: the wind had snapped the banana trees in two as if matchsticks, and the severed trunks seeped pungent sap. The rain had washed down the roads forming deep ridges, making driving easy. All Dennis had to do was lodge the front wheel of his bike into a ridge and we rode along like a tram on its lines. We passed abandoned homes, where branches had fallen against the weathered walls, blocking windows and bringing down water pipes. We passed Ben's wild beans, the neat rows indiscernible, the plants all blown over, and the pods scorched and scattered like seed by the wind. It struck me how volatile the Pitcairn landscape was, and how much a victim to the elements. On the day after my arrival, just one week earlier, Pitcairn had been a sultry, subtropical island, with ordered gardens and stiff, heavily laden banana trees. Now the storm had gouged the earth and ravaged the vegetation. The island I was traveling through was a blighted land.

Dennis was sanguine.

"You never know what is happening on Pitcairn. You can't plan for the future here."

As Dennis spoke, I realized why the Pitcairners' English could sound so stilted. They never used the future tense.

We reached the cliff above St. Paul's Point, a three-story-high megalithic dagger jutting up from the washing water. But the waves were higher still, and as each shattered like a sheet of glass over the tip a bellow arose, slow, deep and dinosaurian, as if a monster had awakened on the ocean bed.

The point was at the end of a promontory that curved back almost

---

* St. Paul's was named by the mutineers, who were reminded of St. Paul's Island, which the *Bounty* had passed when crossing the South Indian Ocean.

to touch the land, forming a lake with a small opening to the sea, which the islanders called Big Pool. Dennis explained that, on a calm day, you could climb down the cliff to bathe in the pool and catch Whistling Daughters by just holding out an open net and chasing them in. But today, Big Pool was seething like a cauldron.*

Dennis and I sat on the cliff edge, looking down on Big Pool and St. Paul's Point, and out toward the ocean. In the distance—it was impossible to tell how far, as the uninterrupted ocean provided no markers—was a break in the clouds, through which the sun beamed onto a calm sea. As the storm howled around us, this shaft of light was as dramatic as a thunderbolt, and I could see how it would be easy to become a believer on Pitcairn.

"How's your house going?" I asked Dennis.

"Good. I put up another wall. Just have to wait until a ship arrives with some windows."

"Can you see the sea from it?" I still hadn't visited Dennis's new home, away on the other side of Adamstown.

"Out the back. But it's not where I want to build," he said. "I want to build up Bill's Ground, close by Dave's and under Ron and Suzanne's."

"Why did you move down to the Edge?"

"Because she chose the spot up Bill's Ground, and I can't look at it anymore."

Dennis told me about his love for Mary from Kansas City. No one knows why she had come to Pitcairn, but she stayed to be with Dennis.

---

* The rocks have been described as "towering pinnacles of residual lava. They are linked to the shore-cliff at one end, and a lower ridge of solid rocks runs from them parallel to the cliff to a far pinnacle. A rocky lagoon is thus formed which, even in normal times, is dangerous, because surges rise unexpectedly through a low gap between the two main pinnacles or over the lower parts of the ridge, and sweep the whole length of the lagoon to escape by the unenclosed lower end. With sheer rock-walls on the landward side, anyone caught here is trapped. Yet it is a popular spot for fishing whenever conditions make it safe enough." (A.S.C. Ross and A. W. Moverley, *The Pitcairnese Language*, London, 1964, p. 184)

Dennis and Mary were going to get married, and Dennis began to lay down foundations for their home below that of his friend Ron Christian, on a piece of land belonging to Ben.

When Mary first went home to visit her parents, the letters were passionate. She remembered afternoons under the pandanus and sunsets on the rocks at Tedside. Dennis ordered some sheets of weatherboard to be delivered on the next supply ship, so he could erect the walls of their new home, and asked if Terry—his best friend and the electrician— would help him with the wiring. But soon Mary had found a part-time job and bought a car, and her letters grew cold. Within a year, she was writing that she was not coming back. Dennis never went up to the site again. Six months later, he began work on a house down at the Edge.

The splinter of light on the sea was still there, teasing us as we sat surrounded by storm. I was wrong about El Niño; the sea didn't join us to the world, it cut us off. How could someone from outside have a vision of settling down on Pitcairn? How could anyone come to the island accepting, as did the Pitcairners, that they might never leave, that this isolated rock and all it provided would soon become the limits of their world? The ocean was a barrier that needed more than a powerful vessel and navigating skills to cross.

Dennis might not find anyone else, not now. There were only two single females on the island—Clarice and Meralda. Clarice—Dennis rolled up his eyes. Clarice, known among many other things as Grumps, was too much for any man to take on. How could he get hitched to tractor driver number one when he was only tractor driver number two? Meralda was nice, but he didn't love her, not like Mary. It was difficult when you'd known someone all your life.

"You don't know what lonely is," he said. "Not where you're from."

He climbed on his bike and revved the engine, though you couldn't hear it for the monstrous bellow from the deep.

. . .

The weather encouraged us to stay indoors, and Irma kept herself busy by rearranging her stocks with the dedication of a supermarket shelf-filler.

She ceased whistling: "You've never baked bread before, dear?"

Irma was amazed. She had presumed I would know something so basic, otherwise what sort of work could I do for her? I apologized, and warned her that, although I could type, she would have to teach me just about everything else.

Irma, Dennis and Ben needed three loaves of bread every two days. Irma gave me the recipe:

Mix   6 teacups warm water
      1 tablespoon surebake
      1 tablespoon standard yeast

Add   1 teaspoon sugar
      1 tablespoon oil
      2 teaspoons salt

Mix all up. Add 7 teacups flour. Knead. Oil 3 tins, roll out paste, cover and leave to rise. Electric oven at 200 degrees for 50 minutes.

My dough puffed up in the tins, and within hours I had three loaves of perfectly browned bread cooling on a wire tray. I was inordinately proud. I may have failed to have understood the method of climbing the ladder to the ship and not have been much use collecting the wood on Henderson, but I could bake a good loaf of bread. I felt as if I had, at last, proved myself to be a useful person on Pitcairn.

The next morning I made biscuits and flapjacks, and cooked the supper. By the following day, it was assumed that I would do all the cooking, and I became responsible for planning and making the meals. Charles and Charlotte, his wiry, nervous wife, came to visit in the late afternoon, and I offered them a homemade biscuit from the tin and made them hot drinks of milo or molasses as if I were entertaining in my own home.

The wind continued to rage, but I had become so used to the sound of shaking walls that I hardly noticed it anymore. Then one late afternoon, just as night came down, it stopped. The bamboos creaked back to upright, the roofs rattled into place and the giant hermit crabs came out again, scuttling around the back of the house and knocking against the side of the duncan.

Now Dennis could put up the antennae for his VHF radio, which had arrived with me on the NCC *Najran*. One of Irma's radio contacts in Houston had heard that a ship was calling at Pitcairn, and put the package on board as a small token of his affection for the island and the Christian family. The Pitcairners were accustomed to receiving gifts of this caliber; most of Irma's electrical equipment was donated by well-wishers.

Dennis nailed up a shelf high in one corner of the kitchen, and placed the VHF on it. It was turned to the emergency channel, 16, so any radio message sent out from a ship could be picked up. But Dennis demonstrated another use for his equipment, which was to talk to other islanders who had a VHF in their kitchen. He picked up the microphone and pressed the button.

"Dave. You se there?" Dave lived opposite Dennis's first site for a home, about three hundred yards up the hill behind us.

"Dennis! Go to twelve."

Dennis switched from the emergency channel, and chatted to Dave about his new machine, which would put him in touch with everyone.

"Over and out."

Dennis turned around to me and beamed. "Em gwen!" Then he switched back to channel 16, and sat down at the table to wait.

Almost two hours later, when not a single peep had come on the VHF, just crackle—"break-break," Dennis called it—he got up from the table and went off to work on his house.

Dennis and Ben went to bed when the electricity supply was turned off at ten o'clock. Irma always stayed up later, either making contact in her radio shack, operating her radio by an old car battery, or just sitting by the glow of a flashlight. Irma's late-night vigils seemed out of place on Pitcairn, where every activity appeared to take place in groups. Irma was unusually still as she sat in the dark, and her hands stayed by her sides. I liked to sit up with her, and then I saw Irma as she might have been if not born in a tiny, intertwined community—troubled, questioning, seeking solitude. Perhaps I was one of the few people ever to see her like this.

We didn't converse, as I rarely spoke, but Irma would give me informal instruction on Pitcairn manners and customs. These lessons, unlike her running commentary throughout the day on practical matters, were of more philosophical content.

"Strangers think that Pitcairn . . ." she would begin, and then followed the lesson for that evening. ". . . that Pitcairners are lazy. They think that life here is easy, that we have everything we want. But you know this is not true."

Irma always credited me with a fraction more wisdom than the average outsider, out of kindness.

"The storm destroys our garden. The bananas are all blown down. We cannot go fishing. Life here is very hard. It's not Paradise at all."

The sea heaved and the palm fronds twittered, but it was calm.

"I like talking to you, dear," she said, and switched off her light.

# 7 · *t a r o   g r o u n d*

"Have a cup of your coffee, dear." Irma was fussing.

"No thanks."

Irma unplugged the deep-fat fryer so she could plug in the billy. I was reading the *Seventh-day Adventist Cookbook,* looking for egg-free recipes. We were low on eggs.

Irma took out a mug and placed it in front of me, nodding toward the big tin of coffee and smiling.

"Please, dear."

To please Irma, I got up and made myself a cup. She seemed satisfied, and went off to check that the sweet rice wasn't burning. Ben continued to grate coconut on his una. *Scrape, scrape, scrape.*

---

*billy*—kettle, even if, as in this case, it is of the modern, plastic kind.

*una*—a wooden stool with a serrated metal point attached to one end. You sit astride the stool and grate pieces of coconut shell on the point.

It was undeniable that the Pitcairners—and Irma's family in particular—had been very welcoming. From Mavis's bear hug on the Landing when I arrived, they had embraced me, to the point at which I could now sit in the kitchen at Irma's reading a cookbook and sipping a cup of coffee as comfortably as I could almost anywhere. Then why had the few outsiders who had come to Pitcairn left under a cloud? Mary's name could only be whispered; I would never mention her in Irma's house. There were the vague, unattributable reports about Perry "not fitting in," when Perry seemed such an ideal outsider and so good at joining in with the islanders' activities. And then, just last night, I had discovered that there had been someone else who had left the island before he had intended to, called Aden.

Irma had set up a radio schedule with Norfolk Island so that the two Norfolk Islanders living on Pitcairn—Glen and Alison—could talk to their families. Glen and Alison had come to Pitcairn on the Temporary Return Scheme, a plan conceived by the Pitcairn Islands Administration in New Zealand to encourage the repopulation of Pitcairn. The scheme would sponsor young people of Pitcairn descent whose families were now resident on Norfolk to return to their ancestral homeland for a minimum period of two years. A free passage and a job on the island would be guaranteed, and the Administration would pay a family to host them. At the end of the two years, should a temporary returnee wish to become a permanent Pitcairn resident, the government would purchase a plot of land on which he or she could build a house. Three young people had been selected so far—Glen, Alison and Aden.

"So where's Aden?" I asked Dennis.

"Se gone home."

"Not 'Pitcairnese' enough for him?"

"Semiswe," said Dennis.

The Norfolk Islanders were renowned for being more Pitcairnese than the Pitcairners. They were descended from those Pitcairn families who had elected to remain on Norfolk after the 1856 evacuation of Pitcairn. They still spoke the Pitcairnese language and greeted one another on the paved roads with "Wut a way you?" They shared the few surnames of the mutineers—Adams, Christian, McCoy, Quintal—some of which had died out long ago on Pitcairn.

Unlike those who had returned to Pitcairn, the Norfolk Islanders had prospered, and there were now almost two thousand of them, still sharing a few last names. To avoid confusion, the Norfolk Island telephone directory listed nicknames: Diddles, Blimp, Hunky and Puss were among the entries. From their phones, Hunky and Puss could dial direct to Tokyo or Turner's Green. A supply ship arrived every week, and there was an airport with daily flights to Auckland and Sydney. Each year, fifteen thousand tourists came to Norfolk, to experience the authentic Pitcairnese way of life.

Alison's surname was Christian, and she spoke Pitcairnese, but she was redheaded and thickly freckled like a Scottish lassie, and smoked like a trooper. She had arrived on the veranda with a cigarette in her hand and Trent, her boyfriend, in tow.

"I'll smoke outside," she said, knowing that Irma's faith forbids tobacco.

"No, no, no," insisted Irma, searching for a saucer that Alison could use as an ashtray. "Please, please," and she offered her a chair. "I don mind."

Alison relaxed into her cigarette while Irma disappeared into her radio shack. Every Wednesday evening Glen and Alison came around for a scheduled talk with Norfolk. It had been more than six weeks since Irma had managed to make contact.

Alison lived at Big Fence, and Glen stayed with Carol and Jay. His job was trainee tractor driver, under Clarice.

"He drives the tractor when Dennis collects the rubbish," said Alison, with cultivated ennui. The tractor had been laid up for some time,

---

*Wut a way you?*—How are you?

having fallen off the Landing when being used to transport goods off-loaded from a ship.

"What about Aden?" I asked.

"He's gone. Well gone." And Alison stubbed her cigarette out on the saucer.

I enjoyed listening to Irma making a contact, because she wasn't Irma at all—wife of Ben Christian, fifth-generation descendant of Fletcher Christian, pillar of the Adventist Church and Pitcairn Islander—but VR6ID, who was chirpy and coquettish. VR6ID even flirted. Suggestive, half-discernible chatter emerged from the crackle.

"You've got a really good signal this evening, Gary. A really good signal."

"Just been D-Xing."

"Thank you for a good one, Gary."

"Would you like a Charley Whisky?"

Then Irma became Irma again. "Meralda. You se there?"

"Meralda will be listening in on her radio," sighed Alison. "To see if I say anything interesting to my mother."

Less than a hundred yards down the hill, outside Mavis's, was Meralda's small wooden shack, from where she liked to work Hawaii. But her ham radio could also be tuned into any other ham radio on the island and, knowing that Wednesday night was when Irma worked Norfolk, she went into her shack just in case there was any news.

Irma's shack was like the rest of her home, tight with electrical equipment, most of which she never used. Irma's brittle frame looked even less substantial among the towers of metallic boxes studded with dials and flickering needles. The walls were covered with what looked like post-cards, but were in fact calling cards sent by contacts who had spoken to Irma, recording the date, time, frequency, duration, equipment used and conditions for the call. Their hope was that Irma would respond with a calling card of her own. The most prized pinup for radio hams worldwide was a calling card from Pitcairn.

Irma beckoned Alison into her shack. Alison went to stub out her cigarette, but Irma shook her head and insisted through hand gestures that Alison bring the cigarette and ashtray with her. Soon the little cupboard was shrouded in smoke, through which Irma emerged like a beaming genie, leaving Alison to talk to her mom.

It was Tuesday, and the post office would be opened by Dennis, just in case anyone wanted to buy any stamps. This was unlikely, as no one knew when the next ship would call and agree to take mail. If news of the imminent arrival of a ship did come through on the radio, the post office would be opened especially so that people could have their mail stamped, whether it was three in the morning or midday. But there were set opening hours: seven o'clock on Sunday evening and seven-thirty on Tuesday morning. And although there were never any customers, Dennis, a dedicated postmaster, always opened up the office at these hours, using them to do his bookkeeping. One of his three assistant postmasters or postmistresses would be there with him.

The Pitcairn Island Post Office was one small room with a counter stretched across the center. A photograph of the Queen and Prince Philip hung on one wall, and behind a sheet of glass some faded Pitcairn first day covers were slipping from the places in which they had been glued. The wall facing them, to the right of the counter, was fitted with wooden sorting boxes, each numbered, to encourage the Pitcairners to use a P.O. box address. With only four last names on Pitcairn, correspondence to Mr. Brown or Miss Warren could be easily misdelivered. In addition, some Pitcairners had been given one of these few last names as a first name, so Betty Christian's father was called Warren Christian. Warren Christian was often confused with Christy Warren, until the latter died a few years earlier. Lately, people had begun to name their sons after themselves; for example, Dave Brown's son was called Dave Brown.

Many letters to Pitcairn were not personally addressed. A card arrived for "Mr. Customer Office Postes and Telecommunications" from a collector of phonecards in Bari, Italy, who wanted an example of a Pitcairn phonecard. Another was written "To the Owner of the Shop Selling Pitcairn Handicrafts." A letter addressed to "Main Tourist Bureau, Pitcairn, Still Ocean" had gone to Irma. As well as being typist and assistant radio operator number two, Irma was public relations officer. Other correspondents simply begged: "To Somebody, Adamstown, Pitcairn Island" or "To a New Friend, Pitcairn, South Sea." This last sender had, as a final plea before posting from Denmark, scribbled on the outside of the envelope, "Please answer this letter."

Dennis showed me a stack of unclaimed mail. There was a brown envelope for "Monsieur John William Gainsborough," who had given someone in France his address as "20 Bounty Street, Adamstown, République des Iles Pitcairn, Colonie Britannique," perhaps because he thought he might settle down on Pitcairn, imagining it to be a place with streets and numbered houses. Or perhaps he just wished to live in a house on Bounty Street, on Pitcairn, and giving that as his future address was halfway toward being there. I searched through the stack for any letters addressed to Tim, in case one had arrived after he had sailed off on his yacht, but found nothing.

Only one of the boxes had any mail in it; it was marked POSTE RESTANTE. There was a letter addressed to Mr. E. E. Bennett, from his mother, Mrs. Bennett of Longmeadow Road, Dartford, Kent, and another to Stephen from his friend in Japan, apologizing that they were unable to rendezvous on Pitcairn as arranged. Mr. Bennett and Stephen were unknown on Pitcairn, and probably always would be. Many young people, painting a route at home of their trip around the world, imagined it would take them to Paris, Amsterdam, London, Bangkok, Hong Kong and Pitcairn Island. So when they gave a list to their friends and family of poste restantes, among them would be the tiny Pacific island, with approximate dates. None of these backpackers ever made it to Adamstown. But Dennis would keep their mail for a year in his poste restante box, then throw it away.

On the counter sat a pair of old-fashioned weighing scales, with great blocks of metal counterweights, and the ink pad and stamp with which Dennis thudded every item of mail that left the island with the Pitcairn Island postmark, the most sought-after postmark in the world.

In one corner behind the counter was a large green safe with a big wheel on the door, the sort of safe that might have been used as a prop in an old Western, for storing the stamps. It was difficult to think who might burst into the Pitcairn Island Post Office and steal its stock. Perhaps the stamps were kept in a safe because they were Pitcairn's only wealth, and held in great value by the islanders. The first set of Pitcairn Island stamps were issued on October 15, 1940, depicting Fletcher Christian and Captain Bligh. Eight years later, the tin-roofed school was built from the profits, perhaps the only schoolhouse to have been built from revenue gained from the sale of postage stamps.

Dennis stood at the counter and ran a finger down columns of figures penciled into a worn leather ledger. Assistant postmistress one, Mavis, sat to one side, counting sheets of stamps. Knowing that I was an official representative from the Royal Mail in England, they both assumed very serious expressions, as if the managing director of Royal Mail himself had come to check the accounts of the Pitcairn Island Post Office.

Dennis showed me a list of postal rates within Pitcairn, pinned behind the counter: letters were two cents; postcards were one cent. Dennis then solemnly informed me that no one had ever sent a letter by internal post on Pitcairn; if you had anything to say to someone, you could go and tell them yourself or pick up the phone.

Literature for the blind was delivered free, but only up to seven kilograms. I imagined some minor civil servant in the Foreign and Commonwealth Office in Whitehall drawing up this last provision, either out of ignorance as to where and what Pitcairn was, or as a joke.

"What about registered mail?" said Mavis, who was still counting stamps. "Em mail gwen missing."

Most of the islanders received requests for curios through the post, and met the orders by sending them back on the next ship that took mail. They were nervous of what might happen to their goods once they left the safety of the island. Robbery was known to be rife outside the waters of

Pitcairn, so the islanders took the precaution of sending their curios by registered post to guarantee their safe arrival. Registered post was put in a sealed sack by Dennis and sent separately from the bulk of correspondence and parcels. For the last few mails, these sacks had been hoisted on board a ship off Bounty Bay and, somewhere between loading and their destination, gone missing. Dennis had calculated the value of the goods lost; it came to $3,686 (New Zealand dollars). Dennis's annual salary as postmaster was $2,347. The Administration in Auckland had been informed, but there had been no mention of compensation. I was from the post office, so I was more responsible than anyone else for this. It was up to me to put it right.

I took down all the details as if conducting an official investigation. I promised that if I passed through Auckland on the return voyage, I would raise the matter with New Zealand Post and ask them to initiate an inquiry. But I felt that, for the second time, Mavis's keen eyes had caught me out.

I walked back up the hill with Dennis, dodging Mavis's dogs. The ground was thick with umbrella-shaped mango leaves, which had fallen in the storms and lain as a loose film on top of red earth, as slippery as a layer of ice. Dennis's bare toes clenched the earth.

I had once met a dedicated rock climber, and Dennis's feet reminded me of this woman's hands. She was young—perhaps in her late twenties—but already her fingers were lined not from age, but from dirt that would never wash out, as if her hands had been dipped in the same sooty substance that police officers use to take fingerprints, and every line was revealed. But what had struck me most was the way in which her hands didn't look like human hands at all, but as if they belonged to an animal, perhaps an eagle, whose safety depended upon them being clamped securely to the side of a rock. They were never straight, but they weren't curved either, as each section of each finger was rigid and at an angle to the one below and above. In the same way, Dennis's feet seemed to be designed not for stepping and walking, but for clawing along the slippery paths of Pitcairn.

I was relieved to reach Irma's, as my legs ached from having to concentrate on keeping upright. "Power-es-e-on," said Ben. I rewarded myself for not falling over by making a cup of coffee, while Dennis helped himself to bean soup and the bread that I had baked the day before. I sat and watched my coffee grow cold, feeling no compulsion to get up and get on. The wind had died, the sea was calm, and there were no trips planned or ships due. But at any moment, a long ring might announce a passing ship or the bell in the Square might peal three times to call the men to public work. The weather might turn, and another sheet of leaves smother the path down to Mavis's.

Irma had suggested that I learn some Pitcairn crafts. The women rarely carved, although they sometimes helped to smooth the sharks or the sails of the model *Bountys* with glass and sandpaper, after the men had cut and rough-shaped them. Royal was the only woman carver, but she was regarded as too tough and very odd. The women painted hattie leaves and wove baskets from pandanus or the strips of plastic ribbon, which was used to secure freight on ships. The pastor's wife, Jenny, had become particularly good at weaving plastic baskets, Irma said, and would have more time than the Pitcairners to teach me, as she had less work to do.

I made my way down to the Mission House midmorning, after Jenny was back from the dispensary, where she worked as resident nurse, with Royal as assistant nurse. The dispensary, between the church and the library, was open every morning except Sabbath from eight o'clock for about twenty minutes. The only other medical personnel on the island was the dental officer, Steve, who had been sent to New Zealand on a three-month dental course. He could do extractions; not one of the adult islanders had any of their own teeth left. Steve's other medical role was neutering the cats and dogs.

By the time I arrived, Jenny's eldest son was at school and her two younger children were playing in the garden, picking maggots out of a dead rat. Their home was unusual, as the veranda was raised, and you had to go up several steps to the front door, which was covered with a mesh of mosquito net. Jenny appeared at the threshold, smiling and serene in a simple skirted dress. I was reminded of the stories of colonial officers' wives in the tropics, fluttering inside their cool houses away from the rampant territory that touched and tickled their carefully pruned gardens.

She had taken out her wooden box frames and some rolls of plastic ribbon, as large as the tires on the three-wheeled bikes. I chose a long oblong frame, which Jenny said was a popular shape for a basket, as it was useful for taking curios out to trade, and blue and pink ribbon.

As Jenny showed me how to tack the first strand to the box, then weave a pattern of blue and pink about it, we talked very little. Jenny asked where I was from, and I said an English seaside town. Jenny was Australian but, unlike her Bondi Beach husband, unnaturally white with hair the color of a pair of tights from the 1950s and slatey eyes. If a color photograph were taken of Jenny, it would appear to be in black and white.

It was customary for the missionary's wife to be a nurse, and I asked Jenny where she had been working before coming to Pitcairn.

"In the theater," she said, and I gulped. Not only was this soft-spoken, placid, matronly woman the antithesis of my image of an actress, but I was shocked that someone should be allowed to run a dispensary and prescribe drugs whose only trade was drama.

"Where?" I asked.

She named an Australian town I had never heard of, and the large, modern Adventist hospital on its fringes.

"I worked in surgery, handling instruments." She corrected my fingers on the ribbon. "I had never been at a birth—except my own children's." She smiled; I flickered back. "Before I came here."

I had heard that Meralda had had a baby who had died at birth, but it was Jenny who told me the full story. Meralda had fallen pregnant, and everyone was delighted. It had been some years since there had been a birth on Pitcairn, and Meralda was devoted to the island. She insisted that her baby be born on Pitcairn.

There is no prenatal clinic, no ultrasound scan, no blood tests on

Pitcairn, but the pregnancy had been untroubled. Meralda was having a bicentenary baby—it was two hundred years since the mutiny on the *Bounty*—and it was as if this child would belong not just to her progenitors, but to Pitcairn. Meralda was breathing life into her tiny, shrinking community. She went into labor around the due date, and a long ring went out: "Yourley there? Yourley? Meralda haven ha baby!" Jenny was in attendance.

Soon it became clear that something was wrong. The baby would not come out; it was stuck. Meralda needed a cesarean. But there are no facilities for surgery on Pitcairn.

Betty raced up to the commercial radio station and sent out a medical distress signal calling any ships in the vicinity with a doctor on board to respond. There was nothing, then a crackle, then a thick Eastern European voice. A Russian vessel was about one hundred miles off Pitcairn with, as was compulsory on all Russian ships, a medical doctor on board. The Captain agreed to make way for Pitcairn, and the longboat was launched to bring the doctor ashore.

The Russian doctor managed to free the baby from Meralda, and saved her life. Then the second long ring went out: "Yourley there? Yourley." Meralda's baby had died. Jayden Jacob Norfolk Warren, six pounds four ounces, was buried the next day.

Jenny related this so quietly, so calmly, with no hint of the agony involved, that I thought her dispassionate, even uncaring, as if her inner emotions were as stony as her casing. Then I realized by the slight, beatific smile that crossed her pale face that she was telling me a religious tale; that, according to Jenny, the story of Meralda's life being saved was not a story of suffering, but a miracle.

I quickly changed the topic of conversation, asking Jenny about the general health of the islanders.

Every outsider who visited Pitcairn had declared the islanders a hearty, wholesome race. In a Colonial Office medical report of 1938, Dr. Duncan Cook had recorded, "The physique of the people is magnificent." Concerns that inbreeding might lead to deformities and idiots had been unfounded. Apart from the scars and limps on the men, they seemed a pretty healthy bunch to me.

"Obesity is the main problem," said Jenny. "It aggravates high blood pressure, heart complaints and diabetes. There's three diabetics on the island."

Rick came in from fishing. His fluorescent microshorts, splattered by the spray, were completely see-through. He walked over to the fridge, took out eight saveloys and put them in the microwave. Then he piled a small mountain of shredded cabbage, chopped tomatoes and lettuce onto a great plate. I thought he was making lunch for his family, but he emptied the eight saveloys onto the same plate and sat down to eat them himself.

"It's all from our own garden," he declared, gesturing at the vegetables.

Rick took some Marmite out of a jar with a knife and smoothed it over the lettuce. He splattered the shredded cabbage with mint sauce. Rick boasted that he had been the first to try Marmite on lettuce, and now all the islanders liked it.

The Pitcairners often had to take what they could get; a ship might be short on flour, but have a spare box of Thousand Island dressing, so that is what they would receive in exchange for their fish. It led to a strange, passing-ship cuisine, which threw ingredients together in odd combinations and led to shortages of essential items and excesses of luxuries. A fruit carrier had recently agreed to pick up *Tub*'s faulty clutch and take it on to New Zealand for repair, as long as she didn't have to stop. So, in a stormy sea, the clumsy lump of machinery had been put in a sack— along with some fresh fruit as a token of thanks—and hoisted by rope from the longboat onto the deck of the moving carrier. In return, the Captain lowered a sack down to the Pitcairners. It contained bottles of tomato ketchup. I suppose the Captain thought it kind to donate an isolated people such delicacies. But we still had no eggs.

"I've been telling Debbie about Meralda's baby," said Jenny, still smiling.

"At least they could get it out," said Rick, tucking into another saveloy.

"Time I went to get some breakfast!" I said cheerily, and, thanking Jenny for her tuition, started to walk home.

Nigger was driving along Main Road on his bike, and stopped when he saw me. He was wearing a tank top T-shirt that showed the full power of his arms.

"Wut a way you?" He spoke languidly and with supreme confidence.

"Good 'un."

The street was empty, apart from me and Nigger. So I asked him a question that I had been wanting to put to him for some time.

"Why are you called Nigger?"

"Cos I se black as a brute," and he laughed.

Nigger was indeed dark, the color of sweet molasses. I wondered how he spent his evenings, with his wife and child away. I couldn't see him sitting on a veranda sanding carvings.

"Do you drink?" he asked, as he had done on Henderson. I sensed that I was being tested, and that there was an answer that I ought to give, a password. But before I could think of what it might be, Nigger kicked his bike into gear and sped off.

I could hear Dennis working on his new house, only yards away, and I wandered over. Terry was helping Dennis out, as he always did, and shrugged when he saw me. He had a rounded, lumbering frame and unnaturally quiet movements, as if his soft flesh cushioned any noise. He was devoted to Dennis (who preferred to call him Toj), and followed him about whether he was working on the longboats down the Landing or collecting the rubbish.* Terry was followed in turn by his dog, Whisky,

---

* All Pitcairners have several nicknames: Terry was Tel, Toj and Thick Lip. The origin of some nicknames are known (e.g. Tom-Worree, Meralda-Daughter), others forgotten. Some say "Toj" comes from the English "toad." The number of different names used in conversation suggests a far larger population than thirty-eight, and at first I thought that Grumps, Expensive and Iglamus were other members of the Pitcairn com-

whom he tied to the handlebars of his bike with a rope as he zoomed up and down Main Road, looking for Dennis.

"You talking to Nig?" Dennis was sawing what could have been a doorpost.

"How do you know?" I said. You couldn't see Main Road from Dennis's house.

"Hear ha bike," said Dennis.

Terry became eloquent. "I can tell all em bikes," he said, in a voice that was as blurred as the edges of his body. "Meralda always drive in one gear. Tom cos em four wheels. And can tell if it one of em girls riding, cos lighter, and make different sound on ha road."

I heard the rattle of an engine. Someone was driving up Main Road in the direction of the Landing.

"That Glen," said Terry confidently. "On Jay's bike. Hear em brakes."

Dennis showed me around his new home, drawing attention to its considerable size and its handy location, so near to the center of town. The house was still a skeleton, with large wooden frames where walls should have been. But the doors had arrived on an earlier shipment, and one had been added to each invisible wall by tacking it into a frame. Dennis, to go from one room to another, rather than simply stepping over the lip of the frame that lay on the ground, held open the free-standing door and bowed me through.

In Buxley Green, Ron had warned me about the three-wheeled all-terrain motorcycles. They were banned, he had said, in every country except Japan. But they were excellent for rough, off-the-road driving, which was the same as on-the-road driving on Pitcairn.

---

munity, not realizing that they were Clarice, Tom and Darrylene. Some of the mutineers, of course, also went by nicknames.

I asked Dennis if he would teach me to ride one. The bikes looked quite stable, with their mighty tractor tires, and Irma and Dennis had no difficulty in buzzing around the island's pitted paths on them. But Dennis suggested that, to ease me in, my first lesson be on level ground. As flat land made up less than 10 percent of Pitcairn's one and a half square miles, there was little choice as to where we could go.

"We gwen up Taro Ground," said Dennis, and I jumped on the back of the broad saddle of his bike.

Taro Ground sat in the very center of the island, on the flattened top of a hill, which was reached by leaving Adamstown by way of Jim's Ground. From here, it was possible not only to sight ships, but to talk to them, and the duty radio operator's job at the commercial radio station, sited in the center of Taro Ground, was to coax a captain to drift offshore, so the islanders could go out to trade. But it was also possible, in certain weather conditions, to speak to an operator in Wellington, New Zealand, and through her book a phone call to anywhere in the world. This process usually took several days, and was rarely successful. If a line did eventually come through to, say, Sydney, it might be five o'clock in the morning in Australia and the call had to be canceled.

Jim's Ground didn't rise up to Taro Ground, it swerved up, as the road was one long sweep around the side of the hill. The dry weather that had smartly followed the rain had transformed the island yet again, and now we were riding over cracked, crimson earth, set so hard it could have been baked in a kiln. Capsizing onto it would be like falling on concrete.

Dennis couldn't remember which Jim Jim's Ground was named after, though he knew Brown's Water was after William Brown, the gardener on the *Bounty*, who had been responsible for potting the breadfruit.

The people of Pitcairn were the Stanleys and Livingstones of their country. They had arrived on an uninhabited island two hundred years earlier, and begun slowly to name everything after themselves. The map of Pitcairn was littered with first names: Nancy Stone, Big George Coconuts, Matts Rocks, Freddie Fall, Minnie Off, Little George Road, Tedside.

In such a small place, every curve in the road, every rock pool, every tree had a distinct identity.

"You know the government orange tree?" said Dennis, when I had asked how to get to Brown's Water. "You know where the road bends past the mango . . ."

Within feet of each other, Ed's Fence became Sour Orange before turning into Skinner's Pen. Any other people would have considered their country well mapped, but the Pitcairners continued to add still further names. If I came off the bike, I imagined "Debbie's Disaster" would be marked on the map.

As we rattled over Jim's Ground it was easy to see why Pitcairn was so subdivided. Dense undergrowth of giant ferns and tangled lantana gave way within yards to a neat, flat garden patch, rather like an English allotment, before the earth dropped dramatically into a deep, volcanic ridge. Just as I became used to throwing my weight forward on the bike to stop us from somersaulting backward as we jolted up a steep path, we would plummet back down into a tiny valley, and I'd throw myself back in the seat to stop us from flipping forward head-over-tail.

Jim's Ground soon became Big Ground, which became McCoy's Valley, which became Taro Ground, into which we bounced over a perfect hill, no more than eight feet high. Taro Ground was like a football field, bright green and astonishingly smooth. The land edging it sloped down so suddenly that you couldn't see it, and Taro Ground seemed to be suspended in the air above Pitcairn.

What you could see was the ocean. It wrapped about Taro Ground like a knitted shawl, one row plain, one row pearl. Whichever way you turned, it was still there, swaddling the island, and smothering her.

A wooden hut sat in the middle of the field, sprouting antennae. This must be the commercial radio station.

Dennis jumped off the bike and told me to shuffle forward.

"Use the pedal to change gear. There's the brake. You accelerate on the handle," and he revved up the engine to demonstrate. "Now go!"

I jerked the bike into gear, accelerated, and released the brake. She roared away, and I was at the other side of Taro Ground, whose flat expanse had seemed so huge, within seconds. I braked to prevent myself from toppling off the edge and into a steep decline. The front wheel rose up like a bronco, throwing me back in the seat.

Dennis was shaking even more violently than me, doubled up with giggles. The bike had seemed such a simple, solid vehicle when I'd sat behind Irma or Dennis, but with me in the saddle it bucked, threw its wheels in the air and stopped in its tracks like a show horse refusing a fence.

The Pitcairners seemed to have a knack of making things look easy, whether climbing the ship's ladder, hoisting heavy logs or driving a three-wheeled all-terrain motorbike. But when I attempted any of these tasks, I failed miserably. It was important that I succeeded in driving a bike. On Pitcairn, only children and the very old rode on the back of someone else's machine.

I handed the reins of the beast back to Dennis, who shrugged his shoulders.

"Try again soon," he said, hopefully.

Dennis was anxious to get back home, to listen to the VHF. We raced down McCoy's Valley, along Jim's Ground and threw aside the banana chandeliers. Ben was sitting at the back of the kitchen, grating coconut on his una, making a soft scraping sound, as if he were a mechanical toy that had been wound up early in the morning and was still grinding away. Ben's gentle scraping provided a steady rhythm against which Irma chattered and whistled. The VHF was silent.

"Any one em?" said Dennis.

"Nitho." Ben wasn't interested in the new gadgetry.

Dennis slouched down in a chair and stared at the VHF. I sat next to him, and watched it, too. I was waiting for something to happen—perhaps Dennis had a hunch that a ship would call, or that someone would try and

---

*nitho*—nothing

make contact. Fifteen minutes later, Dennis and I had not moved, slouched in our chairs and looking at the VHF, only a few feet away.

While I was waiting for something, Dennis was just waiting. If I had asked him for what, I'm certain he would have shrugged. He was just waiting, that's all. Waiting was an activity in itself on Pitcairn, much as reading might be elsewhere. It was a pastime, and one which Dennis was very good at.

"Would you like a Milo?" I asked at last, breaking the vigil. "Shall I put on the billy?"

"No," said Dennis, without moving.

I made myself a cup of coffee and sat back down next to Dennis, returning to the morning's task of trying to think of recipes without eggs. Irma had asked me not to use any of the eggs in the fridge. There were less than three dozen left, with no sign of the next supply ship, and she was worried that we might run out. I welcomed having to bake all the sweets and biscuits without eggs as a mental challenge to be worked upon while I pretended to watch the VHF. These were the recipes I constructed:

| *Flapjacks* | *Jam tarts* |
| --- | --- |
| oats | jam |
| butter | flour |
| sugar | butter |

Dennis rose and went to the veranda, taking with him a half-finished whale carving. He spread out a tattered brochure from Marine World, Florida, at a page that showed a picture on which he was modeling his whale, and on which the curls of red miro shavings fell. Soon Ben put away the una, took out his hand vase from a sack and joined his son. The next time I looked up, Terry was there also. As the sun shut down, with Ben, Dennis and Terry smoothing their carvings with small pieces of sharp glass, a voice whipped onto the VHF. Dennis jumped.

"ZBP, Zulu Bravo Papa. Pitcairn Island Radio. This is Pitcairn Island

Radio. Any ships in the area? Do you have anything for us? This is Zulu Bravo Papa, Pitcairn Island Radio. Closing down."

It was Tom Christian, radio operator, shutting the commercial radio station for the day. Dennis slumped. Perhaps he had hoped the VHF might conjure up voices from outside, the sound of strangers.

That evening Dennis was going down to Steve and Olive Christian's house, known as Big Fence, though nobody could remember why.

"Might be big fence there one time," said Dennis helpfully. Then added, "Do you drink?"

I took a guess at what the password might be. "Yes," I said, and Dennis smiled.

"You comen down Big Fence?" he said.

There was a crowd at Big Fence, but they were accommodated easily, as Big Fence was built like a barn. Each house I visited seemed to be larger than the last, and Steve and Olive's was gigantic, with the same basic design of one huge room with chairs pressed against the walls, and a large table, with a small kitchen in one corner. It was also an excellent example of the local house style in another way: it looked as if it was still under construction. Necessity had become a fashion; sheets of weatherboard simply wouldn't arrive as ordered, or the ship carrying them would sail on past, so walls remained half-built and windows glassless. But Big Fence had one unique, astonishing feature—a vibrant, beautiful mural of dolphins in more shades of blue than I had ever imagined painted along one long wall. The only pictures I had seen decorating the walls in other Pitcairn homes were torn from old calendars.

Steve, Olive, Alison and Nigger were sitting at the table playing canasta, which was shocking, as card playing was forbidden by the Seventh-day Adventist Church. But more shocking than the fan of cards was what Steve held in his other hand: a can of Carlsberg.

Nigger read my surprise. "This is the twentieth century," he said, and went back to studying his hand.

"Want one?" Steve asked.

I nodded to Steve, and Steve cocked his head toward Olive, who went to the fridge and took out a chilled can for me. She was unusually slim for a Pitcairner, but not rakish like Irma. She walked with a skip and a knowledge of being attractive.

Three young girls were sitting cross-legged on the floor, playing rummy and drinking lime juice. Trent and his two teenage brothers were wrapped up in blankets and lying across armchairs in a corner, watching a *Baywatch* video, while the grown-ups drank and played cards. They were a handsome quartet: swarthy Steve, Olive with her fine body, redheaded Alison, and Nigger, dark and mighty.

"Want to join us?" offered Steve, pointing to an empty chair. But Dennis was already cocooned in a blanket next to Trent, transfixed by *Baywatch,* and I couldn't play canasta.

"Sorry, can't play."

Steve shrugged, and turned back to the table.

I hovered about, wondering whether I should settle down to watch the video. I decided instead to play cards with the girls. Rummy was, at least, a game I knew. I sat cross-legged beside them, and soon became absorbed in the game. Only once did I look up and see the adults sitting around the table above me, knocking back beers, throwing back their heads and slapping down cards.


"What did you have to eat, dear?" Irma was feigning a casual question. She was arranging the tomatoes that Charlotte had brought around that evening in return for Irma's gift of beans. There must have been at least two dozen of them, and Irma turned each around and around before placing it gently on top of the last. She seemed to like to finger food, but not to eat it.

"Nitho," I said.

Irma waited a moment before asking, "And to drink?"

I thought of my companions, the girls. "Lime juice," I said. "I was playing—" and I remembered the disapproval of card games. "I was playing with the children."

I didn't know whether to feel glad or sad for the lie. I was pleased to have been introduced into an inner circle of Pitcairn life. But I didn't want to deceive Irma.

She opened the fridge door and, without bothering to look inside, slammed it shut so hard that it shivered.

The following day I went to get myself registered as an alien on Pitcairn. This involved signing my name in a ledger kept at Jay's. As island magistrate, Jay's duty was to check my license to land, but he didn't bother. He had been there when my application had been discussed at Council, so knew my papers were in order.

I flicked through the ledger, reading the earlier entries. They were few and far between. I saw Ron's name. I looked for Tim. He hadn't given me the exact date of his Pitcairn sojourn, but it must have been a couple of years earlier. I traced back several years, looking for Tim and his yacht. Then I went through the entries again more carefully, just in case I had missed him.

"Does everyone sign this book?" I asked Jay. There must have been some mistake, so I asked Jay if he remembered the man with the microlight.

"Wha?"

"A tiny airplane," I said. "I met the man who flew it over Pitcairn. He was called Tim. Remember?"

Charlene put down her fritter.

"Airplane?" she said. "I se nawa see one of dem."

"Not on Pitcairn," said Jay.

If Tim had microlighted over the island, surely people would remember, if it was the first plane they ever saw, the first time they had seen a man with wings, a man who could fly?

"He arrived in a yacht," I continued.

"Plenty do," said Jay.

"Then he microlighted, off Taro Ground, I suppose."

Jay was amused. "Nawa no airplane on Taro Ground."

"Well, at least there's proof that *I* was here," and I signed the ledger.

There were still a couple of hours of power, so Dennis put on a video, *Roses Are for the Rich,* an American miniseries that one of Irma's contacts had sent as a gift. What did Dennis make of the grand Southern mansions, the golden floor-length drapes, the *chink-chink* of cut glass, the teased and perfumed women's bodies on Pitcairn, where they had never seen an airplane and playing cards was a crime?

"Thanks for a nice one. I hope we can meet again. Seventy threes. Seventy threes." VR6ID was in her radio shack.

I slumped in my chair, until, just as the pearly-toothed heroine was directing her first board meeting after gaining the chair of a multimillion-dollar organization, the power went, and the television gobbled her up. Neither Dennis nor I moved, staring blankly at the dot on the screen.

# 8 · down isaac's

Irma and Nola were sitting on the veranda weaving baskets, and Royal was polishing a whale. Reynold, Nola's husband, was working on the fin of his brute fish. Ben was smoothing the duck-shaped head of a walking stick he had cut from coconut palm and orangewood.

Royal often came around like this, in the evenings, rather than sitting alone in her house up the hill with no one to talk to. About once a week Nola and Reynold would also visit after supper, always bringing some work with them. Nola was sitting cross-legged on the bench, with the half-finished basket clenched between her knees. No one was empty-handed; as they talked, their hands were either weaving, sanding or polishing a curio.

I was concentrating on my basket, and found it impossible to chatter at the same time.

"You sa we?" said Ben, as I fumbled with the strands of plastic. I had to master these baskets before moving on to the more intricate and tricky pandanus-leaf weaving.

A plastic basket would be useful for taking curios out to the ships for trade, carrying bananas and going to the store. But a pandanus-leaf basket was the authentic South Pacific item, and could be hawked on board ship.

Irma and Nola were making baskets from pandanus or paioori leaf, which they called thatch. The paioori was not prickled, like pandanus, and grew close to the ground. Paioori bushes were privately owned—Nola had a large one growing just below her house—whereas all pandanus trees were public, and anyone could pick them. Both had broad leaves that had to be dried in the sun, then wound into bundles to preserve them. To make the threads for weaving, the women took a needle and scored the hardened leaves until they broke into fine strands, little thicker than hairs.

They had taken out their half-finished baskets that night, said Nola (who was considered one of the finest weavers on the island), because the wind was blowing from the southeast. This kept the thatch moist. When the wind was blowing from any other direction, the thatch dried out and was too brittle to work.

The wind was very shallow that night, the geckos and mosquitoes both louder than it. From under the faint light bulb that swung on the veranda, outside was black and distant. The veranda was a comforting place of gentle scraping and quacking chatter.

I broke from my weaving.

"Jenella's very pretty." Jenella was one of the girls with whom I had played rummy at Big Fence.

"Yes," said Nola grudgingly. "But not for long. Soon she be fat. Like Thelma." Thelma was Jenella's grandmother.

---

*You sa we?*—"Do you know how to do it?" Perhaps from English "savvy."

Nola, who had a raucous voice and a penchant for jaunty raffia hats, was no nymph. She was the sort of fat you seemed to get on Pitcairn, which was smooth and hard. Although there was an abundance of it, her flesh didn't wobble at all as she walked. She was like an inflatable woman, as solid as if she had been pumped full of air.

"Grumps too," said Irma. "It begin already."

I returned to my weaving.

The men seldom spoke out loud, only nodding when the women said something, or laughing at a small joke they exchanged quietly between themselves. Reynold looked more Polynesian than many of the islanders, and even when he spoke in English had a thick Pitcairn accent. He was as silent as Ben, and considered old-fashioned. When Reynold did talk, it was always with slight hesitation, as if to counter the surety of Nola's squawk.

I asked, "How old are you, Reynold?"

"Sixty, must be I suppose."

He was the only man on the island who didn't use electrical tools for his carvings, which were cruder as a result and fetched less money on board the ships.

"That's fer Tom and Betty," said Irma, as the phone rang short-long-short-short. "Musbe Glen. He calling Sherilene. Wan her go outside. Es too late," and she tutted. That Glen was courting Tom and Betty's daughter was no secret.

The first signs of a definite basketlike shape were appearing from my weave and, proud of reaching this small milestone, I held it up.

"What do you think of my basket?"

"Aw-right." Royal was able to make the most ordinary word sound like an insult. It had to do with the way her mouth twisted like a barley-stick as she talked.

I turned to Nola. "What do you think of my basket?"

"Aw-right."

I banged in some fresh tacks for the next row of weave.

"Em scientists," said Nola, who spoke like a radio turned up to full volume, so everyone jumped. "Should go wipe to England."

There were murmurs of agreement from all around, as if the veranda itself was of one accord with her.

Irma told a tale about how the scientists' equipment and supplies had taken up too much room on the supply ship; Nola drew out parts of it with her ear-cracking voice, and Royal smiled with half of her mouth. Alison had called Irma, Royal and Nola the three witches, and just as I was thinking this, Irma began.

"Alison, she smoke like a hatchet," and her hands started working even faster on the threads of her basket. "This place stink. She se smoke on her sched with Norfolk." Irma cocked her head toward her radio shack in the corner. "I se run and give her one ashtray." Irma was in full stride. "She ought be larn noot fer smoke here on Pitcairn."

The veranda heaved in agreement. My basket was going badly. I had come to the end of a ribbon and must have missed a weave somewhere in the middle because it didn't match the band above it. I had to undo the whole strand and start again.

I remembered Irma's insistence that Alison smoke, her dogged refusal when Alison offered to go outside, her excessive attendance on her with the saucer-ashtray.

"Someone ort fer larn her," said Irma.

I tried to remember the scene more clearly. Had Alison *insisted* on smoking? Or had Irma insisted that Alison smoke? I was trying to concentrate on my weaving—I couldn't be seen undoing a row twice—and couldn't weave with my hands and unravel my thoughts at the same time. And the light and sounds of the veranda had encircled me, making it

---

*go wipe*—used to indicate severe disapproval, impatience or even disgust with someone, suggesting that they should buzz off

*Someone ort fer larn her*—Someone ought to tell her

difficult to imagine somewhere outside of this moment. I just knew something didn't fit.

The weather was brighter now and gardens were being weeded, washing hung out to dry and fishing trips planned.

"Wan go Down Isaac's?" asked Dennis. "Fer fish."

Down Isaac's was a small rocky promontory below the Mission House reached, Dennis warned me, by scrambling down the cliff edge, which might be a bit slippery because of the recent rains. It was the same place where the pastor's youngest child, Ashlee, had fallen, cracked her skull and thought to have died. She had lain in a coma for days, while the islanders kept a vigil of prayer. When she came through, remembering nothing, the pastor declared that his daughter's recovery was a miracle.

Jenny, in an attempt to rescue her daughter, had fallen down the cliff herself and shattered her kneecap. Despite evacuation to New Zealand on the next ship and surgery, her leg had never fully recovered, and she limped and was in constant pain. But Dennis was sure I'd be okay.

Dennis took some crayfish, giant and succulent, from one of Irma's freezers, the sort of seafood a French chef would weep over. These were to be used as bait. Adventism forbids the consumption of food from the sea without scales, which meant that the crustaceans that thrived in the waters around Pitcairn—the island's most abundant and easily harvested form of protein—were chopped up and used to lure mundane fish, in particular the nanwe, the most popular and prolific fish in the waters around Pitcairn.

There had been a huge plate of nanwe—deep fried and whole—at Charlene's general party. I could not imagine a more boring-looking or tasteless fish, with gray skin and off-white, dry flesh, which had to be picked from splintery bones. That crayfish and lobster would be sacrificed for this catch was depressing. Perhaps I could just sit down on the edge and eat a bag of bait instead.

The descent Down Isaac's was as slippery as Dennis had predicted, and I arrived caked in red clay. Jay, Carol, Charlene and Darrylene were already fishing from one side of the promontory, which thrust like a finger out into the sea; Nola and Reynold were on another. Each fisher held the end of a long nylon line in her hand, and was staring out to the point at which it pierced the water.

Royal was farther inland, having decided to dabble for rockfish close to the shore. The colorful rockfish were easy to spot and even easier to catch—you just had to weight your line and throw it down deep by the side of the rock or even in a rock pool, and you'd soon have a bite. They came peacefully, but their flesh was best ground up into fishballs or for trading on board ships. It was the nanwe that everyone wanted—a tugging, biting, whipping, fighting fish the color of rock.

Today the promontory and cliffs behind were steel gray, and the sky and the sea were true blue. On some days, when I had looked down the Edge, the rocks had seemed rose tinted, the sky purple, and it was the sea that was the color of steel. At other times, the shore, sea and sky had melted into one blue gray, broken only by the white ruff of surf around the rocks. The rock pools—Bitey Bitey, Man Pool, Scissors, Hot Water Pool—reflected these shifts in color, becoming brown like a rainwater puddle or as clear and vibrant as a fish tank. They were miniature worlds in our miniature world.

The sea was calm—the calmest it had been for at least two weeks—but it still broke noisily over the rocks, washing white water around the fishers' feet. But even as it whisked up their shins, they stood steady on the rocks, patiently holding their lines.

In some places, the people walk leaning forward at fifteen degrees, as if battling against wind. In others, the inhabitants stand so upright that they look as if the slightest breeze would lift them. But the Pitcairners slouched into the earth as if attached to the rock, as if part of it. It looked as if it would take a hurricane to blow them down. These people were rooted to the island, while I skidded on the surface of Pitcairn, slipping, falling, losing my grip.

Dennis and I climbed out after Jay. Dennis gave me a reel of nylon fishing line, and showed me how to tie a small metal hook onto one end. Then he took out a crayfish, cut off a moist chunk with his knife and pierced it with the hook. He threw the line into the water, where it landed a good twenty feet out, and handed me the reel.

"Hold it like this," he said. "So you can feel a fish."

I took the line lightly between my thumb and fingertips. It seemed to be constantly jerking, tugging away at me so the nylon thread cut into the palms of my hands.

"You know if one em bite," Dennis assured me, and went off to set his line.

I couldn't take my eyes off the water. I watched as a wave, surely higher than those that had come before, rolled toward us, it seemed very slowly. I was ready to make a dash for the cliff, but Jay and Carol, who were farther out on the promontory than I, stood firm, while the water rushed about their legs and sucked back into the ocean, leaving them, to my amazement, still standing on the rocks.

I bent my feet around the hard rock, trying to imitate the talonlike toes of the Pitcairners, and tried to feel my line, but the water was so choppy I couldn't tell whether I had a fish or not. Jay had pulled in two flat gray nanwe since I had arrived, put his thumb behind their gills and broken their necks.

I felt something bite—it was definitely a bite—and tugged at my line, but not sharply enough. The hook was still there, tied to the nylon line, but the fish and bait had gone.

"You muss be very quick," said Dennis.

You never catch one nanwe by itself. Nanwe only appear in great numbers, so Jay's catch indicated that a shoal was nearby. Soon he was hooking fish at an awesome rate; as soon as his line was back in the water, he'd be pulling it in with another. Dennis was slightly slower, with a pile of about half a dozen so far. I had lost some more bait, but not found any fish. But it was good to be standing on the very edge of the ocean with a primitive line in my hand, fishing with the Pitcairners.

*"Run!"* Jay was rushing past me, pushing me toward the cliff. Carol and the children were right behind; Charlene gave me a shove.

*"Run, you se arsehole!"* she screamed.

I turned toward the cliff and started after them, stumbling on the rock that was sometimes slippery, sometimes sharp on my bare feet.

We reached the base of the cliff just as the wave broke over the promontory on which we'd been standing, with a bellow that echoed off the cliffs. The water seemed crazed, foaming as it flooded the rock pools and gurgled down the crevices. My bag of bait was sucked out to sea, as quickly as an ant would disappear down a plug hole.

I'd seen nothing different in that wave. But the Pitcairners had noticed something in that particular surf; its color, perhaps, its speed, even its sound, and knew our rock was no longer safe.

We clambered back out onto the promontory and threw our lines into the sea as if nothing had happened. But I imagined bodies bobbing in the frenzied water, and felt the chill of the ocean creep up on me, and trembled as I fished. Dennis seemed oblivious; his only concern was that I was using up his bait but hadn't caught a single fish. I needed a bite; I had no pile behind me, and I was warned that we would return home with fewer fish than any other family.

Jay decided that we'd been fishing long enough, wound in his line and put his catch in a basket. Royal, Nola and Reynold began to pack up, too; there was, I realized, safety in numbers. Fishing alone would be very, very foolish.

At the base of the cliff, beside the large rock pool named Bitey Bitey—"Cos em cut em feet to shit," squawked Nola—the fish were thrown into one big pile. Royal contributed a rainbow of a catch—blue and yellow striped and lurid orange, as fluorescent as the pastor's shorts, with names like Hoo-oo-oo, Fafaye and Whistling Daughter—which were thrown together with the business-suited nanwe.

Dennis began to sort out the fish, arranging them by size and type. Then Dennis counted us: Royal as one house; Nola and Reynold as another; Jay, Carol and their children the third; and Dennis and I. He set about making four piles, making sure that they had an equal share of each size and type of fish. When he'd finished sorting, he looked up, and everyone turned their faces away from the piles.

"Who's here?" shouted Dennis, pointing at one of the piles of fish.

"Nola," said Jay, whose back was turned, and Nola turned around and put the pile in her plastic basket.

"Who's here?" shouted Dennis again.

"Royal," said Jay, and Royal took her share. And in this way, a pile was allotted to a family without any possibility of favoritism, each receiving an equal share of fish, however good or poor their own catch had been.

I knew I had heard this somewhere before, but it wasn't until several days later that I remembered where—in the log of Captain Bligh.

By Monday, May 25, 1789, the launch into which Captain Bligh and his loyal crew had been forced had been almost a month at sea. Rations had been reduced to one twelfth of a pound of sodden bread—half for breakfast and half for lunch—measured out on scales of coconut shell with a musket ball for a weight. There was no supper.

That day, some noddys swooped close to the launch, so close that one was caught by hand.* It was, observed Bligh, about the size of a small pigeon. The Captain divided it, with entrails, into eighteen parts, "and by the method of 'Who shall have this?' it was distributed with the allowance of bread and water for dinner, and eaten up bones and all, with salt water for sauce." It was the only noddy they caught.

The Pitcairners conducted their affairs as if adrift in a lifeboat, with limited supplies that had to be shared to ensure the survival of all. If a passing ship donated three sheets of sandpaper, each sheet would be cut into eighteen—the number of carvers on the island—even if it meant that they received just a square inch each. When a captain gave a giant tin of

---

* The noddy bird was given its name by seamen, as it was always being caught on the masts and yards of ships.

mixed berry jam, each family took a bowl down to Big Fence with their name written on it, and Meralda and Olive went around the bowls in turn, one spoon at a time in each. My creeping doubts about the islanders' generosity of spirit put me to shame.

"What's that?" I said, as a crab ran across the kitchen floor.

"A crab," said Dennis.

I meant *what sort of* a crab was it. He didn't even think I knew what a crab was.

There was something I wanted to clear up concerning the fishing trip.

"People ever drowned Down Isaac's?" I asked Dennis.

"Plenty," he said cheerily. His acceptance of it annoyed me.

"Then why do you fish there?"

He shrugged. "Wha place else?"

"Tedside?"

"Frankie fell down Tedside," he said.

"St. Paul's?"

"Some time back, two men drown."*

"The Landing?"

"Only get small white fish or buhi down the Landing, cos of oil from em boats."†

Dennis was sitting at the table while I mixed the Alternative Pastry for a chicken and arrowroot pie I was making for supper. I had taken the recipe from Irma's *Picture Cook Book,* another handy publication produced by the Adventist Church, which Irma had received as a gift from a former pastor's wife. I read:

---

*In 1910, Harold Burdett Christian, age seventeen, and Lavis Johnston, age twenty-six, son of a Mangarevan trader, were drowned at St. Paul's.

† A buhi is a moray eel. (I caught one, once.)

*Alternative Pastry*

4 tablespoons water
1 tablespoon lemon juice
4 ozs butter substitute
1 cup whole-meal flour

"Power es-e-on," said Ben, as he did every day, even though the power came on at the same time each morning and each afternoon. Perhaps Ben made this comment because, in a place where the supply of everything was so uncertain, he feared that, one day, the electricity would fail. It just wouldn't be there—the freezers wouldn't begin to growl, the arrowroot pie wouldn't be baked and the billy wouldn't boil. And each morning, Ben expressed his surprise and relief with "Power es-e-on."

"The power is on, Debbie, for your coffee," said Irma. She had interrupted herself delivering a monologue about the hardships of living on Pitcairn, due to one of the two televisions in the big room blowing up in the middle of a miniseries.

"It's such a problem on a small island. You can't get things fixed," she said, echoing "small island," "small island," "small island" as she searched for the comfort of a surface to clear.

"Steve. Steve. You se there?" The sound of Glen's voice on the VHF brought Irma to a standstill, as if she were playing musical chairs and the music had just stopped.

Steve came through. "Glen. Go to twelve."

Dennis reached the VHF just before Irma, and switched to channel 12. They both stood looking at the machine. Steve and Glen exchanged information about a fishing trip. I carried on with my recipe.

1 cup white flour
$^1/_2$ teaspoon salt

Heat water and lemon juice. Gradually pour over chopped shortening in basin. Stir briskly until mixture is light and creamy. Add the combined dry ingredients. Mix lightly with fork to form a soft dough. Bake in a very hot oven.

Which oven? I thought, looking about Irma's electrical appliance store.

I had been baking without eggs for about a month now, although there were still three dozen eggs in the fridge closest to the kitchen. Irma had checked them occasionally, congratulating me on not using up her last supply. But I was beginning to wonder what we were saving the eggs for, if not to eat them. So the next day, while Irma was at the commercial radio station, following *The Picture Cook Book* I decided to make upside-down sponge cake, which required two eggs.

I cracked open the first. The yolk bobbed black in the bowl, and the stench was overwhelming. I opened a second, then a third, then a fourth, and all came out stinking and rotten. I kept on cracking eggs, finding just three good ones in the first dozen. Thinking they would all go bad pretty soon, I decided to crack open the second dozen as well, and at least eat the few good ones while we could. In all, I managed to save six eggs. I abandoned my plans to bake upside-down sponge cake, and decided instead to make the eggs into an omelette for supper.

When Irma came home I was chopping peppers. She saw the bowl of yellow yolks on the table.

"What's that for, dear?"

"An omelette!" I said. "When I cracked open the eggs, they were nearly all rotten. I managed to save half a dozen. So I thought we could have an omelette with them!"

"But now we have no eggs, dear."

"They were rotten," I said, thinking she hadn't understood.

Irma opened the fridge door and peered inside, as if she could conjure up the rows of eggs just by wanting them to be there. But there was just an empty shelf. It struck me that I had never seen a shelf at Irma's that wasn't jam-packed.

Irma's distress was obvious in the tightening of her mouth and the untypically slow, soft way in which she closed the fridge door.

"We. Have. No. Eggs," she said.

"We didn't *have* any eggs. We only had *rotten* eggs. This"—and I held up the bowl of yellow yolks—"is all we've got left."

I was trying to make things better, by explaining, but I was only making things worse. A lack, a shortage loomed up before Irma and made her anxious. It hadn't mattered that the eggs were rotten; at least they were there, lining the shelf of her fridge. Empty spaces frightened her. You never knew when you would be able to fill them again.

"It se aw-right, dear," she said, "I'm not hungry," and went out to the duncan, looking as if she might be sick.

I'd fallen into a pattern of spending my days cooking, weeding, washing and joining occasional fishing trips, and in the evenings sitting on the veranda working on my basket and listening to the conversation. One morning my gentle routine had been broken by a call to public work. Public work was an alternative tax system. Instead of having islanders pay a percentage of their income to the Administration, which would have been impossible to enforce and in most cases amounted only to cents, men between the ages of sixteen and sixty were required to answer any call to public work—repairing the longboat, clearing the roads or maintaining the molasses and arrowroot-making equipment. Recently the men had begun to grumble: now women were earning a wage (*Look at Olive! She'd been island secretary for five years, earning more than two thousand dollars!*), they should have to do public work.

Irma, as always, was the most articulate on this controversial issue.

"Women's lib on this island, you see, dear," she explained, "has gone all wrong. Now the women have some of the highest-paid government jobs, but don't have to do public work. Royal, for example. She earns a lot. She has a widow's pension and her government job. Yet she doesn't have to do public work. She makes a lot of carvings. While the men are doing public work, she can make carvings and earn money. The women can trade on the ships while the men have to unload cargo. It's not right."

Terry, who was working on a carving as Irma did the washing and I kneaded the dough, suggested that everyone should pay tax on their government job, but not on the sale of their curios.

"The women have it easy," said Irma. "While the men work, they can do anything!" She raised her arms, wet from wringing the clothes, to emphasize this astonishing, and appalling, truth.

"It's the same in New Zealand," said Irma. "They have this thing called doll."

"The dole," I said.

"Well," she explained. "People who work have to pay tax for those who don't work. It's not fair. So I think they should put a stop to it."

Irma—as assistant radio officer number two, public relations officer, and typist—had a taxable income. But she was near retirement, and too old to help clear roads. So I offered to do public work in her place.

Often Irma seemed grateful, but I never knew whether she wanted me to think I was pleasing her or whether I really was. But her delight at my offer to work was genuine. The burrows on her face stretched and turned upward, and, for the first time outside her shack, she looked like VR6ID.

"People will *see you*," she said. "I like people to know that you work, dear. It's good for them to see. No one can say I don't want to work." And she smiled so unaffectedly that I smiled, too, pleased that I was behaving proper Pitcairn.

When the bell in the Square struck three times one morning, Ben, although seventy and no longer making money except from the sale of his carvings, quietly went and picked up his hoe, pulled on his taumata and waited on the veranda for Dennis and me. He shuffled up behind me on the back of Dennis's bike, and we headed west up a path I hadn't taken

---

*taumata*—archaic Tahitian word for a hat made from plaited coconut leaves. On Pitcairn, the word is used for any pull-on hat, such as Ben's.

before. The road curved up to Garnet's Ridge, at 1,100 feet the highest point on the island.

We arrived at a huge road, at least ten feet across, a real superhighway. Some of the island men were leaning on wooden implements at the road edge, talking to others who, at the most, seemed only to be playing with the vegetation.

Ben slid off the saddle—he couldn't jump—and went to the verge, where he began to *snip-snip* away at the fern and weed. Each time his bamboo handle brushed against the lantana, the small yellow and scarlet flowers released a strong, sweet scent. But the head of his hoe was so small and the crunchy vegetation so stalwart that Ben just tickled it. But he kept on patiently *snip-snip*ping away at each defiant fern, until a few inches of verge were cleared and there was a clear drain down the side of the road for when the rain came.

Once the islanders, nearly three hundred strong, controlled the vegetation. There were large areas of cleared land, well-defined gardens, sharp-edged roads where the red clay met the green vegetation. But now, with the population down to fewer than fifty, the vegetation was in control. Leaves, twine, stems and branches grew over roads, almost obscuring them. Hibiscus and lantana rapidly claimed buildings not continually shorn; the lower walls of the courthouse were smothered in it. Rose apple trees, which grew like weeds, had dammed Brown's Water. Gardens were continually encroached upon, so that corn would lose the light and the beans be choked. If the vegetation wanted something—an islander's food, an islander's home—it could take it.

Ben weeded in silence, never halting the *tap-tap* of his hoe. But the young bucks had a more aggressive technique, swinging their tools and cracking bawdy jokes.

"It make em stiff," said Trent. "All em digging."

"I se stiff all ha time," said Nigger, obviously not referring to his muscles. I noticed that a slight sweat had spread over his forearms, like dew. It seemed a long time ago and far away that I had brushed another's damp flesh, comforted by human touch.

The good joke provided an excuse to stop work, and all the men had
lowered their tools and looked toward Nigger, ready to catch the next one-
liner.

"Might be why Worree no do public work," chipped in Glen. "He
nawa stiff!"

Worree was the nickname for Tom Christian. Tom, the island intel-
lectual, disliked getting his hands dirty. But Perry was there working in his
stead, attacking the lantana systematically and with vigor.

To my surprise, the pastor joined in the ribaldry, even putting up a
name for inclusion in a list of Pitcairn men who were "nawa stiff." Sometimes he lifted up his video recorder from the front basket on his bike and
filmed those of us who were working; but most of the time he was
propped up on his hoe, laughing at someone else's story or telling one
himself. Most of his tales were about fishing, to which he was devoted. He
would often spend a day Down Rope or at Tedside with Nigger, Len and
Glen, a line in hand. He was also known to be a voracious nanwe eater,
having beaten all previous Pitcairn records by devouring twelve whole fish
in one sitting.

Talk turned from sex to ships. Someone said that a Swedish ship was
going to call Sunday noon, and again I wondered what made them say
this. Information on Pitcairn seemed to emerge from sources I had not yet
fathomed, as if plucked from the heavy air.

Terry, who had said nothing so far, mumbled, "Last time one Swedish ship call third June, 1989. Ha captain good 'un. He give me big waterproof. But ha Filipino steward mean as a brute," and everyone stopped to
listen, because Terry was always right about the ships.

There were a few lengths of clear verge at the edge of the road when
Steve decided that our work was done for the day. It was about midday,
and time for breakfast.

Perry ambled up, throwing one bare muscular leg in front of the
other instead of stepping. He was naked from the waist up, tanned and
glistening with a light sweat, which made his hairless chest seem as if it
had been oiled. His skin was so flawless, his tan so even and his smile so

fixed that, although his shape was that of a perfect male, he was not sexy. I no more wanted to touch his perfect body than if it had been molded from plastic.

"Would you like to walk back with me?" he said in perfect English and, although an invitation, coldly.

"Sure."

My legs were pockmarked with mosquito bites, some still ripe, others tipped with a tiny scab. My hands were blistered from the hoe, my hair dirty from the earth. My sweat didn't sit on me in a thin film, like oil; it soaked my clothes, it ran down my legs. It made me feel uncomfortable. Unlike Perry, I wasn't able to cultivate the appearance of someone who was lounging on a South Pacific idyll. I looked battered and harassed. I looked like I had spent the morning working on a road.

Perry strode confidently down the path.

"Are you enjoying Pitcairn?" he asked.

"Sure."

"I am enjoying Pitcairn. It is what I expected." He said this with more than a soupçon of self-congratulation.

"Not the videos, naturally," he said. "I was not expecting the videos. But the rest. Yes. Certainly."

It had taken Perry more than three years to reach Pitcairn and, if nothing else, he should have been given a prize for persistence. His license to land had been referred back several times. For Perry was an unashamed Paradise-seeker, and had put this on his application. He had been searching for a primitive island where he and his girlfriend could buy a piece of land, build their own home and settle down. Perry was twenty-five, although he looked like a teenager; his girlfriend was fifteen.

She had remained behind in Germany while Perry had paid a yacht three thousand dollars to take him from Tahiti to Pitcairn. He was to lay the foundations for their new life together, and then return to Germany to claim his bride. By that time, she would have celebrated her sixteenth birthday and be old enough legally to marry him. He showed me a picture of her that he carried in his pocket. She was indeed a schoolgirl, and a very pretty one. With long blond hair and a coquettish smile, she was the picture of an ideal partner for the perfect Perry in Paradise.

When his application had been turned down for the third time by the Council, wary of Paradise-seekers, Perry decided to write an open letter to the Pitcairners. The letter—in which he offered to work full-time for any family who would agree to invite him to the island—was pinned up outside the courthouse. Tom Christian snatched up the offer.

Now Perry lived with Tom and Betty, fishing, weeding, trading, do-ing Tom's public work and helping to dig their new well. He was a good worker, and freed Tom from the manual, menial tasks he so disliked, to talk on his ham radio and write his diary. Perry also helped Betty in her garden every afternoon. I had heard that the broccoli he had planted just a month earlier was beginning to sprout.

"How do you find fitting in here?" I asked, tentatively. Perhaps he would confess to me, a fellow stranger, a slight feeling of unease, a knowledge of the difficulty of being accepted in such a small place. Despite all outward appearances, Perry might yet prove to be a con-fidant.

Perry declared, in a matter-of-fact manner, that he had had no prob-lem at all. He had found it remarkably easy to be accepted into the com-munity, and had found everyone most welcoming.

"Yes. Most welcoming," I echoed softly.

We were walking down Jack's Tatties, passing Royal's house. She lived on the edge of town and her home had a suburban feel about it, set back from the road with a big front garden leading up to her door.

As if from nowhere, Royal appeared in her driveway.

"Wut a way you?" she greeted. She looked us up and down, and strained her neck so she could see back up the path.

"Good 'un," we chorused.

"Wa sing yourley doing?" Royal should have been a police interro-

---

*Wa sing yourley doing?*—What are you doing? What are you up to?

gator. She was always so disconcertingly direct that it made me startle, then flounder, and then feel guilty for no more than not having an immediate answer, and then blush, and then appear as if I were trying to hide some crime I had just committed, or was even in the throes of committing.

"Making babies," said Perry, thinking to crack a Pitcairn-style joke, and we walked on.

"God!" I said, hoping we were out of Royal's earshot.

Perry laughed, although it was very dry for a laugh.

"God!" I said again. I had visions of Royal mounting her bike, speeding down to Irma's, throwing herself through the bananas and declaring to anyone who might be on the veranda—Nola? Charles? Charlotte? Terry? Dennis?—"I bin see Debbie and Perry comen fer Garnet's Ridge. They se fucking!"

It was just as Ben was saying grace for supper that a ship came through on the VHF. We put down our forks and stared up at the machine.

"Pitcairni. Pitcairni. Pitcairni."

No reply.

"Pitcairni. Pitcairni. Pitcairni."

We heard Jay answer. "Pitcairn Island here."

She was a Balkan ship, a 36,000-ton bulk carrier, passing seven miles off Pitcairn.

"Are you a Pitcairner or from England?" asked the duty officer.

"I am a Pitcairner," said Jay.

"Your name must be Adams, then!" The officer was pleased.

"I am Warren," said Jay. "Jay Warren. From a whaling captain in the last century."

The officer was undeterred. "How many of you on Pitcairn? Do you have a school? Do you have electricity?" He laughed after each question, as if telling a joke.

It was already dark, and gusting up to forty knots. In four days' time, it would be the shortest day of the year. But the Pitcairners would go out to ships in the dark, and in bad weather.

Jay asked for the ship's name, and where she was bound, to be recorded for the *Miscellany*'s shipping news. Then he said, "Would you like to call at the island?"

The thought of going out in this swell was terrifying. But the opportunity to trade could not be missed; ships were rare these days. And if Jay's invitation was accepted, the bell would be sounded, the bike engines started, and I'd gather up the curios and jump up behind Dennis and make for the Landing.

Dennis and I stared at the VHF, waiting for the officer's reply.

"No, thank you very much. We must make Auckland by the end of the month." And the ship sailed by.

The meeting to discuss the proposed Pitcairn Island Museum was eventually going to take place. It had already been postponed several times due to bad weather, but this day had broken fine and the recent gusts might pass within an hour. Though you never knew on Pitcairn.

Irma had given me a rundown of the issues involved. The main problem with establishing a museum to house examples of local crafts and the relics from the *Bounty* was that no one wanted to surrender their goods. Most families had a piece of the *Bounty* legend; one of the *Bounty*'s cannons lounged in the Elwyn grass in front of Len and Thelma's; Tom Christian's house was built on stones taken from the home of Thursday October Christian, Fletcher Christian's son; every home had a few of the *Bounty*'s nails wrapped up in old newspaper; and hanging above the island secretary's desk, where Olive counted out the wages for paid work, was the head of the *Bounty* hatchet, pinned up on a board below last year's "Simms Diesel 8 Turbocharger Service Ltd." calendar.

A museum to house these artifacts and protect, preserve and catalog them, where visitors could be taken for a charge, had been muted several years earlier. But Tony had breathed new life into the idea; the Pitcairn Island Museum was his favorite project. And he had overcome the second major hurdle—where it should be located, and on whose land—by offering the school's art room, which was no longer used.

Still, Irma had many reservations. Why should anyone donate their things to a museum? How would they know that they would be safe? And who would get the money from the visitors? I had heard Royal and Irma on the veranda, arguing over these matters, although never with each other. The conflict was with some third, unnamed force—"them," "you knows." I was looking forward to a lively meeting in the courthouse.

The whole island turned out, and sat down on benches that were arranged around the walls, looking like overgrown teenagers at a school dance, waiting to be asked. Tony sat in the middle of the ring and outlined his plans before throwing the project open to discussion. There was none. Even Nola tilted her head gently in agreement when Tony mentioned how much better it would be if nails from the *Bounty*, for example, were altogether in one place, safely under lock and key. A museum committee was appointed by one person suggesting another, who mimed a "What? Me?" and then graciously accepted. There were no objections to any appointment and no contended posts. The meeting was drawn to a close.

People shuffled out into the night, which had turned balmy, and began to fill the single long bench that ran all the way along one side of the Square. I sat on the courthouse steps and watched the uncomplaining, compliant audience at the meeting transform itself into a loud, debating, objecting, opinionated throng. Now their nods were emphatic; of course it was right to have doubts. Who had the time to run a museum? Why should they hand over their things for visitors to gawk at? What was in it for the Pitcairners?

They *were* right to have doubts. Despite a law forbidding the removal of any relic of the *Bounty* from the island, much of Pitcairn's *Bounty* heritage had been plundered by outsiders. As early as 1850, Walter Brodie reported, "Little is now left of the *Bounty*, as everyone that touches there tries to get a part of her. I got a small piece of wood, which I have made into a box, and a part of her keel." The rudder is in a museum in Suva, Fiji, fished out of the waters around Pitcairn in 1933. In the 1950s, a *National Geographic* expedition, claiming to have uncovered the wreck for the first time, carried off yet more segments of the ship. The *Bounty's* copper kettle, used by seaman William McCoy to distill alcohol, was now on Norfolk Island. Other artifacts had been openly sold by the islanders. Twenty dollars could get you a nail from HMAV *Bounty*.

Perry was sitting on one end of the bench. I made my way toward him, then stopped. Royal was there with Nola, and, perhaps, if I sat too close to Perry, they would become suspicious. I had played it very cool with Tony, just nodding at him when I went into the meeting so as not to rekindle any rumors. Was Irma watching me to see where I would sit? Of course not! I was being ridiculous! I walked home to make myself a cup of coffee and retreat to my room.

I had been on Pitcairn for eight weeks, so thought I might celebrate by opening one of the small packets that my friend had given me before leaving: *It will be like having a conversation with me; you can react to each thing. Otherwise you won't realize that there's another world back here, which is carrying on and changing, just like where you are.*

Most of my Afrique-Trunk was just as I had packed it; the typewriter, paper and boxes of ribbons and corrector fluid seemed such strange baggage on Pitcairn. I found the packets and chose one, peeling back the gift paper. Whatever was once in the parcel had disintegrated. It was crawling with maggots.

I tried to think what it could have been. It must have been meat. It *was* meat. Nothing else would attract maggots in that way. And—of course—it wasn't just meat. It was *pork*. What had it been? Dried pork? Pork pâté? My friend had known that pork was forbidden flesh on Pitcairn, so had packed a little parcel of it for me as a treat.

Whatever possessed her to do that? Didn't she understand that to travel was to fit in with, not to flout, the beliefs of your host? I had been careful to do nothing to offend Pitcairn sensibilities; I had been particu-larly careful not to offend Irma.

My friend was right: even at this distance, the parcel made it seem as if we were talking to each other. Except we weren't talking, we were argu-ing. I was so furious that I had to stop myself from shouting out loud.

9 · *t e d s i d e*

The fair weather encouraged everyone to work in their gardens. Perry could be found among Betty's watermelons most afternoons, weeding and pruning. Betty was hot favorite to win the annual watermelon contest, and expected to weigh in a fine specimen of more than fifty pounds. Ben, dressed in nothing more than a pair of shorts and his taumata, walked up to his garden at Big Grass, using his upside-down hoe as a walking stick. He had cleared the ground and was planting manioc by breaking the stalks and thrusting them into the earth. When it looked like rain, Ben would put his raincoat on over the top of his shorts, so with just his bare legs and feet showing, he could have been naked underneath.

Everyone had their own garden. Ben's was separate from Irma's, which was just above our house. Dennis had a patch farther down the hill.

At last count, several years earlier, there were more than 150 garden plots on Pitcairn. The very largest was said to be one third of an acre, the size of a decent English backyard, although I never found one that large. There was a spot of ground below Dennis's new house at the Edge, strangled with waist-high weeds and grass, that, Dennis said, could be mine.

On arrival at Pitcairn, Fletcher Christian had set about dividing up his new kingdom according to European land laws, drawing neat lines across a primitive map. Even rocky promontories had to be appropriated, so that Down Isaac's was named after Isaac Martin, the mutineer who owned it. Christian allocated land by means of a lottery, believing it to be the fairest method. But there were only nine names in the draw—those of the mutineers. Those who knew how to cultivate the land—the Polynesian men and women—had none of their own to work. They could only be employed to dig, weed and grow for the Europeans.

Over two centuries, these nine plots had been divided and subdivided as children inherited from their parents. Even if left unused, land was not forfeited but could be passed on down through absent generations. So those who had left the island fifty years earlier could bequeath their land to their children, who would divide the postage-stamp plots of earth before bequeathing the ever smaller patches to their children, none of whom had even been to Pitcairn.

Every piece of the island, whether cultivated or not, was owned by somebody—an ordnance survey of the island would be crisscrossed tightly with lines—and everyone knew who owned which piece of land. And it wasn't only the patches of land that were name-tagged. Each fruit tree—jackfruit, orange, mango, fe'i—belonged to someone, even if it appeared to be growing wild, and every Pitcairner knew which they were allowed to chop down and which they were not. I had discovered this when, one day, I had brought back an orange I had found lying under a

---

fe'i—plantain, from the Polynesian *fayee.* But *plun,* although derived from the word *plantain,* is "banana" in Pitcairnese.

tree on the path. By the time I had reached Irma's, I had eaten half of its sweet flesh.

"Lovely orange," I announced to Irma. "Want some?"

"Where did you get it, dear?"

I gave vague directions, somewhere up a path near the first site for Dennis's house. I was unable to pinpoint trees with Pitcairn accuracy.

"Was it close to five rows of lab-lab?"

I couldn't remember having seen any wild beans sown nearby. Anyway, Irma's questions were beginning to irritate me. She always seemed to want to know so much about everything I did or saw, or anyone I met, in such detail. Only the night before she had asked me if Alison was at Big Fence. *Of course* she was at Big Fence; it was where she lived.

"Dear, it's only that you must not eat someone else's orange."

"But it was a tree in the middle of nowhere. There wasn't a house in sight."

"Every tree belongs," said Irma. "That sour orange Up Pulau is Bernice's." This confused me, as Bernice lived on the other side of town, and the orange tree was right in front of the school building, so should by rights be harvested by the schoolteacher.

"That patch of fe'i past Brown's Water, on the way to Tedside, that Bla Bla's. The one next to it is the government orange tree." The government also owned trees, Irma explained, all over the island. The schoolteacher, as the governor's representative, was the only one who could pick the fruit there.

"Only plun," said Irma, "belongs to the people." She wandered around the kitchen, consulting her mental map of Pitcairn.

"It was on the ground," I said. "I didn't take it."

"Might be," said Irma, turning over the idea. "If on the ground, might be anyone can take it. But dunne larn bout you found it. Es better that way."

The creation of my garden was an imposing task: first the ground had to be cleared. Dennis found me a spade and fork, and I began to dig. Irma warned that the earth would have to be well turned, to allow the seeds to take root, and arranged in raised ridges as if plowed, so that there were mounds and troughs and clear divisions between the corn, the beans, the cabbages and whatever else I chose to plant. Rick came over from the Mission House one day and said he had too many lettuce seedlings. As soon as my mounds and troughs were ready, he would let me have some. It was a miracle, he said, how well things grew on Pitcairn.

Sometimes I would take a break from gardening to give Dennis a hand. He had enough weatherboard to pin up the walls of one room, so he chose the bedroom, and I painted it bright blue, the only color of paint he had. One finished room inside Dennis's home made it seem even more like a life-sized doll's house, and Dennis and I the dolls that could be plucked out by a giant hand from above.

So the pattern of my day shifted slightly: I cooked and cleaned in the morning, and dug and hoed in the afternoon to the sound of Dennis working on his house—*bang, bang, bang.* Terry worked alongside him, but made no sound as he laid the wires. In the early evening, I would either sit on the veranda, still working on the basket, which was almost complete, or go down to Big Fence or Tamanu, where Nigger Brown lived.

Tamanu was a favorite haunt for the young people of Pitcairn— about half a dozen of them—who would come and play cards, listen to music and, if the pastor, who was a great friend of Nigger's, wasn't there, drink beer. Alison taught me to play canasta at Nigger's one night, and asked if I wanted to come over the next day, while Nig was out fishing, and learn how to paint hattie leaves.

Nigger's home was unlike any other. It had few electrical appliances, was sparse and open, with tasteful, simple, Scandinavian-style furniture. Nigger's home could have been anywhere, or anywhere but Pitcairn. It was the most inappropriate setting on the whole island for learning native crafts.

---

*hattie leaves*—the leaf of the *Bauhinia purpurea.* The name "hattie" probably came from Hattie Andre, a missionary teacher on the island from 1893 to 1896.

Alison had been soaking the hattie leaves in a bucket of water for over a week "til em smell like shit," stripped them of their flesh and dried them in the sun. Those she showed me were saucer size and shaped like a pair of lungs. Their fine web of white veins held together nothing but the warm air in Nigger's big room.

Alison took out her paints and brushes. You had to paint the leaves layer by layer, she warned, and one color at a time. If you tried to paint the whole picture onto them at once, then the colors would smudge into each other. She suggested that we paint flowers, as, although they didn't sell as well as pictures of the *Bounty*, they were far easier.

Alison's job under the Temporary Return Scheme was cleaner of John Adams's grave, and as such she was responsible for the upkeep of the resting place of a mutineer from HMAV *Bounty*. It must be thrilling to be such a guardian of history, I thought.

"Interesting?" I offered.

Alison snorted. "Boring," she said. "Fucking boring. Extremely fucking boring for twenty dollars a month."

I asked Alison how old she was, and she said nineteen, which surprised me; I had thought her much older. Not because of her looks, which were difficult to put an age to, but because she seemed to have lost her innocence. Not sexual innocence, but an unfiltered response to her environment. She was no longer easily awed, excited or upset. She was wise to how wily the world could be.

She was particularly acute about Pitcairn.

"It's unique," she said. "There's no place like it. And that itself makes me very happy for being here. Happier than I could be anywhere else. But it also makes me terribly depressed."

I drew an outline of a flower onto the muslin leaf with a pencil. It was supposed to be a hibiscus—a wide-open flower with large flat petals that overlapped, and a long black stamen. I mixed a little pink paint and colored in some of the petals in broad strokes, leaving gaps where a darker shade of pink could be added. Then I waited for the paint to dry.

I thought I knew what Alison meant. Sometimes I would be cheered by the simple fact that I was here, on Pitcairn, that most impossible of places to be. I knew that everything I did and saw and every person I talked to could only be done, seen and talked to on Pitcairn. Pitcairn didn't belong to a set of types of places. It wasn't just another American Midwestern town, or south of Spain beach resort, or even South Pacific isle. It was incomparable; it was Pitcairn.

But sometimes, this knowledge was overbearing, because its uniqueness was predicated on its isolation. You couldn't move on to the next town, try another resort up the coast road. This was it—all you saw, all you did, everyone you met were all you were going to see, do and meet until you left the island, or probably forever.

Alison had a dozen or more leaves spread out before her, and was putting a green leaf below the flower on each. She was known to be good at hattie leaves whereas Nola, who was such a nimble-fingered weaver, was notoriously clumsy with the paints. It was considered a good joke when a passing sailor was seduced into buying one of her leaves.

While waiting for her petals to dry, Alison added the final touches to some leaves that already had a large pink flower painted on them: she dipped a very fine brush in black paint and wrote "Pitcairn Island Home of the Mutineers of the H.M.S. Bounty Landed January 23rd, 1790."


I liked to be the last to go to sleep, savoring the darkness. But often when I returned from Big Fence or Tamanu after the power had gone, I had to battle for the solitude of the night with Irma. She would be in her radio shack, cruising, listening in on other people's conversations—Heidi in Hawaii contacting Rick in Romney Marsh, Bob in Boston giving German George a Charley Whisky. I would go to my room and, by the light of my flashlight, read or write. The sounds we made were small—the crackling of Irma's radio, the creak of my bed—but we could hear each other, and knew that we were in a place on Pitcairn that existed only at this hour. If the atmospheric conditions were bad, and there was no one to listen to on her radio, Irma would give me another one of her lessons.

Once, when I came back from an evening at Tamanu, Irma was sitting up in a chair in the dark kitchen. She did not jump up when I came in and asked me no questions, and her hands were, as they always were at these special times, at rest. I sat down in a chair on the other side of the room, fearful that she would detect the beer on my breath, and waited for her lesson.

"This island," she began, "is going right back where it started from."

It was best to wait for Irma to explain.

"In the beginning, al-co-hol—" she had difficulty saying the word out loud "—al-co-hol caused our problems."

In many accounts of the mutineers' early days on the island, alcohol is given as the reason for driving them to suicide and murder. William McCoy was said to have experimented with fermenting the tee-root to produce spirits. Matthew Quintal, impressed with his neighbor's success, turned his own kettle into a still. From then on, the two men were in a constant state of intoxication.

One day McCoy, in a drunken delirium, threw himself from the cliffs. Quintal is blamed as the instigator of the feud that ended with the violent deaths of all but one of the remaining mutineers.

"You see, dear, what it did in the early days. It is doing the same now," said Irma.

I never debated in the dark with Irma; it did not seem appropriate.

"Al-co-hol," the very word stung, "is destroying our island. It is turning children on their parents. It is evil."

There was a pause and, although I remained mute, Irma waited.

I never knew with Irma how disingenuous she was being. Was she accusing or confiding? Was she claiming an intimacy with me, two stubborn women who enjoyed the dark? Or was I being scolded for misbehaving, like a child?

"Ben and me, we do not like Dennis drinking."

A cockroach ran over my foot.

"Please, do not mention this to Dennis. Do not say we have talked about it."

I shook my head. Irma could not see me, but, in such quiet, she could hear the smallest movement.

"Good night, dear." It was my cue to leave. I raised myself carefully from the chair, and left Irma to the night.

It had been several weeks since any news had gotten back to me about having an affair with Tony. Still, I went to Up Pulau only during school hours, when Tony would be in the classroom teaching. Chris gave me a cup of tea and a homemade scone, and sat me down in a small study to one side of her sitting room where Tony conceived his projects and where the world's only complete collection of *Pitcairn Miscellany*s was stored. Tony had made a project of putting them all in binders, so it was easy to find the issue you required.

The monthly newsletter listed everything you could want to know about the island—the weather (total rainfall, sunshine hours, average pressure, rain days), shipping news showing ships that had made contact with the island during the previous month, a pastor's piece, a fishing report and a couple of articles, mostly written by the editor, who was Tony. If an islander contributed, it was almost always anonymously.

I looked through the bound back copies, from the first issue of April 1959, and found that two things had changed in the style of the *Miscellany:* the paper had expanded from a single sheet to two, and for the past couple of years there had been Mary's new masthead. It was a striking picture of the *Bounty,* sailing toward Pitcairn on a calm sea under a cloudy sky.

"Good, isn't it?" said Chris. "She was a great artist. She did that mural at Big Fence, with the dolphins. She used to give the children art lessons in the school. I think she was some sort of artist in America. Would you like another scone?"

The *Miscellany*s gave me a glimpse of what Pitcairn might have been: proposals for a Pitcairn Island Souvenir Agency to market and sell the curios, recycling schemes, packaging of Pitcairn oranges for export to New

Zealand, plans to harvest Pitcairn's wild coffee, which the editor had roasted and drunk, and a solar power project. Jim Akers, a physics teacher at Crescenta Valley High School, California, had dreamed of building a solar generator for the island, naming it Sunfire One. The saving on fuel costs would be enormous. The fridges and freezers were run by kerosene, which was not only expensive but extremely energy inefficient: it took seventy barrels of fuel to deliver one cask to the island. The editor expressed the general delight of the islanders at the possibility of unlimited light. "All we can say here on Pitcairn is 'Welcome Project Sunfire.'"

Mr. Akers, aided by some friends, dedicated himself to the construction of Sunfire One. The group were not solar power specialists, but enthusiasts, using Pitcairn as a playground for amateur designs, much as a backyard might be. Perhaps Sunfire One was built but they couldn't find a shipping company to transport it, or perhaps the experiment never worked, but Sunfire One did not reach Pitcairn's shores.

I turned to another year; there was Tony's project, the Pitcairn Island Museum. It was reported that a committee had been formed to raise a museum on Pitcairn. They painted the old library, made cabinets and collected items. The editorial read:

"At last it is near completion."
"What is?"
"Don't you know? The Pitcairn Museum of course."

The issue was dated 1967.


By the time I arrived home it was night, and Royal had come around with her carvings.

"Perry quit Betty and Tom's," she announced. "He se gone to Nigger's."

Irma was still agitated about the broken TV, which she had never watched. This news perked her up.

"Perry se quit Betty's?"

"Semiswe."

"Paan."

"Betty larn he no work."

"Wa sing he doing this place anyway?" said Irma, even more animated.

"You down Nig's last night?" Royal said, turning to me.

"Yes. He's got a lovely home."

"You stay there all night?" she smiled, with just half of her mouth.

"No. I come home to my own bed."


Outside the courthouse was the public notice board, where Perry's appeal for a home on Pitcairn had been pinned. There were rarely any notices there, and when there were it was usually to announce, well in advance, the arrival of a cruise ship.

The decline of the cruise ship had affected Pitcairn severely; selling souvenirs to passengers was the islanders' main way of earning cash. Royal boasted that one of her flying-bird carvings, usually sold for twelve dollars on a cargo ship, could fetch one hundred dollars from a paying passenger. And a shark, whose regular price was ten dollars, could go for the same. Islanders had been known to make four thousand dollars from a cruise ship in just one day.

Forty years earlier, an average of four passenger ships called a month. The luxury Shaw Savill ships *Corinthic* and *Athenic* made regular stops off Bounty Bay; liners like the New Zealand Shipping Company's *Rangitiki* brought 450 passengers; the Dutch liner *Willem Ruys* slept more than one thousand. In 1963, the New Zealand Shipping Company made its last call at Pitcairn. Now ships were not only seldom, they were smaller.

---

*paan*—an expression of surprise, from old English "pon my word."

The last cruise ship to call—more than eighteen months earlier—was the *Society Explorer*, she had berths for just eighty passengers.

There had been only one notice on the board outside the courthouse since I arrived: next year, the cruise ship *Maxim Gorky* would stop on her way from Easter Island, bound for Tahiti. People were speculating on who would make use of the onboard hairdressing salon, go shopping in the duty-free shops or get a manicure. And, although it was eight months until she was due to call, already sharks were being smoothed and baskets woven for the passengers. Even Dennis, a reluctant carver, had a dozen sharks laid up and was cutting more. Our trip to Henderson, some said, was to gather the extra wood needed to satisfy the passengers' demands.

The ETA was 1800 hours on February 6. She would stay till the following evening. The sixth of February was a Friday, so the *Maxim Gorky* would be anchored off Pitcairn for the entire Sabbath, from dusk to dusk.

The islanders were bound not to cook, clean, garden, fish or trade on Sabbath. But the profits from selling curios to the passengers of a cruise ship meant the temptation was great.

I asked Tom, a church elder, if he would trade with the *Maxim Gorky*. He gave the question some thought.

"I am praying that she will not arrive on Sabbath. But if she does, then it is because God wants it that way. He wants us to trade."


It was Wednesday evening, when the library was open from seven o'clock to seven-thirty, so I went down to see if there was anything interesting to borrow. I was looking for a reliable history of Pitcairn.

The library was next door to the post office, but a quarter of the size. Nola, the librarian, sat in one corner weaving. She was surprised to see me.

"Debbie," she shrieked. "You wan som tin?"

---

*som tin*—something

"A book," I said.

She was even more surprised.

"Where's the history section?"

Nola guffawed.

The cataloging system was chaotic. Books were stacked in piles on the floor or in cardboard boxes. The book which I had sent to Dennis before I arrived was balanced on top of one of the piles. Those on the shelves had clearly been left undisturbed for some time, as they were thick with dust.

"Do you enjoy reading?" I asked Nola, who was concentrating on her thatch.

"No," she said. "Nawa read. All ha books full of shit. People write bad things about Pitcairn in books," and she tutted toward one corner, as if a particularly offensive volume was to be found there.

"Them people who go write books on Pitcairn should go wipe." When Nola said "go wipe," it was with the force of a bullet and as frightening as having a gun held to your head.

Adamstown seemed quite populated. There were at least a couple of dozen tin roofs, not including the buildings around the Square and the school.

Driving along Main Road from the top of the Hill of Difficulties I would first pass Big Fence on the right, then Vula's and a few more houses before the store. After the Square, there were houses set back on either side of the road until the curve through the huge banyan trees, which blocked out the light even on sunny days. Past Big Tree, as the banyans were called, was Len and Thelma's and the burial ground, then Tom and Betty's and a scattering of houses all the way up to the school.

When Dennis and I drove together, Dennis would point out whose house was whose.

"That place Steve and Olive's. That place Vula's. That place Christie's. That place Bla Bla's. That place Bernice's. That place Nigger's. Nigger's is like one of your homes."

I had not met—or even seen—half the people whom Dennis mentioned.

"Where's Christie?" I asked.

"In New Zealand."

"When he coming back?"

"Nawa. He se gone thirty years."

"Where's Bla Bla?" I asked.

"He se dead as a hatchet," said Dennis. But his house stood along Main Road, with the tin roof collecting water and the curtains drawn.

One fine afternoon Dennis and I went exploring. I wouldn't say that we had grown close, but we had become companions. He said I should call him Sambo, his nickname, which all his friends used. We spent a lot of time in each other's company, and I found him easy to be around, shadowed by Terry.

There was a house just by the Square that Dennis had said was Elwyn's. It had been abandoned for more than twenty years, since Elwyn had died and his wife had gone to live in New Zealand.

The house was made of wood and built on stilts of rock, so that there were steps up to the veranda and the door. The steps were covered in weeds, and we had to tread carefully as in places the wood had rotted through. It occurred to me that many of the building materials Dennis had ordered from New Zealand could be found here.

"Why don't you use these windows?" I asked him. "They look okay."

Dennis was shocked. "Dem es fer Elwyn."

Perhaps the confusion of tenses was no linguistic accident; perhaps there was no past for Pitcairners. Everything occurred around about now, and every islander was still here with us. And Dennis could not take the

---

*dead as a hatchet*—a favorite Pitcairnese phrase, often used to mean incapacitated, whacked out, not good for anything. Perhaps it originated with the *Bounty* hatchet hanging in the island secretary's office, futilely nailed to a board on the wall, but this is only my speculation.

windows because they belonged to Elwyn, who had died a quarter of a century earlier, and in whose rotting big room we now stood.

There was a hint of self-deception in the Pitcairners' refusal to demolish the abandoned homes. As long as they still stood, driving along Main Road was like driving along a real street, with real homes every fifty or so yards.

Elwyn's big room looked as if it was still in use, with a huge amount of furniture and ornaments everywhere, and a can of butter on top of the tablecloth, as if Elwyn might walk in at any moment. But in places, plants had crawled in through cracks, their tentacles winding around a chair leg and their curled leaves lining the floor. This was the only color in the room, as even the wood had faded to gray.

There were verdigrised brass lamps on almost every surface, their cut-glass shades dulled by mold. There were so many brass lamps that I wondered at first if Elwyn and his wife had made it a hobby to collect them. But then it struck me: the room looked just like Irma's, except in the place of every electric kettle was a brass lamp. Polish them up, and Elwyn's would sparkle with gadgetry. Fifty years earlier, these brass lamps must have arrived as donations from well-wishers, too.

The islanders have always been an object of charity, believed destitute and deserving. When HMS *Blossom,* under the command of Captain Beechey, stopped off Pitcairn in 1825, the seamen donated their breeches to the ill-clothed islanders. Captain Beechey made representations to His Majesty's government, who responded by sending out "a proportion for sixty persons of the following articles: sailor's blue jackets and trousers, flannel waistcoats, pairs of stockings and shoes, women's dresses, spades, mattocks, shovels, pickaxes, trowels, rakes," all of which were taken in His Majesty's ship *Seringapatam.* The ship's commander, Captain Waldegrave, declared to the assembled islanders, "I have brought you clothes and other articles which King George has sent you."

Captain Beechey's mission established a precedent for the supply of Pitcairn's needs. When some Swedes saw a video of the Pitcairn children running around barefoot, they misread this as a sign of poverty, not

practicality, and sent a huge consignment of sneakers. But the most gener-
ous shipment arrived on the last day of 1959—seventeen bales of good-
quality used clothing from Seventh-day Adventist congregations in the
United States. Pitcairn was prettified: the younger girls received more than
twenty dresses each.

We creaked back down the stairs, leaving everything as it was.

"We mus na touch em," said Dennis. "Dem es fer Elwyn."


I was having a bath in just two inches of water. The fine weather had left
the tank less than half full. Irma had warned me, water was getting scarce.

I heard Royal arrive; she had brought Irma some beans from her
garden. Irma was going to soak them overnight and mash them into
fritters.

"She drink coffee. That be all she drink. That be fut she so thin."
Irma didn't sound angry. She sounded as if the person she was talking
about was someone whom she would rather have nothing to do with, was
a nuisance and a scourge. She was talking about me.

"It se no good," she said, not from despair at failed attempts to
reform me, but in utter disgust.

"She no good 'un," agreed Royal.

I stood up in the puddle of tepid water, shaking myself dry like a
dog. The night had arrived while I'd been in the bath, and the sounds of
the geckos and the surf rose to fill the absence of light. I pulled my
Pitcairn Island sweatshirt on over my shorts, the picture of the *Bounty*
under full sail making way across my chest.

As I walked carefully into the kitchen, Irma gave me a huge smile.

"Everything aw-right, dear?"

"Fine. Just tired. I'm off to bed." And I walked step by step past
Irma, past Royal, to my room.

---

*fut*—"why," maybe from English "for what."

I had been comforted by Irma's hospitality, always making sure that I had a cup of coffee, as she knew I liked. It had never occurred to me until now that Irma's eagerness to please was to draw attention to what I was doing—not to condone it.

I thought of all the other things that Irma had so gently, kindly egged me on to do. Were all these incidents of her quiet insistence in fact reprimands? I remembered how persistent she had been with Alison: "Do smoke, dear." Everything I had strived for, everything I thought I had understood, every approval I had sought and gained was called into question.

I looked through the torn mesh on my window down into the rustling valley. Perhaps I could jump out and sneak over to Big Fence or Nigger's? But the window was too high and I was too scared—of the drop and of Irma.

One of the tiny lizards had defecated on my bed, leaving a sticky trail across the single sheet. I tossed it off and lay down in the darkness, wondering when the light would come.

One afternoon, after all my baking was done and I had left the bread dough to rise for when the power came back on, I set out for Tedside, on the far west of the island. I was looking forward to the walk; since learning to drive the bike, Pitcairn had become even smaller. Now Taro Ground, a quarter-of-an-hour amble, could be reached in five minutes and McCoy's Valley, once a half-hour adventure on foot, was a bumpy but brief bike ride away.

I knew that you could get down to the sea at Tedside, as Dennis had mentioned that it was a popular place for rockfishing when the weather was fine. It was also the best spot on the island to see the setting sun. It was the only place where there was any hint of transition from day to night, any mention of dusk. Everywhere else, it was either dark or light. Dennis had told me that he and Mary had gone down there often at the end of the day.

I took the westward path running up behind our house, a direction I had never taken before. In places it was dug deep into the clay, with steep embankments on either side hung with ferns. In others, the path turned sharply upward and broke through into the soupy sunlight, and I was standing on some sort of summit, and ahead of me the path plunged down into another tunnel of vegetation. The undergrowth rustled as the lizards and fruit rats that I couldn't see scuttled about, giving me the sense that I was being watched.

I crossed a damp, shallow ditch where it seemed water had run just a few days before, which must be Brown's Water, the island's only natural spring. Once it flowed freely, and it provided the first few generations of Pitcairners with all the fresh water they needed. But now it was reduced to little more than a trickle, and often was dried up altogether, although along its narrow banks the leaves still shone an even more vibrant green than along the edges of the paths. One valley was studded with tall plantain trees, heavy with fruit. I wondered whose they were.

The only inhabitant on the west of the island was a terrapin. Dennis had said I could easily spot if it was around, as it tanked a path through the bush. It was as large as a Shetland pony and a native of the Galápagos Islands, from where it had come over thirty years earlier. He, or maybe she, was the sole survivor of a project to introduce the species to the island. Now the terrapin wandered around alone, with no possibility of ever finding a mate. I saw a line of broken Elwyn grass, but perhaps it was caused by the wind.

The path went up and down, then up, up, up before winding down the cliffs and tumbling into Tedside. At the crest of the cliff there was a shack, rather like a large garden shed, looking as if it had been constructed from wood and iron sheets scavenged from the shore below. But there was little scavenging on Pitcairn; we were too far away and too small for much to reach us. Charles said that he had once found a bottle with a message in it, but the seawater had seeped inside and by the time it arrived on the island the words had been washed away. But this could have just been one of Charles's tales.

When I walked up to the shack, it became clear why it appeared so ramshackle. It had been abandoned for some time. Inside there were two rooms, both very small. One had a table that was sitting up like a dog on its two remaining legs. There was a tin mug, an empty can of lambs' tongues and a fork on the floor, as if someone had been eating at the table just before it had collapsed. In the second room was a mattress. And on the floor was a shirt, a man's shirt.

Even in the disuse and decay, the shack felt as if something had happened here that was wanton; and for the first time on Pitcairn, I was reminded of the sort of life a European might imagine living on a South Pacific isle—primitive, remote, elemental and passionate. This small place, on such a small place, was the stuff of fantasies. That sour-sweet scent hung in the air, suggested in the way the shirt was tossed on the ground, beside the bare mattress that so unashamedly filled the floor. The shack seemed designed to serve the most basic, encompassing desires.

Now the fruit rats had left their droppings. But the stain of that scent was unmistakable.

I walked backward through the entrance, where I imagined there had never been any need for a door. I was standing on some rocks, about twenty yards away from the water's edge. From the cliffs behind, palm trees shot out horizontally, their roots embedded in the red clay, looking just like the guns used by clowns in the circus that sprout feathers when fired. Below, the sea hit the rocks sharply, frothing about the hard shore. Between the cliffs behind and the rocks in front stood one huge pandanus tree, whose leaves had shed a crackly blanket, which was comfortable to sit on.

I looked down at my legs: they were spotted with rancid mosquito bites and blotched with bruises. The coral cuts still oozed. I had scratches on my arms from clearing the lantana for my garden. I remembered reading the astonishment of historians in the British Library—it seemed so long ago—that the Tahitian women found the toothless, pockmarked, scarred-from-knife-fights mutineers attractive. Captain Bligh had given a description of Fletcher Christian after he had spent five months on Tahiti, in order to facilitate his master mate's capture: "blackish, or very dark complexion, dark brown hair, strong made; a star tatowed on his left breast, tatowed on his backside; his knees stand a little out, and he may be called rather bow legged. He is subject to violent perspirations, and particularly in his hands, so that he soils any thing he handles."

The South Pacific had not made me attractive; I had not become a tanned, supple, unscarred sylph. Pitcairn had attacked my body and changed it. Already my bare toes were beginning to spread.

The pandanus above me was a strange-looking tree, with each long tortured branch carrying only a few large leaves. It wasn't really a tree at all, but a plant in tree's clothing. Its strength was deceptive; if you needed something to hold when walking along a slippery path and reached out for one of its leaves, it would pluck easily from the branch, and you would fall with the leaf still in your hand. The plant-tree's bark looked as silvery and hard as the coconut palm's, but it was spongy to touch, and you could dig your nail right into it. And if you leaned on a branch, it would snap in two like a strip of raw carrot.

The sun was slipping behind the ocean, like a golden coin being pressed into a steely slot machine, but there was no flashing of lights, just night. I took out my diary. I felt awkward writing in public, sitting on the veranda, as writing was not welcomed. Spending time by myself in my room was also regarded with some suspicion. I relished the thought of writing alone here, and being able to record whatever I wanted. I wrote:

> I haven't drunk any coffee for three days now.
> I thought Irma liked me. I thought I was doing okay. Why didn't she say something to me about the coffee?
> How can I make myself more Pitcairn? I think I should learn just to do exactly what everyone else does. Perhaps however small the difference, like drinking coffee, you need to be part of a team here, to pull together.
> Pitcairn is a Pandora's box of unspoken emotion. But what if it

*were spoken—then what? How can you cool down when you live to-*
*gether under a cloche?*

It was the smallness of the island that had attracted me to it. I had
thought it would be far easier to get to know, understand and become part
of a handful of people on a spit of rock; now I was not so sure.

I pulled a leaf from a low-lying branch. It was surprisingly sharp,
and scratched the tip of my finger.

*It's not like Africa. I could always find someone like me there.*
*Even if hundreds of miles away. I could get on a bus. Here there is no*
*one, and nowhere to go.*

I began to walk back, feeling the earth under my bare feet grow
colder with the dark. I could barely see the path, but it had become a
tunnel of sound as the small animals of the night ran among the undergrowth on either side, as if drawing a track of noises for me to follow. I
was enjoying the walk.

*Mmmmeeeeeeeeeeeeeee.* The glare of the headlight blinded me.

"Debbie! You okay?" Dennis looked frantic.

"Fine," I said, feeling desolate. "Anything wrong?"

"Mum sent me out—she se worree. We se all worree. Bout you bin?"

"Down Tedside. I went to watch the sunset."

"Alone?" Dennis was astonished.

*Mmmmeeeeeeeeeeeeeee.* Another headlight dazzled me, then bounced
off. It was Irma.

"Bout you bin?" she asked, frantic.

"Down Tedside."

"Who with?"

"No one."

It was clear that Irma didn't believe me. She continued talking under
her breath, never looking at me, never actually accusing me, but making
me feel wretched.

I was escorted back to the house like a runaway child being returned to her home.

"It dangerous," said Irma. "No one gwen down Tedside by emself. It dangerous."

Perhaps Irma thought I might take a false path and get lost, fall down a valley or be bitten by a rat. But it was clear that the dangers Irma was referring to were not from the dark or the road or the nocturnal animals, but other people. And it wasn't in the form of physical threats, but of disapproval. It was dangerous to go by yourself for a walk down Tedside in the late afternoon, because people would disapprove. There might be rumors that you were making a secret, romantic assignation. But more, it was an individual, adult act and was seen, therefore, as an act of defiance.

# 10 · up tibi

It had been more than two months since the *Tundra Queen* had called, and there had been no more ships. Pitcairn had turned inward. We had no one to talk about except one another, and even Ben and Irma were beginning to squabble. So when I finished all my housework and gardening, I would go and visit Dennis in his new house and give him a hand painting, or hold a door frame while he marked the place.

The exceptionally calm weather, which would have been ideal for a ship, was also good for swimming in Bounty Bay. The water down the Landing was oily from the boat engines, but it was the only place on the island where you could enter the water safely. Yet I was still afraid of someone casually suggesting "Let's go nawe" because of the sharks.

---

*nawe*—swim

Whenever I remarked, as nonchalantly as possible, that I was just a little anxious about bathing in shark-infested waters, I was openly laughed at. Sharks can't harm you, I was assured, and was told the story of when Nigger, for a dare, thrust his fist inside a shark's jaw.

It was Alison who said it was a good day for a swim. And—although I never knew how word traveled on Pitcairn and the will of one became the will of all—by the time we reached the Landing half the island was there, the men stripped down to their shorts and the women fully clothed, jumping in and out of the water as if undergoing baptism by total immersion.

There was a ladder on the side of the jetty, which was the easiest way into the greasy water. The current was surprisingly strong, pulling me out toward the open ocean. I splashed my arms and pretended to be enjoying myself, but I was frightened by the power of the sea. As soon as I thought I could, without letting people know that I was afraid, I began to swim in toward the slipway. But I was getting nowhere; although facing toward the shore, I was still heading out to sea. Then a wave broke just behind me and took me, crashing, onto the slipway. Before I could stand up, it hauled me out again, on my spine and headfirst. The backs of my ankles scraped against the rusty metal runners down which the longboats ran, and began to bleed. No one was paying the slightest bit of attention to me; I think they thought I was having fun.

The sea played with me for a while, hauling me up onto the slipway, then tearing me off again, until my legs were slashed in several places. I wondered whether to cry out, but instead just looked up at Alison and Kari, dangling their legs over the side of the jetty. I surrendered to the wave; it took me, tossed me, whirled me around, then dumped me so high up on the slipway that the next, lesser surge could not reach me. I wanted to weep, but I called over to Alison.

"Great!"

She waved back. "Good 'un!"

I returned the cheer—"Good 'un!"—trying to be as Pitcairn as possible.

. . .

When I returned home there was a stamped envelope lying on the table. It was addressed "Debbie, c/o Post Office Box 2, Pitcairn Island, South Pacific Ocean." For a moment, I forgot that it could not have come from outside, that it could not be from a distant friend, my mother or my boyfriend. It had to come from Pitcairn.

"Have you had your coffee, dear?" Irma was repacking the freezer. She was particularly frenetic, even for Irma. She had no Irish tatties. They were in short supply all over the island, and the few Irma had left she had given to Rick.

"No, thanks. Don't feel like one today." I slouched before the VHF, hoping for a message.

Irish tatties was the name given by the Pitcairners to the simple potato—small, round and brown-skinned. We had home-grown kumara (sweet potatoes), yams and pumpkins, but Irma was right; the sack of Irish tatties was empty.

"We've got kumara . . ." I murmured (I preferred the peachy flesh of the sweet potato).

"What are we going to *eat?*" she snapped, slamming shut a full freezer.

I opened my letter. It was short and very sweet.

*You are very nice company and I want to be your friend.*
*Sambo*

The franked, two-cent stamp on the envelope showed a painting of HMS *Blossom*. I was the first recipient of a local letter on Pitcairn since the post office had been founded more than fifty years earlier.

It began to rain heavily, battering the roof and drowning Irma's cries.

. . .

My garden was coming along well. I had planted corn, beans and cucumbers. Already the beans and corn were sprouting, and little green question marks were rising up through the red soil. The corn was crowded together at one end of the clearing, in a box of rows, as Irma had told me that if corn is spread too thinly it will be blown down by the wind, but if planted tightly, the stems will protect one another. Beans, on the other hand, needed a lot of room, and I had planted them sparsely in long thin rows, so they would not get tangled and suffocate one another.

From my garden at the Edge, the land sloped gently up to Main Road, curtained off by a copse of head-high coconut palms. I could hear the bikes going up and down the street, detect which direction they were traveling in, and recognize Terry at least, because of the woofs and yelps from Whisky as he pulled him along. Below, the land reached to the cliff down which Ashlee had fallen, and tumbled to the ocean. On this day, the water spread out like a sheet on a well-made bed. But it was often deceptive from the Edge; you could see if the crests broke into whitecaps, but from higher up it was easier to judge the size of the swell.

Dennis assured me that the sea was calm, which was why we were going to take out the canoes, which were hauled up in a small shed alongside the longboats down the Landing. They didn't look like canoes at all, but were stubby and oblong, with sides that rose at right angles to their bottoms. They resembled shallow shoe boxes, but Terry said they were modeled on Boston whalers, after a ship had called carrying one, and were very stable in the water.

Fishing from the canoes was of two types: you either dragged a line behind you for wahoo—a giant fish with a prehistoric spine whose tough flesh the islanders ground up for fishballs—or you drifted gently with a line dropped over the side, to catch any red snapper that were around.* The snapper could be fried, although it wasn't as popular as nanwe. Most of the snapper was frozen and taken out to the ships.

---

* This is not the same as our red snapper, but a grouper *(epinephelus fasciatus)*.

Every family had a canoe, and every other canoe had an outboard motor, so only half of the canoes were taken out at any one time. I had read in a *Miscellany* Up Pulau that the motors had come from a Japanese fishing consortium, in return for fishing rights in the rich Pitcairn waters. But even in their motorized canoes, the Pitcairners were lucky to catch half a dozen fish. Dennis was happy if he caught one wahoo every three or four trips. He often came home empty-handed.

The canoes edged easily down the slipway. I jumped in from the jetty, Dennis pulled the throttle and we set out to sea in a shoe box. The boat rocked, but not unpleasantly or with any menace; it was more like being cradled than shaken.

There were no obvious arrangements made before we cast off, but we were always in sight of another canoe, carrying Clarice and Meralda. It tickled Dennis to no end, seeing two women fishing together, and it was clear from their obscene gestures that Clarice and Meralda found something amusing in seeing me and Dennis alone in a canoe.

Because the canoes were so small, and the Pitcairners so huge, no more than two people could go out in a single craft without the risk of being overloaded and capsizing. But it was rare for anyone to go out alone. You needed one person to keep an eye on the line, and the other to keep an eye on the water. You never went out for wahoo without a partner, as the fish was so heavy that you needed two people to drag it in.

We sped around to the south side of the island, to a spot Dennis knew was a favorite snapper haunt. We turned off the engine, dropped a line and waited. Our line must have been thirty feet long, but it still didn't touch the ocean bed. This was startling only because I could *see* the bottom, see the dark and differing shades of coral and rock, and notice where they broke and where there was sand. It was as distinct as a painting-by-numbers.

We waited for about ten minutes—it was difficult to tell exactly how long—rocking back and forth in our box, and Meralda and Clarice about a hundred yards away, rocking back and forth in theirs. Then Dennis waved over to the other canoe, and we set out for a different spot, even farther around to Ginger Valley; perhaps we would have more luck there.

Len Brown, Dennis said, was the best when it came to fishing. He knew all the good grounds, and had an uncanny knack for finding the shoal. From the rocks he pulled nanwe as if they were made of steel and he had a magnet for a hook. In the canoe, he just had to switch off the engine and a shoal of snapper would congregate around him. Some people simply had the knack, said Dennis, and others didn't. Dennis was not renowned for his fishing skills.

He handed me the line. We rocked and talked. The first Pitcairn Island internal mail delivery, which Dennis had so carefully stamped, was never mentioned.

"What's the shack down Tedside?" I asked.

"You mean the summer house? That's Nigger's."

"Summer house?" The idea seemed absurd.

"Fer holiday. Weekend away. Es ha other side of island," said Dennis.

Of course, it was almost as far as you could get away from Adamstown, the opposite end of the country.

"Nigger no bin go that place this time."

"Why?"

"Ka fut," said Dennis.

The line went taut. *God*—it was a big 'un. Dennis helped me pull, but down in the depths this fish was thrashing. Dennis threw on the engine, and we were off, racing along as I held on to the line.

"That kill em," said Dennis, with relish. We bounced along in our box until the line went limp. I drew in a handsome gray fish, about twice the size of a salmon.

"Kingfish!" cried Dennis.

---

*ka fut*—don't know why

When I held it up high in my hand, the broad flukes of its tail touched the bottom of the boat. It was a prize of which any hunter would be proud.*

When we lured another, Dennis was even more excited. Clarice and Meralda's boat was empty. They signaled over to turn back toward the island.

I was thrilled to be speeding into Bounty Bay with the silver in our hold. The fish arched in the basket as I negotiated the Hill of Difficulties, with Dennis leaning forward to counteract his weight on the back and shouting orders.

"Mind em ditch! Turn em wheel!"

But I knew that he was pleased that I could handle a bike, and that he had taught me.

We spent another evening at Nigger's. Rick was strumming vigorously on his guitar: *There is joy, joy, joy in our hearts . . .* Perry was there, and, despite the temporary setback with Tom and Betty, buoyant about his prospects on Pitcairn.

"I will ask permission to build my own house," he said. "That will be much more easy than staying with a family. Then my girlfriend and I will be able to live together."

Many of the others were tired from a day's fishing, and left early. I stayed behind to finish my beer, talking lazily with Nigger. We both, and especially Nigger, knew the risk of being alone together. That in itself was enough to accuse.

He told me he had thought of setting up a fishing venture, somehow

---

* There is some dispute among the scientific experts as to which fish the kingfish actually is. They can broadly agree on the color (whitish, yellow toward the fin) and the length (from one to six feet), but it could be either a tuna or Carangidae. Of course, the Pitcairners are quite certain about the fish's identity: it's a kingfish.

getting the money to buy a boat with refrigeration, so he could fish Pitcairn waters commercially, taking the catch on to Tahiti for sale. Prices were high in Tahiti.

"But . . ." he said, and that was all.

Since a teenager, he had been carving. He was known as a fine carver—his flying fish on a stand were the best on the island—but now he rarely took up his tools.

"When I was twenty," he said, "I didn't care that I would be doing the same thing for the rest of my life. Now it's a horrible thought: that I will never do anything else than what I'm doing now."

He drove me home through the orchestra of the night: the rats scuttling, the bamboo creaking, the whistle of the surf.

I came out of my room when I heard Royal and Irma arrive back from picking beans. I asked Royal if geckos rubbed their back legs together, like grasshoppers do. For several nights, there had been squeaking behind the Afrique-Trunk in the corner of my room, with the untouched typewriter and unopened correction fluid still packed inside, followed by the dry sound of something scampering away. I thought it must be one of the harmless lizards.

"Rat," said Royal. "Es one rat squeak."

She was delighted to share her knowledge with me, keeping her eyes fixed upon my face as she did so.

"Oh, a rat," I said, as cheerily as possible. "It's only a fruit rat. Oh, that's harmless."

"Toj this place?" said Irma.

"No." I hadn't heard anyone.

"Oh, it's just that someone doing souvenirs, dear."

I noticed a shower of shavings by the chair on the veranda, so fresh you could smell them. Terry must have been sitting there, as quiet as a cat, scraping his carving while I read in my room. Even though I had been at home, and Irma had not, it was Irma who knew this.

There was a long ring; it was definitely a long ring, and, without thinking, I picked up the phone.

"Yourley there? Yourley? Yourley, ship es comen. Five P.M. This day."

From all around Adamstown, the listeners responded to the news.

"Wha place she es comen from?"

"Filipinos? Filipinos no good fer trade."

"Paan!"

"Long time no ship."

*"Erickson Frost."*

"Might be she no gwen stop."

"Surf good fer em boats."

"Paan!"

I put down the phone. Irma and Royal were standing feet away from me.

"It's a ship," I said.

"Paan!" said Irma, lunging for the phone.

Royal snorted.

Irma added her comments to the countrywide chorus.

"You se say Filipino? . . . Ha Captain good 'un. . . . He se big as a hatchet."

Dennis strode in. He was going to open the post office in case people had any mail, in the hope that the Captain might agree to take it on board for posting at his next port of call. In exchange for the courtesy of carrying the mail bags, Dennis would give the Captain some bananas.

The chandeliers of fruit in front of the veranda were wearing thin, and some were turning black. Down McCoy's Valley, Dennis had spotted some good bunches, so we tied two tarbs to the back of the bike and set out to claim them for the Captain.

We rode past Fred's Mango, up Jim's Ground, through Hulianda

---

*tarb*—a machete, used to slash and cut. Origin of the word is unknown, but may be Polynesian.

into a valley as big as a ditch with a cluster of banana trees to one side. Some had been blown down in the storm, and the snapped trunks lay on the ground. From the center of the standing stumps, a thick white stem thrust out, as fresh and shiny as a spring onion. Already the new stem was two feet high; within months a new tree would be formed.

The bunches were hanging far above us—perhaps twenty to thirty feet—and I wondered by what method, and involving how many dangers, the tree had to be climbed and the bananas cut down. But Dennis swung his tarb at one of the highest trunks and the blade sank into the trunk, splattering him with sap. Dennis swung again, and the tree creaked and, slowly, fell, and a bunch of bananas, as big as a man, thudded onto the leaf-cushioned earth. There was just a stump, as high as Dennis's waist, where the tree had stood.

I took my tarb and struck another tree. The trunk was soft and crisp, and the blade slashed deep into it, showering me with sweet, sticky juice as clear as water. I pulled out the blade and slashed again, and again and again, until the tree groaned and fell. The stump was a raw wound, bleeding juice, with a snow-white center ready to thrust forth again: already, it seemed, a new shoot was erupting, searching through the umbrella of leaves for the sky.

The bike could take no more than four bunches, three strapped to the back behind where I sat and one in front of Dennis. We drove home gingerly; if we hit a ridge on the path at a bad angle, the extra weight behind would make us capsize, somersaulting backward.

It was enormously pleasing to see Irma so delighted with our load, and Royal unable to comment.

"You cut em?" she eventually asked.

"Sure did." I felt better than I had for days. I went to make some milo. As I switched on the electric kettle, I noticed that my hands were turning brown, the color of a Pitcairner, but in patches, like a piebald horse. And stains were emerging from my sweatshirt and shorts. It was like witnessing the special effects of a sci-fi movie take place on my own body. One minute I was white and clean, and the next a brown cloud was spreading over my skin and clothes, and at such speed that, if I put my hands behind my back then brought them forward again, I would have lost another one of my fingers to this mysterious creeping disease.

I looked around to see if anyone else was being overtaken in this way, but their skin was dark and their clothes so stained already that I couldn't tell.

I held my hands up in front of me, hoping that, if I kept them as far away as possible from the rest of my body, it wouldn't spread. Royal, watching my horror, laughed.

"Se juice," she said. "From em plun."

The sap from the banana tree, although colorless when first struck, slowly turns dark brown and stains. It would not, Royal informed me, wash out for several days, and she pointed to my face. Fine brown spots were erupting on my cheeks.

"Don mind," said Dennis, who was sitting in a seat opposite the VHF. The ship might call at any time, giving her position.

It was time to get ready, so I went to change into some clean shorts and my Pitcairn Island sweatshirt, part of the team.

"Can't plan for the future here," said Ben, working on the fingernails of his hand vase. We had been sitting on the veranda all afternoon, and still no news of when the ship would call.

"Can't plan for future on Pitcairn." Ben often said the same sentence twice, slightly rephrased, as if he expected to be misunderstood, or ignored.

Terry was listening, but made no outward sign of having heard.

Then he began. "*Willem Ruys* due to stop twenty-sixth April, a Friday, 1963, with one thousand passengers. We work very hard on souvenirs. Day before she due, Thursday twenty-fifth, news come through: weather so bad that ha ship far behind. She no stopping."

We sat for a further five minutes or more without speaking.

"What you doing, Terry?" I asked.

"Jus waiting."

Ben looked up. "When ha ship comen, you jus wait around."

The following afternoon the bell struck five times. We had been waiting on the veranda, the bike loaded with bananas, since the previous day. But now the starting gun had been fired and we were off. Within minutes we were down at the Landing and we jumped into *Tub,* followed by our baskets of curios and Dennis's mail bags containing my postcard home.

Wrapped in newspaper in my new curio basket was one of Ben's hand vases, with his signature scratched on the base by Irma, and three small sharks from Dennis. I had a notion to see if the chief steward had any garlic, to swap for some postcards or stamps.

The *Erickson Frost* rose over the horizon and roller-coastered toward us, as broad and high as a tidal wave. Yet Steve kept us bobbing toward her, the engine on full throttle, as if this were a meeting of equals, not a tiny longboat heading for a rampart of steel. When all we could see was the side of the ship, Steve dance-stepped *Tub* sideways, and we attached ourselves to her.

The wall of faces at the top of the rope ladder was a familiar formation—one group short, dark and round faced, smiling and constantly moving; the other tall, silver-blond, with arms crossed and sage expressions. Filipino crew and Scandinavian officers, standing either side at the top of the rope ladder.

The sea was so calm that I skipped onto the rung, and skittered up.

"That's dangerous," said an officer, crossing his arms even tighter and rocking from side to side on large, flat, booted feet. When he stopped speaking, the rocking was arrested and he became a statue of Viking virtues again.

I sniffed. "You just have to watch for the swell. Where're you bound?"

"New Zealand." The officer was not a talkative man.

"What are you carrying?" I tried to counter his taciturnity with a light skip in my voice.

"Ba-na-nas." *Bananas* acted as a rhythm for the officer's rocking—right *(ba)*, left *(na)*, right *(nas)*.

"Anything else?"

"No. Only ba-na-nas."

"Would you show me to the galley, please?"

He thumbed aft, then recrossed his arms.

"Thanks."

The *Erickson Frost* seemed very large, much larger than I remembered the *Tundra Queen*. But perhaps my vision had shrunk. Fish and people came in extra-large on Pitcairn, but everything else was a child-sized portion.

I must have walked to Tedside and back just reaching the galley. And the galley itself was not one big room, but a series of utilitarian, uncluttered spaces, through several of which was the chief steward by a row of cold stores.

"Hello. How do you do?" I fanned out some postcards. "Do you have any garlic, please?"

He nodded enthusiastically—"Please, please"—unbolted a cold store and showed me inside. Although it was no bigger than a large cupboard, he followed me in and stood close to me among the sacks of vegetables—red onions, sweet peppers, cabbages whose leaves were already curling and Irish tatties. There was a netting bag of garlic bulbs, tied together in bunches; the chief steward reached in and picked out a big bunch for me. He waved the bunch before his face as if displaying a shrunken head, then closed the door.

My first thought was *It's very cold in here.* My second: *You're smaller than me,* as the chief steward made a lunge toward me. He pulled me to his chest and attempted to kiss me, jerking my head toward his. I tugged my head away and kicked his shins. He stood back a moment, and we confronted each other in the cold room, like boxers just before the bell for the next round.

*Ding!* And the chief steward lunged toward me again, this time adopting the tactic of holding my arms down and pushing me up against the cold steel door.

I shouted, "What the fuck—," freed an arm and walloped him in the face. It was the shock, not the force of my blow that made him totter away from me. And, as if insulted, he touched his struck cheek softly. Then he smiled at me.

"Please," he said, grinning broadly, making the word as long as a snake. He was still holding the bunch of garlic in one hand, and waved it at me, as if enticing a dog with a bit of fine meat. Then he pointed toward a sack of onions.

"You would like?"

"No, I would not like your fucking onions!"

*Ding!* He pushed at my shoulder so I fell back. He kissed my shoulder, then started to make a line of kisses toward my mouth. It felt like a cockroach crawling up my neck. I wriggled and kicked, but it didn't deter him. It began to dawn on me that he actually liked it. I could feel the bunch of garlic—clasped in his hand—banging against the top of my leg.

I began to draw circles away from myself; first, there was the cold room with its sack of red onions, its peppers, its Irish tatties, all stacked about me as the chief steward splattered my neck with kisses. Beyond that was the galley, where Jay would be striking a bargain for his frozen snapper. Beyond that was the deck, where Royal, Nola, Kari and Meralda had their curios spread out on a sheet before them. There was Dennis on the bridge offering the Captain our bunches of bananas, while the hold below held thousands of tons of the same fruit. Glen would be keeping the helm in the longboat as she floated alongside. Beyond that was the reach of sea to Bounty Bay, the pimple of rock called Pitcairn and then the great ocean. Three thousand miles away was New Zealand, where the *Erickson Frost* with her chief steward on board was bound.

With renewed energy, I threw the chief steward off. We tussled with each other: I pulled his hair, kicked him, and he sneaked kisses whenever a piece of my flesh was close enough to his. I had the sense that he thought this was all part of a game, and that despite my show of resistance, a bargain had been struck: I would let him have rough-'n'-tumble sex with me in exchange for a bunch of garlic bulbs. I wondered how long this would go on; would we continue for hours, throwing each other against the sacks of onions until the red peels began to crumble? Would we, exhausted by the fight, collapse in a heap, panting and dewed from the cold? Would the longboat leave without me, as I sailed on in the cold room to Auckland?"

"*Fuck youuuuuuuu!*" I delivered one last blow. It hit the chief steward on the forearm, and his hand shot up smartly as if from an electric shock.

"Ooooh." It was more an expression of surprise than pain. He looked at me with utter disgust, sized up what our encounter had been worth, picked off one bulb of garlic from the bunch and threw it at me. It hit my chest and fell on the floor. I walked over to the sacks, held out my sweatshirt like an apron and filled it with onions. I nodded toward the door, and the chief steward drew it back and let me through.

It was warm and bright in the galley. Jay was offering some fish for a drum of sunflower oil. He saw my hammock of onions and the chief steward close behind, and winked.

We were making ready to leave. Baskets and the drum of sunflower oil were lowered on ropes, knocking against the side. Steve was handling a large television, which he had exchanged for twelve Pitcairn T-shirts. Large plastic sacks marked "Hazardous Waste" were bundled into the longboat.

"What's that?" I asked Kari, hanging over the deck rail.

"Later. I tell you later," and she reached for a rope for her curio basket.

I climbed down the ladder as the longboat lounged on a quiet sea. Trade had been good, so the singing was heartfelt.

*We part, but hope to meet again*
*Goodbye, Goodbye, Goodbye.*

I turned to Randy, Trent's younger brother, who was sitting next to me. "The ship looks so huge," I said. "There's nothing that size on Pitcairn."

"The island," he said bluntly.

Although there was a swell, the mood on board was buoyant and not even Betty was seasick.

"Onions!" said Royal, peering into my bag.

"Fucking onions," I said, and Royal laughed. It was the first time I had cracked a joke on Pitcairn.

I had been told that Kari kept pretty much to herself. As her husband, Brian Young, was away, she just stayed at home with the kids, read books and worked her ham radio. Her house—Up Tibi—was out of town anyway, a couple of hundred yards up the hill behind the Square, so it wasn't surprising that she rarely came into town. Not even her brother-in-law Terry went out of his way to visit her.

Up Tibi was a short, steep climb from Adamstown, and within minutes of leaving Irma's I had driven Dennis and myself up to Kari's back door. She was sitting in a deck chair on the veranda, from where she could look down over the town, the Edge and the heaving sea.

"You can hear the ocean from everywhere on Pitcairn" was the first thing she said. Her words were part advertisement, part declaration of affection and part warning. She was in love with this lone rock in the ocean and would not betray it.

Kari was sun-bleached blond, wiry, middle-aged and as attractive as an athlete, exuding healthy living. Despite twenty years on the island, she remained physically distinct.

We went inside for the shade. Kari's home was far more Pitcairnese than Nigger Brown's. It was cluttered, and furnished with simple chairs and tables. On the wall was a floor-to-ceiling handwritten chart, showing important historical dates.

4000 B.C. THE CREATION
2349 B.C. NOAH'S ARK
1871 B.C. ABRAHAM OFFERED UP HIS SON
1491 B.C. MOSES ON THE MOUNTAIN . . .

Kari reached into a "Hazardous Waste" sack and pulled out a beer.

"From the ship," she said. "It is necessary to let yourself go once in a while. Simply studying the Bible is not enough on this island."

Dennis neither spoke nor moved.

"How do you reconcile it, then? Being an Adventist and drinking?" I asked.

Dennis rubbed his nose with the flat of his hand, so his whole face was obscured.

"Where in the Bible," she asked, "does it say that you can't drink?"

I nodded in agreement, believing the question was being used to confirm an opinion rather than examine it.

But Kari wanted to know. *"Where?"*

After so long on Pitcairn, a genuine question, with discursive possibilities, sounded rather odd. I didn't know where to begin, but Kari took out her New International Bible and looked up "drink" in the index. It referred her to Proverbs 31:6.

Give beer to those who are perishing wine to those who are in anguish let them drink and forget their poverty and remember their misery no more.

Kari read it out loud, over and over. Then she said, "Let's go down to Rick."

"I count I gwen start fer home," said Dennis. I had almost forgotten that he was in the room with us.

Kari wouldn't let him. "You comen long fer aklen," she said.

Kari went to brush her teeth, so Rick would not be able to smell the beer, picked up her Bible, and we walked down to the Mission House. At every junction, Dennis discovered a reason why he had to just go and visit Jay, pop back home to see if Terry was there, help Ben weed his garden, but Kari dragged him along like a child being taken shopping.

Rick welcomed us warmly, as if overcome with joy at Kari, Dennis and I so unexpectedly popping in to see him. Kari was blunt: she said we had come to ask where exactly in the Bible it forbade drinking. Dennis had not yet come in through the door and hung around outside, looking for a chance to escape.

Kari opened her big black Bible and pointed to Proverbs 31:6. She read it out loud, " '. . . and remember their misery no more.' "

Rick fidgeted in his seat, pulling on the hem of his see-through fluorescent shorts as if suddenly aware that they were indecently brief. After a pause, during which he seemed to be wanting us to think he was praying, he said, "You've just come up to me with this; I need some time to think about it, to look at the commentaries on that section. Give me a week, will you?

"Give me a week," he repeated.

Then he told us his life story, beginning at the very beginning. This was his testimony: as a young man, Rick used to drink, a lot. He wasted his life. Although God was talking to him, he could not hear. Then Jesus Christ came to him and said, "Your body is the temple of God." And he stopped drinking, and turned to the Savior of Mankind.

It was a simple tale, emotionally put, but the emotion had the feeling of being well worn. I suspected that it was a story Rick had told many

---

*aklen*—"us" or "we." Although very common and in everyday usage, the source of this strange word is entirely unknown.

times before, and to far larger audiences than the few lost souls that now sat around his kitchen table. He stood up as he spoke, as if addressing a rally.

"What about dancing?" I asked.

Kari added that dancing was the only safe form of exercise available to people on this island, and that it was excellent physical release.

Rick said nothing. He looked very carefully at his hands, as if some words of guidance from above might be written there. Then he looked toward Jenny.

"It's seduction," she said. She was quite sure of that. The fact that dancing was seductive meant that it was, without question, a sin.

Bolstered by Jenny's words, Rick felt on surer ground, and his fidgeting ceased. Now it was only Dennis who looked uncomfortable.

"Good," said Kari, apparently well pleased with our discussion. "We will be seeing you next week, then, Rick," and we left—Kari leading, I in the middle and Dennis behind, pretending he wasn't really with us.


"Because this is such a small place," said Irma, ironing a pair of trousers with her hands, "you see the problems." It was all she had to say. She picked up a hoe and went out to her garden.

I hadn't thought of it quite as succinctly as that. In other places, the problems were faceless. Drug addiction, child abuse, violent crime were all statistics, committed by people without known names. They weren't people we knew. All transgressions remained unattributable.

But nothing was anonymous on Pitcairn. If one man got drunk, we all knew who he was. "Drunkenness" was not free-floating, but always attached. It was also very visible. One incident could assume the importance of a social trend. And it was our neighbors, our own family who were the perpetrators.

. . .

"Would you like to come to dinner?" It didn't sound like Dennis at all. His voice was different; and he spoke slowly and carefully, as if his words had been rehearsed.

"Would you like to come to a candlelit dinner in my house?"

"Well . . ." I didn't know what to say.

"Perhaps on Wednesday?"

It was the first time I had heard a Pitcairner refer to the day of the week, with the exception of Sabbath.

"Just the two of us."

He was sounding more and more like a character from one of the American miniseries we watched until the power went. I said nothing.

"Do I take it that means yes?"

I tried to picture it. Dennis and I, in my best seersucker skirt and top, sitting at a table in the skeleton of his house, without any walls, with a carpet of red earth below and a ceiling of stars above. I couldn't imagine a more public place for an intimate dinner for two.

"Yes? Is that yes?"

Perhaps Dennis had misinterpreted my ease with him. Or perhaps I refused to recognize that it meant any more than that; perhaps the misinterpretation was by me, of myself.

"No," I said slowly. "I'm afraid I can't."

Dennis became Dennis again, and his soft face winced.

"Oh," he said, but it was more like an ouch. "Might be some time else."

"Might be," I said.

# 11 · t a m a n u

*C*harlene, Darrylene, Darlene and Sherilene were leading the singing, directed by Rick. They stood at the front of the church, all dressed up, their feet planted firmly on the ground, but smiling and hand-jiving, as if performing for a congregation of deaf people.

*One, two, three, four, five*

*Jesus Christ is still alive*

*Six, seven, eight, nine, ten*

*He's coming down to earth again*

The rest of us were clapping, but not in time to the music. We were trying to swat the swarms of mosquitoes that hovered around the pews.

The sound of our stamping and slapping set an alternative rhythm to the count of the song, so the total effect was of a percussion section hopelessly out of sync.

The service drew to a close with Tom announcing the time of the next Sabbath's sunset, and the children filed out. I had been at church for more than an hour already, attending the Sabbath school, which took place before each morning service, to please Irma, who was leading today's lesson. Only Tom and Betty, Charles and Charlotte, Jacob and Mavis, Irma and Ben, Carol and Jay, Kari, Royal and I had been there. But we had scattered ourselves like seeds around the pews, as if by refusing to bunch up the church would appear to be full.

Rick had stuck close to the program in the Adult Sabbath School Lessons Book, a copy of which we each held. It gave the program for the lessons for July, August and September—last year. The pamphlets had arrived too late on Pitcairn to allow us to pray in unison with the world-wide Seventh-day Adventist community, but we still worked systematically through them. We were at lesson four, for the week commencing July 21, although it was the following August.

The lesson was entitled "The Gospel Identified." Rick helped to elucidate the text for us.

"It's no good putting a plant in the soil without roots. You might as well throw it away. It's the same with people. They are always looking for their roots, where they come from. So it is with the Gospel. The Gospel has roots—it comes from God."

Irma stood up. She was holding the teacher's edition of the lesson-book, from which she read what *Gospel* stood for.

"G-O-S-P-E-L." She spelled out the letters as if the name of an import-export company.

"G-O-S-P-E-L. *Gospel*," she said. "God's Only Son Perished Eternal Life. That is what *G-O-S-P-E-L* stands for."

Charles was asleep. He looked both the smartest and most American I had seen him, wearing jeans and a plaid shirt.

Rick told us some more astonishing facts. There were, he said,

300,000 Christian martyrs a year in the world today. *Three hundred thousand.* That was more than five thousand times the population of Pitcairn meeting grizzly deaths in the name of the Lord. And did we know that Seventh-day Adventism was the fastest growing church in the world? Two and a half million people had joined the Adventist church in the past five years. *Two and a half million.* We might want to remember that in our prayers.

I flicked through our lesson book. At the back was an order form— "Half Price Specials for Kids from the Producer of 'Kids Are Christians Too.' " This week's worldwide collection target was $5,000, to pay for twenty thousand "Power to Cope Bible Guides for Handling Stress," to be distributed in the streets of New York. That worked out to twenty-five cents apiece, so if we collected as much as last week, Pitcairn alone would be able to provide the harassed of Wall Street with almost two hundred copies.

The lesson book set us a number of tasks. There was a short piece of text from the Bible that we had to learn by heart, and a list of suggestions for further study and meditation. Then there were questions, as if we were participants in a TV game show: "Name at least four of the special reforms that are part of the three angels" messages as recorded in Revelation 14." Lastly, we had to do a quiz on "Practical Considerations."

Please check the correct answer:
- Christ's role in the gospel effort is more important than that of God. True False.
- The resurrection is just as important as the crucifixion to the gospel plan. True False.
- The Holy Spirit is even now moving up the church with early rain power. True False.

I envied the Pitcairners their unquestioning faith. Christ was coming again, of this there was no doubt. There was truth and falsehood, and you could distinguish one from the other by a check in the box. And the day of the week in which we ceased working and came to church was not *the* Sabbath, but Sabbath, with no definite article necessary, as sure as it was Tuesday or Wednesday or Thursday.

Irma had explained quite clearly why Sabbath fell on Saturday. She had taken an old "NJS Electronics Manufacturers of Industrial and Professional Products" calendar down from the wall and pointed to how the weeks were divided up into rows, and how the first day of each week was Sunday.

"Some people are trying to change the calendars," she said. "They're trying to make *Monday* the first day of the week."

I looked baffled, so Ben chipped in. "It's the Catholics. They want to make everyone like them."

"But God blessed the seventh day and made it holy, so that must be Sabbath," said Irma. She handed me the calendar, her finger still resting on the rows.

The pastor was standing up before us again, his legs shrouded in Sabbath trousers. He announced that we were going to watch a Global Mission video and switched on a huge TV, which he had wheeled into the center of the aisle on a trolley.

The screen was filled by a face that looked just like our pastor's; he was the same age, had the same wispy blond hair, the same earnest eyes, the same emphatic method of delivering his words. But it wasn't our pastor; his name was Dwight, and Dwight was another pastor in another small place, surrounded by people different to and darker than he, who did not speak themselves but were spoken about a great deal by the pastor. As we saw these people go about their everyday tasks—eating, gardening, attending school—their pastor's commentary informed us that they had converted and had been saved. Then Dwight wept.

Until that moment, I had not realized what Rick's calling as a missionary meant, and that the Pitcairners were to him what these silent people were to the Rick look-alike pastor on the video. I remembered Rick videoing us at the store, fishing, loading the longboat, climbing the ladder and trading on the ships. Which distant Seventh-day Adventist congregation, so much larger than ours, would one day see this?

Rick was sitting down, not watching the video but watching us. I wondered at how the chameleon-charactered pastor, who was so willing to please and so eager to be liked, had come to be the representative of the one certainty on Pitcairn: their faith.

As no one worked on Sabbath, we would often go for a walk. Rick encouraged this, for the same reason as *National Geographic* was the only permissible reading material on Sabbath: a walk was an expression of appreciation for the wonderful world God had created. Last Sabbath, I had explored the far side of the island, where the land was deeply ridged, with Reynold.

Reynold refused to learn to drive a bike, walking over the island's paths in his broad, stained feet. When a route was too long, he cut a new path with his tarb. He had taken me along one of his highways, stretching from Long Ridge through Water Valley, which he had opened to save an arduous walk across the rocks if he wanted to go fishing in West Harbour.

When we went, the lantana had reclaimed part of his path, but it was still easy to follow. Across a small valley, he had rolled a boulder as a bridge. We had eaten huge juicy oranges and Reynold showed me how to peel a twig from the burau tree, plentiful in Water Valley, scrape the wood underneath and apply it to a bleeding wound to stop the flow. He peeled me a guava, so unpromising outside, so pink, fleshy and sweet inside. We foraged for candlenuts and found one that the rats hadn't hollowed out and eaten. Reynold cracked it, and inside was a cream-colored waxy sub-

---

*burau*—can be written *booroa, porou, paraow, purau, pulau*. These variant spellings have confused scientists when they have attempted to identify a particular tree, as different Pitcairners will claim that it is a purau, not a burau, which outsiders, seeing the alternative written name, have read as a different plant.

stance. He said that he used the unbroken ones under his copper to keep it burning well.* At Irma's, we used diesel-soaked sawdust. No one except Reynold, I imagined, continued to collect candlenuts.†

On the way back down to Adamstown, at the turning for Highest Point, we met Charlene, Sherilene and Darlene, who were on a Pathfinders Sabbath walk, led by the pastor. Charlene, wearing her "His and Her Tournament Chub Cay 1983" T-shirt, was examining the path for tracks.

"That's Dave the Mouth. He must have walked back." She searched the moist mud, and spotted another interesting specimen. "And there se Darrylene. She se wearing my shoes!" And the tire marks made shortly afterward, she observed, clearly belonged to Glen. Reynold's bare feet and nimble steps were by far the most difficult to track.

This Sabbath, Dennis suggested that we climb up to Christian's Cave. Meralda was to join us, but she was unwell.

"Meralda fever as fer Archie's cock," said Dennis.‡ Following the visit of the *Erickson Frost*, several islanders, particularly susceptible to illnesses from the outside, had gone down with the flu. But Terry would still be coming along with us.

The cave had been Fletcher Christian's retreat on Pitcairn. He must have hoped he would never have needed such a place, that he would want to remain in the midst of his fledgling community, the seed of nirvana he had planted. Yet from the very early days on the island, it is said that

---

    * *copper*—once a huge copper pot but now a tank set in stone with a fire underneath. Irma's was out the back of the house.

    † It is generally believed, outside Pitcairn, that the candlenut is extinct, but, although not nearly as common as it once was, a Pitcairner can easily find one. Before the generator, they were used for lighting.

    ‡ Archibald Warren, a long-dead Pitcairner, had a rooster famed for its miserable, bedraggled looks. So if an islander has "da fever" (the flu), they are likened to Archie's bird.

    Pitcairnese is full of words and phrases that use personal names, and nearly every Pitcairner has contributed to the language in this way. Most recently, Royal's teenage granddaughter Shelley had hidden down Tedside when the ship that was to take her back to New Zealand had arrived off Bounty Bay. Now if someone disappears, it is said that they "do Shelley."

Fletcher used to climb up to this cave below a place that perhaps was not yet known as Lookout Point. He kept a small store of provisions there, and erected a small hut. From its shelter, he could look down over the settlement at Adamstown (although it would not have been named such), Bounty Bay and out to sea, and be forewarned of the approach of a ship— either to hail or hide from it, who knows?

The cave was reached by a steep flank of rock, so could be easily defended from strangers, or indeed his own people. For the Polynesian men, some of whom were from aristocratic families, had grown resentful and restless, and sought revenge.* Not only had they been robbed of any stake in this new land, but they had been short-changed on the women. Of the twelve women, nine were claimed by the mutineers (one each) and the remaining three were to be shared among the six Polynesians.

Some accounts say that it was just nine months before Christian was killed in a fight over who should be whose wife; others give him a full three years before being bludgeoned to death. By the end of 1793, only four mutineers had survived the massacres—Quintal, McCoy, Young and Adams.† In fear of their lives, McCoy and Quintal are said to have gone to live in the bush. It wasn't long after that McCoy, a former employee in a Scottish distillery, discovered how to make spirits from tee-root and, in a

---

* Little is known about the Polynesians who joined the *Bounty* mutineers. Frequent misspellings of their names has also led to confusion surrounding their identities, although Only the women were given European names. Niau (sometimes Newhow or Nehou) was from Tahiti, and is said to have been murdered by Edward Young after the brutal deaths of all but two of the European men. Oha (sometimes Oher or Ohoo) was from Tubuai. Tararo was from Raiatea, and may have been a chief. Teimua (sometimes Teirnua or Temua) and Titahiti (or Ta'aroamiva, the young brother of a chief) were from Tahiti. It is generally asserted that none of the Polynesian men fathered any children on Pitcairn, but it is impossible to substantiate this claim.

† The mutineers' names are also spelled in different ways in different places, and there is no accepted standard. McCoy is sometimes McKoy or Mickoy. Thomas Burkett can be spelled Burkitt or, as my own name, Birkett. Able-bodied seaman Birkett remained on Tahiti, where he was captured, taken back to Britain on board HMS *Pandora* and hanged.

state of intoxication, threw himself from a cliff. Young and Adams chopped up Quintal with a hatchet. Young died one year later, either from asthma or consumption. By 1800, less than ten years after the *Bounty* had been burned, only Adams and the women remained.

When Pitcairners walked around town (which was rarely) or ambled across the Square, they looked awkward and large. But when they made their way over a rocky mountainside, they skipped like goats. Even Terry, who was big even by Pitcairn standards and whose body was as soft as a duvet, skittered across the shingle and glided up the scree. It was I, tight and small, who looked ungainly, grabbing for the lantana, whose spindly branches broke off in my hand and sent me down the loose pebbles of clay on my bottom.

Dennis and Terry showed me how to tackle the slope sideways, running, not walking, diagonally across the shingle. This way, Terry said, you didn't slip. I grabbed hold of Dennis's hand, and together we zigzagged up the hill as if dodging bullets.

The slope ended in a sharp and sudden ledge, which Terry and Dennis hauled me up onto. A huge rock towered hundreds of feet above us, and in this rock was a hundred-foot-high dent, as if a giant chisel had chipped a piece out of the side of Lookout Point. It formed a sort of shelf in the rock face, only a few feet deep, which was Christian's Cave.

We sat in the shallow cave and dangled our legs over the ledge. Captain Beechey had written, "So difficult was the approach to this cave, that even if a party was successful in crossing the ridge, he [Christian] might have bid defiance, as long as his ammunition lasted, to any force." But it seemed a poor hiding place, with no shelter from the wind or rain, and no warmth. Already in the early afternoon we were in the shadow of Lookout Point, and the cave—or dent—was damp and smelled rank from rarely feeling the sun. But it would have been an excellent place to spy from. Adamstown rolled out below us like a map, with Main Road a red streak through the green, the square a gray-white clearing, and the tin roofs twinkling through the trees.

What an extraordinary place to be sitting, on a ledge overlooking a settlement of men and women descended from British mutineers and Tahitian women.

"What do you feel like?" As soon as I spoke, I realized that my question sounded ridiculous. I covered myself by giving a list of possible answers, like the quiz in the lesson book.

"Polynesian? Pitcairnese? British?"

Dennis kicked his legs against the ledge. "We are British," he said.

"I know you're British—technically—but what do you *feel?*" Perhaps it was such a silly question that it had no answer.

Dennis continued to kick, and Terry joined in his rhythm, like two people who walk along a road next to each other, falling into step.

"Britain will never give this place up," Dennis said. "But we'd be better off with France."

Pitcairn was on the edge of French Polynesia. If under the French, the Pitcairners could share facilities and supply ships with Mangareva. Britain, Dennis said, is a long way away.

"But what do you *feel?*" I refused to give up this line of questioning, although it was obviously irritating Dennis.

He spoke quickly. "We're black islanders. That's what we are. Black islanders." And that, Dennis's kicking legs and hunched shoulders said, was the end of that.

"That's Nig," said Terry. "On his way to Len and Thelma's." I could hear the sound of an engine, although I could see nothing. Most of the paths, apart from Main Road, were arched over by trees and, although you could tell where they were by the pattern of the vegetation, the path itself and anyone traveling along it was obscured. But I could tell it was Nigger, too. Some bikes buzzed like wasps, sounding like giant insects winging around Adamstown. But Nigger's roared, and if there had been no rain and the path was dry and hard, it would make the earth shudder.

Terns swooped in front of us, crossing back and forth from one side of the cave to the other. I had seen them swooping like this from Adamstown, their brilliant white wings clear against the black gape in the rock.

"We can go down an easier way," said Dennis.

Terry took the lead, jumping over the side of the ledge in a different direction from the one in which we had arrived. There was a patch of slippery shingle, and then what seemed to be a sheer cliff, falling for about thirty feet. I turned to Dennis, hoping he would say that the way was impassable, but he waved his hand toward the edge and, when I turned back around, I could just see the tip of Terry's head disappearing downward.

"You next," said Dennis. "Down the Hole."

I looked over the cliff edge again. There was a crack running down it, making a shaft the size and shape of the chutes used to take food from a restaurant kitchen to the tables upstairs, except this chute had only three sides. Someway down the chute was the top of Terry's head, moving away from us.

"Keep your arms out straight in front of you, press your arse against one side, and your feet against the other," said Dennis, coaxing me down the Hole. I thought I had seen something like this being done by a hero in a movie, accompanied by explosions and a three-headed tentacled creature peering over the top of the shaft. I lowered myself into the Hole so I was sideways against the cliff face, thrust out my arms and pushed out my bottom, but did not get a good grip with the soles of my feet, and I dangled at the top of a thirty-foot drop.

"Legs up! Legs up!" shouted Dennis, and I raised my knees, pushed my legs out, so I was wedged into the shaft. I slid my bare feet down a few inches, wiggled my bottom and edged down my palms, and by this method, inched my way down the Hole. Feet, bottom, hands. Feet, bottom, hands. Dennis was just a few feet above. One wrong footing and he would be on top of me, and we'd both be tumbling down the Hole. Feet, bottom, hands. Feet, bottom, hands.

Was this Fletcher Christian's escape route? If he saw someone skipping sideways up the shingle, did he make for the Hole? Whom would he be escaping from?

And as I was thinking this, and feet-bottom-handing down the Hole,

I realized that I was no longer afraid. My mind was not concentrated on the physical task alone, but, feeling confident in it, had begun to wander to other things. For the first time, the Pitcairn terrain had not cowed me. And I was no longer a child; I didn't need to be chivvied through even the simplest task and carried on the back of someone else's bike.

I crabbed down the rest of the Hole, the gap between Dennis and I widening, and led the way back down to the school.

Later that day a stranger came to the island: a black albatross. It walked along the jetty like an inspector of works, judging the concreting the men had done, and snapped its beak at anyone who tried to interrupt the procession. Up and down it went, up and down, occasionally venturing over toward the boat shed and inspecting *Tin* and *Tub*, nodding its long head at their hulls as if saying, "Fine work, lads. Fine work."

There was a constant crowd on the Landing, the children an oozing and ebbing wave as they crept up as close as possible to the bird, then retreated with a scream as it clapperboarded its beak at them. Charles, who seemed to know about these sorts of things, said it had flown from New Zealand, and was on its way to the South Pole.

"To breed!" chirped Charlene, who found this very funny.

"Long way fer fuck," said Dave Brown.

For days, the albatross paraded the Landing. It was a mystery why he stayed and didn't fly off to find a mate. There was nothing for him on Pitcairn. Then, one day, there was a long ring.

"Yourley there? Yourley. Ha albatross bin fly yonder."

"Paan!" said Irma. It would be more than a month before any more strangers came to Pitcairn.

I was gradually working through the old *Miscellany*s at the schoolhouse, taking notes of anything interesting, although I wasn't quite sure why. I

would record any startling statistics, such as the alarming number of acci-
dental deaths on the island. Between 1864 and 1934, the most common
cause of death had been by accident, more than one fifth of the total. I
then saw that most *Miscellanys* contained news of some fatal or near-fatal
fall or drowning. Just three weeks before I had landed, a yacht had arrived
from Easter Island and anchored in Bounty Bay. During the windy night,
her mooring had broken and she had ridden up onto the rocks at Old
Man, by St. Paul's Rock. The woman on board had been drowned. It was
Glen who had brought in the body. She was buried by the Pitcairners in
the burial ground next to tiny Jayden Jacob Norfolk Warren. Her grave
was unmarked, a mound of fresh red mud, not yet fallen in but already
smothered in light mauve flowers.

Alongside the shelves of newsletters, there was an unbound volume
of the *Laws of Pitcairn, Henderson, Ducie and Oeno Islands,* and a ledger
that had been headed "Local News," seeming to have been kept by a
former schoolteacher. It had irregular entries. 5 June, 1971 read:

> *First bomb in French nuclear series. Double feature film. "Surf
> Party"—"Laughing 20s."*

Pitcairn is less than six hundred miles to the southeast of Mururoa atoll,
the French nuclear testing site. During the testing period, monitors had
been stationed on the island to record the fallout and blast effect. Forty-
five minutes after a bomb was detonated, a dull roar, like a wave, would
sweep over Taro Ground and the weatherboard houses would shake. A
French naval vessel was reported to have once anchored off Bounty Bay all
through the night, ready to evacuate the island. Terry said that he had seen
a seabird drop dead right out of the sky. Many islanders said that other
islanders had a photograph of a mushroom in the sky, although I never
saw one. The double-feature film was in the days before the arrival of
videos on the island, when once or twice a week the whole population
would gather in the courthouse and a film reel was shown. A few entries
later read:

*8 August, 1971. Fourth bomb in French nuclear series. Boys went in long boat for barracuta—caught 13.*

The two bombs between the first and fourth had not been worthy of an entry—although several fishing trips had.

There was one more surprise: an abandoned house had been broken into and some medical supplies that had been stored there were missing. Following this brief report, the schoolteacher had scrawled in a large and angry hand, "BLOODY THIEVES ON THE ISLAND."

I tried to get down to the store every Thursday night, when it was open from seven o'clock. I meandered around the near-empty shelves, taking as long as possible to decide what to buy. Of course, nothing was going to have been put on display since the last time I was there; no new stock could have been delivered from the warehouse or another shipment of eggs have arrived. Whatever was there last Thursday would be there this Thursday except, perhaps, less of it.

Still, shoppers wandered around the store with genuine interest as if they might, somehow, stumble across something they had missed last time, even though there can have been no more than a couple of dozen different items altogether.

Irma's walk-in larders were all full, and there were stacks of tins piled up on the floor. Yet every week, I bought as much as possible at the store. I put the items in my basket, tied it to the back of the bike and drove up the short hill home. I'd place them out on the kitchen table one by one, pretending to check that I had everything I needed.

"Two tinned lambs' tongues, one Irish stew, three glutton scallops, one peach halves in syrup . . ."

I wanted Irma to see; I wanted to prove that I was contributing to this household; I wanted Irma to think well of me.

.   .   .

We were sitting in deck chairs on Kari's veranda. Kari was wearing shorts and a bikini top and swigging a beer, as if on holiday in the Costa Brava. I had dropped in to see her on the way back from Taro Ground; Tom had rung to say that a call was coming through for me at the commercial radio station.

On June 17, 1985, Lady Young, Minister of State for Foreign and Commonwealth Affairs in London, had officially declared open the Pitcairn-New Zealand radio link. The link was soon found to be unreliable and any attempt at conversation on it was usually indecipherable, but it gave great hope. From the link to Wellington Radio ZLW, onward via landlines to Telecom International in Auckland, callers could—in theory—be connected to anywhere in the world. But by the time I had arrived at Taro Ground, for the second time this week, all contact had been lost. I had no idea who was going to such lengths to get in touch with me, or why.

Kari shrugged; it happened all the time.

I stretched back in the syrupy sun. "I think Irma regrets inviting me to stay with her."

Kari rolled her glass between her hands and wiggled her feet. After a few minutes, she began to talk, pretending to have changed the topic of conversation.

"Most visitors come here with a preconceived idea about what they think Pitcairn and the Pitcairners to be: this is a community with no crime, no jealousies, no problems. When people think like this, no wonder people come here and expect us to be sprouting wings."

She took another swig of beer and gazed out from her veranda. "Isn't this island beautiful? I heard you went up Christian's Cave on Sabbath?"

She returned to the conversation. "Outsiders have been hard on Pitcairn. They have judged the islanders harshly, angry that their own dreams have not been realized."

She paused. "Visitors have also been ungrateful. They live with an island family, share their home, see what they eat, how they dress, peer inside their cupboards . . ."

Through the door into Kari and Brian's bedroom, I saw a life-size cutout of Clark Gable towering over the unmade bed.

". . . They then take these intimacies and tell a world that wanted to hear something else. And the world, disappointed that their imposed dream did not exist, blames the Pitcairners for shattering it."

She had one more thing to say. "It is wrong to pry."

I tried to erase the picture of Clark Gable, forget he was there, looming over the roughed-up sheets on Kari's bed. But the life-size cutout wouldn't leave me.

It was quiet at Tamanu. The pastor wasn't there, and just a few people were folded into Nigger's few chairs listening to the stereo. Nigger's house was close to the sea, and the surf was loud. It seemed as if the wind was brewing up, and the fine weather would turn.

One by one people drifted away, until only Nigger and I were slumped opposite each other around the table. Nigger seemed to be waiting for me to leave.

I didn't. I wanted to engage Nigger in conversation, to find out things, inquire, learn and, through understanding, become part of this place. I tried to talk, using my hands to start a sentence, but they fell back onto the table. Nigger didn't say anything, but we looked at each other. Perhaps there was another way to bridge that gulf, to reach out to a Pitcairner.

We just sat there opposite each other, occasionally glancing up at the other's face, waiting. Neither of us had the courage to make the first move; neither of us wanted to be responsible. Our hands danced across the tabletop. I don't know if it was Nigger, or if it was me, that first raised up, but the other followed.

It was a long, slow, silent night. The only noise was the steady rhythm of the wind and water breathing. Nigger had told me how, as a boy, he had often fished from the rocks below his new home, where now the waves must be washing white against the darkened rocks. Somewhere, out to sea, there would be the lights of a ship, beyond Henderson, beyond uninhabited Ducie, beyond anywhere I could imagine at this moment.

Nigger breathed with the water. Once, he started at a sharp sound through the window, like the crack of a pandanus twig.

I sat up on the edge of the bed. It would be light soon, arriving like an overhead bulb being switched on.

"I'll drive you back," he said.

I thought of the sound of Nigger's bike roaring through Adamstown just before dawn on the way up to Irma's.

"No, thanks."

And I walked past Tom and Betty's, past the burial ground, under Big Tree, past the road that led to Royal's, and turned up the hill toward home.

# part three

〜　〜

# 12 · john adams's grave

-----

$\mathcal{I}$rma looked very odd; she was lying down. I had never seen Irma horizontal before, and that—more than her rasping breath and the damp flannel laid over her face—was shocking.

Irma had been taken ill earlier in the day; she had been washing up at the sink, held a hand to her head and said, "Ha world es illy-illy," and keeled over. She said that every time she tried to get up, the world about her started to reel. A makeshift bed had been prepared for her from the bench on the veranda. The lightness of her body made it seem as if she were levitating over rather than lying on it, already halfway to heaven.

-----

*illy-illy*—usually said of the sea, meaning "rough," probably from the English "hilly." However, Polynesian often uses the same word twice, to indicate superlative.

It was never suggested that Irma, who was so weak that she could not sit up or hold a cup of water, would have been better off sent to bed in her room. She lay on the veranda as if in state, and received guests, who arrived with gifts of food and words of comfort. Charles and Charlotte brought tomatoes, peppers and lettuce from their garden. Rick clasped Irma's hand and helped himself to some arrowroot pie from the fridge. Royal sat by Irma, bolstered by her dual role of sister-in-law and assistant nurse, but talked to whoever was around rather than to the invalid herself, although Irma was her topic of conversation.

"She se work too hard. And she nawa eat."

Royal was right: Irma was incapable of rest. Jenny had come around after the dispensary had shut and diagnosed Irma's condition as exhaustion, compounded by a poor diet. Irma ate no protein—shunning meat because of her faith—and little else apart from the odd leaf of lettuce. It was amazing that she had kept going for so long. The only cure, Jenny said, was rest and food.

I began to cook furiously. Perhaps, somehow, I was responsible for Irma's collapse. But I had crept in so quietly, she could not possibly have known what had happened the night before.

I baked more arrowroot pie, and banana bread, and molasses flapjacks. As the evening came and Irma, her face still hidden under the damp flannel, was no better, I increased my efforts. I prepared dough for four loaves of bread. I prepared a large salad, which I knew Irma would like. I made cups of milo for all the visitors.

That night the thunderstorm came, the tails of lightning lashing Pitcairn, whipping the paths and gardens. Ben was worried about Irma's tomato plants, which were too young to withstand strong winds and heavy rain. My garden sloped slightly toward the sea, and a sudden downpour would wash away much of the red earth. Ben, Dennis and I sat on the veranda, guarding Irma and watching the storm.

The next morning the air was unnaturally still and the sun shone in a half-hearted way, as if it hadn't quite woken up, giving each moist leaf an eerie sheen. Irma was no better; she had taken only water since the previous day, and could still not sit up. Ben had slept in the chair next to her.

I placed a plate of sweet rice next to him, and went out to my garden. The trenches had been cut deeper by the storm, and some of my corn had been uprooted. Right down at the edge, overhanging Down Isaac's, a yard or so of my garden had disappeared, washed into the sea. The storms and winds were constantly changing the shape of Pitcairn; since I had arrived, parts of the cliff above the Hill of Difficulties had broken away and fallen down toward the Landing. At St. Paul's, the red earth had become so exposed that in places it blew about like sand, forming little dunes where once there had been wooded valleys. When Jacob had been forester, he had tried to plant some miro seedlings to save the soil, but they had refused to root in the tender, bald patches. Little by little, this tiny country was being absorbed by the ocean.

I walked over to the Mission House to gather the lettuce and cabbage seedlings that Rick had promised me, and took them back to my garden. The moist soil absorbed the roots easily, and the seedlings sprung up, as if they were already growing in the red earth. I could hear Dennis and Terry down at the new house, but stayed working in my garden, until night threatened and I went home.

Dirty plates and cups were piled up next to the sink, and I began to wash them. Dennis came in and put on the video, slouching in front of the TV screen. Ben was reading the real estate section of the *Sydney Morning Herald* from two years earlier. The rustle of the pages and the whine from the video were the only indoor sounds; Irma was still silent.

Dennis picked up his half-finished mug of milo and slammed it down on the draining board. His face remolded into a grimace, and he hissed, "You se . . ." The last, indistinct word was surely "bitch." And I realized that beneath Dennis's puckish, plasticine face lurked many other Dennises, ready to be formed.

I surprised even myself at how loudly I shouted.

*"Don't you dare to speak to me like that!"*

"Like what?" said another Dennis, gently. "I don't know what you mean."

Then he used his most powerful expression of defiance—slothfulness—in the slow, slow way in which he ambled off. From under the flannel, someone coughed, one small, sharp crack of a cough. Ben looked up, then returned to reading the newspaper. I washed the dishes noisily and left them to dry.

"Fuck, fuck," I spluttered, just under my breath, but no longer caring. I could feel my face twisting, battling to stay straight, and I remembered with a breath of a laugh that the Pitcairnese word for "angry" was "ugly."

For three days Irma lay on the veranda. Although there were plenty of visitors, they chatted among themselves and we—Ben, Dennis and I—hardly spoke. Then, when I woke on Sabbath morning and went to make myself a cup of milo, there was Irma, walking around the kitchen in her flowery dress, whistling. Her reappearance was so sudden that it was less like a recovery and more like a miraculous cure. The makeshift bed had disappeared.

"Are you coming to church, dear?" she asked.

"Yep," and I went to change into my seersucker skirt and top.

After the service, the Sabbath walk to celebrate the wonderful natural world that God had created would have to be by myself. Dennis was ignoring me, watching a Norwegian home video on Pitcairn.

I set out for John Adams's grave, under the banyans at Big Tree and up a track opposite Tom and Betty's, where he was buried next to his wife, Mary, and a daughter, unnamed.* I reached a simple headstone shadowed

---

* "Mary" was Teio, the only woman to have brought a child to Pitcairn with her. Captain Beechey formally married Teio and Adams when he called at the island in 1825. She died only nine days after her husband, on March 14, 1829.

by coconut palms. It appeared as if it had been erected just weeks before, as the edges had been concreted to make them sharp and the inscription rechiseled with a heavy hand, and that it had been kicked over and broken in half, showing a crack where the top had been crudely cemented to the bottom. And although the path to it had been cleared, the grave itself was tickled by ferns. Behind the burial site rose Lookout Point, the white terns sweeping back and forth before the dark dent of Christian's Cave.

I felt the letters on the headstone.

SACRED

TO THE MEMORY OF

MR JOHN ADAMS

DIED MARCH 5 1829

AGED 65 YEARS

IN HOPE

There had been no John Adams on the muster list for HMAV *Bounty*. The man who became John Adams, father of the Pitcairn community, had signed on as Alexander Smith, known as Aleck. He had said he was twenty years old, and came from London.

John Adams's real name is still unknown. Some scholars suggest that Alexander was his true first name, and Adams his true surname, which he changed to Smith when joining the *Bounty,* perhaps because he had deserted from another ship. On Pitcairn, he reverted to his true surname of Adams, but assumed a new first name of John. Why and exactly when he did this, nobody knows.

When Captain Mayhew Folger, sailing from Boston in command of the *Topaz,* set off with two boats at dawn on February 6, 1808, intending to search for seals around the shores of Pitcairn, he was astonished to see smoke rising from the land and a boat paddling toward them with three men in her. The skipper from Nantucket had unwittingly discovered the fate of the *Bounty* mutineers. At the time of this discovery, the former able-bodied seaman was still calling himself Smith.

"Aleck" was quick to build up a fine reputation with the visitors. He assured them that he had been a reluctant mutineer, seeking only to support and act with the majority; he had been a follower, not a leader, in the revolt. And the American skipper recorded, with approval, that whenever Smith spoke of his former mate, he never omitted to say *Mr.* Christian.

Captain Folger eagerly collected Smith's tales of the early days on the island. Now in his forties, much tattooed and pitted with smallpox, Smith told the Captain that Mr. Christian had become severely depressed shortly after arriving on the island, throwing himself off the rocks into the sea. Four years later, the Polynesian men had revolted and killed every remaining English man except Edward Young (known as Ned) and himself, who had been severely wounded in the neck by a pistol ball. Then, the widows of the deceased rose in the night and murdered all the Polynesian men, leaving Young and Smith, with eight or nine women and several children.

As Ned, once *Bounty*'s midshipman, lay dying of a respiratory complaint, he determined to teach the illiterate Adams to read, using their only books—a prayer book and Bible salvaged from the *Bounty*. Adams absorbed and embraced the teachings. Some religious commentators suggest it was then that, in a personal remaking and repudiation of his past sins, he abandoned the name Alexander Smith and reverted to his true name, John Adams.

When Young passed away on Christmas Day 1800, he was the first man to die a natural death on Pitcairn. Adams, as the only man left on the island, became undisputed leader, determined to teach his people the way of piety and virtue. He now scorned all alcohol, and introduced daily morning and evening holy services. His only text was the *Bounty* Bible. Clasping this, he officiated at weddings and christenings. Captain Folger declared him "Commander in Chief of Pitcairn's Island."

Captain Folger reported this extraordinary find to the Admiralty at Greenwich. After all, following Bligh's account of the mutiny, the Admiralty, at great expense, had sent out the *Pandora* in an attempt to locate, capture and bring the mutineers back to face British justice. Although succeeding in imprisoning those mutineers who had stayed on Tahiti, the whereabouts of the remaining nine men remained unknown. On her return voyage, in March 1791, the *Pandora* had unknowingly passed just one hundred miles north of Pitcairn.

In a detailed letter, Captain Folger described Pitcairn's thirty-five-strong population as "very humane and hospitable people." But the findings of a Nantucket skipper did not even warrant a reply. Folger, concerned that his discovery had been ignored for more than two years, wrote directly to Rear Admiral Hotham, enclosing the *Bounty*'s azimuth compass, which Adams had given him on Pitcairn. Not even this stirred the Admirals.

Five years after Folger's visit, the British warships *Briton* and *Tagus,* traveling in convoy, chanced upon Pitcairn in the early morning of September 17, 1814. Captain Philip Pipon of the *Tagus* found a population of forty-five, all "finely formed, athletic and handsome" with teeth like ivory, and living under the rule of "a venerable old man named John Adams." The island, Captain Pipon estimated, was of a substantial size, perhaps six miles long and four miles broad.

Adams now had more details to add to the events of 1789: he told Captain Pipon that he had been sick in bed when the insurrection had broken out, and had been forced to take a musket in his hand. After the mutiny, Christian had become "always sullen and morose; and committed so many acts of wanton oppression, as very soon incurred the hatred and detestation of his companions in crime, over whom he practiced the same overbearing conduct, of which he accused his commander Bligh." After forcibly seizing one of the women, Christian had been killed by a Polynesian man. After listening to Adams's tale, the *Briton* and *Tagus* sailed the same night.

By the time the *Sultan* called in 1817, the fourth ship to touch at Pitcairn, Adams felt confident enough to try and write his autobiography for Captain Reynolds. He made four attempts, each varying in style and content. Perhaps the most successful was:

The Life of John Adams Born November the 4 or 5 in the Year Sixty Six at Stanford Hill in the parrish of St John Hackney My father was sarvent to Danel Bell Cole Marchant My father was drowed in the River Theames.

That was all John Adams could recall of his former life.

But it has been suggested that Adams wasn't Alexander Smith at all, but Fletcher Christian. Perhaps Adams, not Christian, had been slain, and the leader of the mutineers assumed the able-bodied seaman's name. His identity masked, he could not be accused of masterminding the mutiny, reducing himself to the role of a reluctant participant. Perhaps he thought this might save him from the gallows.

It was eight more years until the *Blossom,* under the command of Captain Beechey, anchored off Bounty Bay. Estimating the island at just four square miles, Captain Beechey was mightily impressed with the fledgling community. "The perfect harmony and contentment in which they appear to live together, the innocence and simplicity of their manners, their conjugal and parental affection, their moral, religious, and virtuous conduct, and their exemption from any serious vice, are all to be ascribed to the exemplary conduct and instruction of old John Adams." Adams now looked far more favorably on the first leader of his flock; he told Captain Beechey that Christian had been always cheerful, naturally of a happy disposition, and had won the good opinion and respect of all who served under him.

Among the Polynesian women and the children, there was no one to challenge the patriarch Adams's portrait of their first two decades on the island. The man with no name also became the purveyor of truth. I liked to think that this man was neither John nor Alexander, neither Adams nor Smith nor even Christian, but someone quite different. Perhaps a ship-wrecked whaler named Larsen or a deserter called Jones was buried in this overgrown grave.

Kari was sitting in her big room, reading a novel; although it was only the early afternoon, it was already chilly outside. The weather arrived like the night—suddenly—and you were plunged into it without warning. When I woke, I never knew what color the sky would be or the pattern of the sea. Each evening, I recorded the day's weather in my diary. The last few consecutive entries read:

> very stormy day
> sunny but mountainous sea
> fair
> lovely day
> sea gray and rough as a brute

The swings in the climate confused the passage of time. We weren't moving from spring to summer, or summer to autumn, but skipping from one disjointed day to the next. It was no good planning to plant beans on a calm warm July afternoon, to avoid the worst of the winter weather, because the next day a strong wind would blow them down or a downpour wash them away. The only forewarning, Ben told me, was if a yacht passed; that was a sure sign that a storm was to come.

There was something I had wanted to ask Kari for some time, but as I spoke, I heard the sound of my own voice with the same self-consciousness that I did when I was abroad, and I was the only person with an English accent. It must be because I had forgotten how I sounded, as I hadn't talked to anyone for almost three days.

I asked Kari if, as a councillor, she would accept her own application for a license to land if it came before the Council today.

She smiled. "No. We have to protect Pitcairn from ladies like that. Would you like a beer? Which reminds me . . . of unfinished business."

Rick was eating lunch when we arrived at the Mission House. He was pleased to see us; he had, he said, been consulting the biblical commentaries.

"Wine does not mean wine," he said.

"What does it mean, then?" I was in no mood for humoring Rick.

"Well, when the Bible was written, wine meant a drink that was not alcoholic."

"But what about beer?" Kari remembered the verse, *Give beer to those who are perishing* . . .

Rick had not thought about the beer. He pulled on each of his fingers, clicking them out of their sockets.

"The passage refers to people who are *sick*," he said. "You can give beer to people as *medicine*."

"Beer as medicine?" I tried to imagine the sort of affliction that could be cured by a bottle of Beck's.

"They don't mean *beer* like we mean *beer*," said Rick. "When the Bible was written, it was a different sort of beer."

I glanced at Kari, waiting for her to challenge this blatant absurdity. *Different wine! Different beer!* Kari was nodding at Rick, mulling over his words.

"Uuuuum," she said. I turned my back to Rick and stared at Kari, rolling my eyes. But she wasn't looking at me, still considering what Rick had said.

Then she spoke. "Yes, that does make sense."

I looked at Kari again, but she was absorbed, really concentrating on understanding Rick and the verse from the Bible.

"The Bible says your body is the temple of God," said Rick.

"Yes," she said. "Thank you very much, Rick. Thank you," and got up to leave.

On the walk to Up Tibi, Kari was contemplative.

"I used to think Rick was a wimp," she said. "But now I have a lot more respect for him."

I walked beside her until we had passed through the Square and came to the road that forked toward Irma's. I didn't say anything. I examined Kari's face, searching for something, but it was like looking at a portrait hanging in an art gallery; it was interesting, but distant.

"Kari?" I heard my voice again, strained, unfamiliar even to myself. *Kari, Kari. Please talk to me.*

She didn't reply.

Then, "Glad we did that," she said. "I feel much better now." And we parted.

As I walked over the veranda, Dennis called to me, "Want to go fer shark?" It was the puckish Dennis, the Dennis with whom I'd driven to St. Paul's, gone out in the canoe, zigzagged up to Christian's Cave.

I couldn't answer.

"Shark hunting. We laid the lines yesterday. Might be som tin."

There was a pattern to Pitcairn that I could not see, a rhythm that I could not hear, like a dog's whistle when I wasn't a dog. I could see no reason for Dennis's violent change of attitude toward me. I had not confided in anyone, so surely no one could have known that I had been at Nigger's until so late, or what we had done there. Perhaps it had been my mistake about the coffee—although I hadn't drunk any for some time—or Irma's illness that had put everyone in a bad mood. I was glad that things were back to normal.

"Great. I've never caught a shark."

The *Miscellany* of March 1978 reported that there had been yet another explosion in the rat population. People were tackling the problem by laying traps or poison. But when Nigger Brown discovered a rat trying to climb in through his bedroom window, he shot it between the eyes. The editor added a postscript: "Anyone calling at the Browns' house at night should call out in a loud clear voice before entering."

I was munching on some of Chris's dried bananas, when Tony interrupted me. He wondered if I would write an article about going to Henderson for the next *Miscellany*.

I called the piece "The Price of a Carving." I described the boat voyage to the island, the heavy and demanding work of cutting and collecting the miro, and briefly mentioned the mishap on the way home. The piece ended with an appeal for understanding.

I arrived back on Pitcairn, for only my second day on the island, already convinced that life here is anything but easy, and Pitcairn is no paradise isle. The fruit may hang in abundance from the trees, but how many people take to the ocean in open boats and work from sunrise to sunset for a $10 carving of a shark?

"It's good. They'll like it," said Tony.

I was so pleased. I could see Irma showing the article to Royal, who would particularly like the reference to hard work, and Royal nodding and passing it on to Charles, who would pretend he could read it. Dennis would like the bit about the steadfast and reliable crew. Rick would congratulate me, and it might be mentioned one night down Big Fence or Tamanu.

"But I won't put your name on it," said Tony.

"Why not?"

"Better not to, round here," he said. "You never know. I'll put 'By *Miscellany* Subscriber.' "

"*Miscellany* Subscriber?"

"It's better that people don't think that you write."

The shark lay on its bloated stomach on the Landing, the same sheen and color as the wet concrete. The long, unscathed body, as big as my own, bled from a butchered mouth. Dennis had taken the knife from his right buttock and cut out the jaw. Now he and Glen were trying to roll the mighty fish back into the bay. If it was left on the Landing, it would begin to stink.

The shark had been caught in Dennis's lines off Tatinani. It had drowned, unable to breathe unless free to swim, and was dead by the time we had reached it, just after dawn. Dennis and I had hauled it up into the canoe, and Dennis had examined its teeth. They were minuscule triangles, with tips as sharp as a needle, almost a hundred altogether. Dennis would wash the severed jaw and, when the flesh had rotted away, remove the teeth with tweezers and use them in his shark carvings. The rest of the carcass was thrown away.

It was still very early when we arrived back at the house, and Dennis hung up the jaw on the veranda next to the bunches of bananas. A letter had been thrust under my door. Perhaps I hadn't noticed it when I had stumbled out of bed that morning, or perhaps someone else had put it there while we'd been out in the canoe. It read:

> *Dear Debbie*
> *Things look a lot better now. Can you please come down to the house for a chat and a late night beer.*
> *Please think about it please.*
>
> > *Your friend I hope*
> > *Sambo*

Although the letter was in an airmail envelope, there was no stamp on it, just a hand-drawn heart struck through by a red arrow, and my juvenile name, Debbie.

When the weather had been fair for a few days, an expedition Down Rope was planned. If there had been any recent rain, the rocks and loose clay fell away in lumps in your palms. But in dry weather, as long as you went carefully down the cliff face, facing inward and using your hands, it was not so treacherous. And once you reached the bottom, you would be on Pitcairn's only beach, a narrow strand fringed with pandanus trees and backed by a mighty cliff. Engraved upon the cliff face were the Polynesian rock paintings.

More than five hundred years before the *Bounty* mutineers sailed into the bay, there were Pitcairners. They came from neighboring Polynesian islands in their powerful wooden canoes, laden with foreign plants and with the wily fruit rat stowed away in the hold. Then, almost four hundred years later, they abandoned their island home, maybe in haste, as they had left plenty behind them.

Unlike the latter-day inhabitants, the Polynesians had spread their homes throughout the island. Their small cutting stones fashioned from pitchstone have been discovered Down Rope, and volcanic oven stones at Tedside. *Tridacna* shell adzes to shape wood were found at Tautama; they left awls made of bird bone, for piercing tiny holes; pearl-shell fishhooks; coral abrading tools, for rubbing and scraping; and one incised human tooth. But there had been more—massive red lava statues, the stone gods guarding their shore. When the new Pitcairners arrived on the *Bounty*, they declared the statues of the earlier inhabitants "idol images" and rolled them into the sea. The Polynesians' burial mounds—piles of stones covering human remains—were disassembled. But the rock paintings Down Rope remain, although the rope that had given the cliff face its name, used to help climbers, is gone.

I approached the cliff's edge with caution, but not with fear. The feel of the red clay was familiar to me; I knew how it looked solid, like pink granite, but took impressions of your fingertips and broke like putty. I also knew not to trust the tortured branches of the pandanus, not to hang on to them but to break through when they blocked the way.

With the mighty cliff rising sharply behind us, the stretch of beach was a secluded spot. The sand was shockingly yellow, a color not to be found anywhere else on the island. Smooth, dark boulders lay on the sand. At first I thought they looked like washed-up whales, but their form was more human, or even godlike. Perhaps they had been pushed over the edge of the cliff.

The beach Down Rope was the only place on Pitcairn where the sea did not do battle with the land. Here, it stroked the edge of the island. There was no violence. And, in this rare, calm meeting place, the strands that bound people together for a moment unwound. Something happened on the beach Down Rope that I had not seen happen anywhere else: each Pitcairner wandered off in a different direction. Terry sat down under a big pandanus to watch the water, leaning against one of the huge boulders, which was almost the same shape as him. Dennis strolled along the icing-sugar sand, examining the rock pools and kicking up showers of small stones. Dave collected coconuts, placing them under the big pandanus. I wandered off to look at the rock paintings.

They were scratched white onto the gray side of the cliff, like graffiti. A man, the size of a child, was holding his arms up, fingers spread, as if surrendering, and with a look of terror on his worn face. Above him in the sky was a star, and to the left a half-human, half-animal figure and a series of symbols like hieroglyphics, which no one has been able to read. On his other side was a disembodied phallus, as long as his trunk. The phallus appeared to have two legs, and to be dancing.

It was clear that these were not a series of random scratches, but a story. I sat on a rock and examined the circular eyes that were dents, the long scar of a mouth, the button nose. What was this story about? What was the artist trying to tell us?

People were beginning to weave their footprints back to the big pandanus, re-forming the tightly knitted ball. Dave cut off the tops of the coconuts so we could drink the clear, cold juice.

"Heap of shit," said Terry. Dennis had been explaining how, next year, there were plans by the Pitcairn Islands Administration in New Zealand to issue a set of Bligh stamps. It was to celebrate 175 years of something, but he wasn't sure what.

"Bligh's got nothing to do with us," said Terry. In March 1972, he said, a descendant of Bligh's had applied for a license to land. He had wanted to make a brief visit to the island. The Council had unanimously refused.

"Might cause trouble," said Terry.

"Trouble?" I couldn't think what Terry might have in mind.

"He might stir things up."

Another Bligh descendant had been a passenger on a passing ship that stopped off Bounty Bay, and had attempted to visit the island, said Terry. He had not been allowed to come ashore and left the same day.*

---

* This was not Morris Bligh, who did go ashore for a few hours in 1991.

The next trick, Terry said, was that Bligh's bones were offered to Pitcairn. These had been rejected outright by the Council, too. Bligh was now buried in Britain somewhere. They were going to build a highway through his grave.*

I told Irma that, now I could drive a bike, I needed to get a license to make it legal. It was the police officer's job to issue the licenses, for which he charged fifty cents.

Irma became even more frenzied in her cleaning of the bolt.†

"You no got one then, dear. I think you got license?"

"No."

"Oh." Irma searched for another reason why I should not go, lifting the bars on the bolt as if she might find one hidden underneath them.

"I gwen down Tamanu," I said, and parted the bananas.

There were no other bikes outside Nigger's—I had checked without thinking. He must be alone.

The morning power was still on, and the stereo was shouting, *"What's love got to do, got to do with it . . ."* Unlike other Adamstown houses, Tamanu was set well back from the road and had no neighbors, so the stereo was not in earshot of anyone else's home. Nigger was sitting in an armchair, smoking a cigarette. His head was thrown back and his eyes were closed. He was wearing his tank top T-shirt.

"Hi." I spoke softly, and the music was loud. Nigger's eyes remained closed, drowned in the song.

Nigger's big room was very large and I was standing right in the middle of it. I played with my hands, rubbing my fingertips together, feeling ridiculously nervous.

---

* Bligh is buried in the family grave in Lambeth Churchyard, London. There are not, and never have been, any plans to destroy the site.

† A bolt is the open fire over which fish is fried, the pan resting on metal bars supported at either end by stones.

I had heard his bike, and been in his company, several times, but we had not been by ourselves since that night. Being alone with anyone on Pitcairn was difficult; only Kari and Christine, both outsiders, were people with whom I sat by myself—apart from when Irma was giving me one of her lessons in the dark. I knew that what we had done was unacceptable in this small, interwoven place, but I was reluctant to surrender my chance of intimacy.

I shouted louder, attempting to sound relaxed and cheery. *"Hi!"*

Nigger lifted his head before opening his eyes, slowly.

"Hi."

"I've come"—I tried a smile—"I've come for my driving license."

Nigger was not smiling. I had overestimated his difference from other Pitcairners, in his stylish home, his languid manner and easy conversation, even his taut body. I had thought that he had wanted to step out of Pitcairn, as I had wanted to step in, and, together we could meet in a place of understanding. I had seen these small differences as signs of loneliness reflecting my own.

But Nigger was a Pitcairner; and on Pitcairn such liaisons were forbidden. He wasn't being unfaithful only to his family but to his people.

Nigger Brown, descendant of William Brown, gardener and mutineer, had, only in a moment of weakness, succumbed to becoming part of my wild, misguided fantasy. Now he knew better.

He raised himself from the chair, pulled open a drawer and took out a folder. I began to move toward him, no more than a suggestion by lifting my hands.

Nigger's eyes remained fixed on the folder, studying the documents carefully. The "Pitcairn, Henderson, Ducie and Oeno Island Driving License" (there had never been any vehicles on any other island in the group apart from Pitcairn) was a piece of blue cardboard, the size of a postcard, which Nigger folded in half. It entitled me to drive the tractor as well as the bikes, and any cars on the island, although there weren't any. On the cover it said, "THIS LICENCE MUST BE PRODUCED ON DEMAND"; the only person who could make such a demand was the police officer, Nigger.

"It costs fifty cents," said Nigger.

I walked over to the kitchen counter and placed down the coin, then backed away. Nigger walked over and picked the coin up. He took it back to the folder and wrote out a pink slip as a receipt. He took the license and receipt, and placed them where the coin had been on the counter. It was as if we were conducting an exchange of prisoners, and the counter was our No Man's Land. I didn't want to pick up the coin. Then there would be no more exchanges to be made, and I would have to leave, alone.

I had wanted to touch a Pitcairner. But now at Tamanu I was trespassing, a stranger. Nigger raised his eyes, part in confusion, part in horror: I had to go.

I made one more gentle attempt to stay, to continue.

"Is it the end?" I asked.

"The end of *what?*" said Nigger.

Of course. Nigger was right; it had been my fantasy, not his. I picked up my license and drove home.


Jenny decided she was going to tackle the problem of obesity head on; she pinned up a notice on the board outside the courthouse.

Coming This Sunday at 7:30pm
Jane Sansone's
Walk Aerobics
The too Busy to Workout, Workout


The video had arrived on the last supply ship, and she would borrow the video player from the church and lead the class herself.

Perry came up to look at the notice; the last one on the board had been his.

"Would you like to come to dinner?" It was a casual invitation, made formal by Perry's overprecise English.

"Because," he added, "I am leaving." He was planning to go as soon as possible, on the first ship that agreed to take him. That could be tomorrow, next week, Christmas or even next year. It all depended upon when the vessel called.

Once the decision to leave was made, the emigrant's bags were permanently packed. He had to be ready; he might get less than one hour's warning, and if he missed that ship, he might wait four or five months until he had another chance. He would be as good as gone for weeks and weeks before actually leaving.

Perry suggested supper the following day, adding, ". . . if I'm still here."

When I arrived home Dennis was watching the VHF, as intently as if it were his favorite video. No one else was in.

"Any trips planned?" I asked. "Surf's good."

It was a lovely day, and I knew that Dennis was low on bait. Perhaps he intended to go down to Tedside to search for catfish between the rocks with his arro. Once I had done some of the washing, I could join him.

"Nice day to go for bait," I said a little louder just in case he hadn't heard me. "Want some milo?"

Dennis stood up, and went and sat on the veranda. I walked out after him, and looked down at him while he glowered down at his broad, naked feet.

"What the . . ." but I gave up, and went and shut myself in my room.

With Perry gone, there would be thirty-seven left on the island. I had thought, before I arrived, that the population was forty. That was the figure given in the most recently published statistics from the Pitcairn

---

catfish—the name used for a small octopus, perhaps coming from "cuttlefish," as pronounced by one of the mutineers.

arro—a pike about twelve feet long with a metal prong on the end, used for spearing bait between the rocks.

Islands Administration. But by the time I had arrived, there were only thirty-eight. Every time a figure was given for the population of Pitcairn, it was smaller than the previous one. And every time the number was quoted, it was with a sense of pessimism and panic.

However many people lived on Pitcairn, it was rarely considered enough. In March 1960, the *Miscellany* put the population at 147, occupying fifty-seven houses, with twenty-nine vacant homes. Two years later, the *Miscellany* reported that the population was down to 115, most of whom were either very old or very young. With only twenty-two adult males, "What a predicament Pitcairn Island is in," the editor wrote. "For on this small body of men rests the maintenance of the roads and tracks, the boats and the other dozen and one jobs which are required to be done. It is little wonder that slowly but surely island vegetation is taking over much of the island." Two years later, 1964, the population had dropped further, to ninety-four. The Norfolk Island Council made an open invitation: if Pitcairn had to be abandoned, the islanders would be most welcome to join their distant relatives on Norfolk. With British passports that were invalid for settlement in Britain, and marooned on the edge of French Polynesia, there would have been nowhere else for the Pitcairners to go.

A decade later, a visiting journalist, Ian Ball, found eighty-five Pitcairners, "hardly greater than the number of passengers who can be squeezed into a city bus at rush hour." He noted, as had many before him, that the birthrate among the islanders was low: more than two children was rare, and a family with an only child was common.

Ball calculated that a minimum of twenty-seven able men and boys were needed to launch and crew the longboats, and that this number could not be sustained for much longer. "The tiny Pitcairn commune, the living evidence of the mutiny in the South Seas aboard His Majesty's Armed Transport *Bounty* on April 28, 1789, is close to an undistinguished extinction," he wrote.

Now, more than twenty years later, there were twelve men—including Ben, who was third oldest after Jacob and Warren, Betty's father—and including Trent and Glen, who were teenagers. These men pulled the longboat from the shed, went out to trade on ships, offloaded the supply ship, maintained the roads with the help of a few women and, when a rainstorm caused a landslide that blocked the Hill of Difficulties, blasted the rock face and cleared the debris. Against all odds and every prediction, the Pitcairners had carried on.

Rick was sitting on the bench outside the commercial radio station at Taro Ground. Another unsuccessful attempt had been made by someone to reach me on the radio.

"Pitcairn won't die because everyone leaves," he said. "There will always be some people who stay here. It will die because they abandon God. That's why."

Whenever I left my room, I never knew how I would be greeted. Neither Dennis nor Irma had spoken to me for two days, and when I'd seen Alison in the store, she had ignored me, too. When I cracked a joke, I didn't know if it would be received with silence or a hearty laugh. When I cooked a meal, I didn't know if it would be welcomed with faint praise or, as Irma had done the night before, with a damning remark: "Not even this lettuce is wash. It dirty as a brute!"

If I had been told the cause of the hostility, I could have attempted to put up a defense. If it was connected with Nigger, then someone must have been spying on us that night, through the window. But anyway, there was no cause for gossip or complaint now: I assiduously avoided him, even dodging up a side road when I heard his bike approaching.

But far worse than being unable to find a reason for my banishment was its randomness. The brief daily entries in my diary concerning my social life had become as unpredictable as those for the weather:

*no one spoken to me*
*said Good Morning to Dennis, but didn't answer*
*lovely day, went fishing with Dennis*

*long talk with Irma in the dark*
*Irma not speaking to me now. No idea why not*

The uncertainty surrounding every encounter was unbearable; would I be embraced or shunned? The very worst time was when someone was being nice to me, especially Dennis or Irma. It lulled me into thinking that everything was all right now, that there had been some unspoken misunderstanding, which had, thankfully, at last been cleared up. Then, the next day, they would refuse to eat with me, Dennis carrying his breakfast out onto the veranda. It was impossible to avoid these meetings, as there was only one thing that was clearly and consistently disapproved of—staying in my room.

I longed to go away, not permanently, not to leave the island, but long enough to break this random pattern. I longed to emerge from my room one morning, a small bag slung over my shoulder, and announce, "I'm off for the weekend. See you soon!" part the curtain of bananas, push aside the drying shark's jaw, and walk away. But there was nowhere to go.

The Pitcairners had created day trips to Down Rope or St. Paul's, and even built weekend homes at Tedside and Flatland. But it was all a lie. Everywhere you went, you were on Pitcairn. It was the same heavy air, the same tangled weed and trees, the same clawing mud on every corner of the island. The only route you could draw on your travels was circular.

Of any part of the island, Flatland was considered farthest from Adamstown. This was not strictly the case in terms of distance—in fact, Flatland was no more than a five-minute drive up the hill behind Irma's— but in atmosphere. A small plateau with fine views over the capital, mosquito-free Flatland had been designated Pitcairn's favorite holiday resort. The Christians from Big Fence had a holiday home there, as had Irma.

"Bout you gwen?" called out Royal, running up behind me on her bike on her way home to Jack's Tatties.

"Tedside," I lied.

"What you doing?" asked Charles, sitting in front of Charlotte as they drove to Aute Valley on forestry work, to look at a pine tree. Charles was assistant forester to Reynold, forester.

I fingered a bush at the side of the road laden with Job's tears, the seeds of a tall bushy grass that were collected by children and threaded onto fishing line to make bracelets and necklaces.

"Picking Job's tears," I said.

But, by now, everyone would know that I was at Flatland.

Flatland looked out toward the northeast, over the school at Up Pulau and up to the Edge above the Hill of Difficulties. There were white-caps on the water beyond.

I sat on what was left of Irma's holiday home—the raised wooden floor. The walls had collapsed and been buried under the surrounding grass, so you had to walk carefully or your foot might get trapped between two planks. If my leg had become stuck, I could have stayed there for hours before Irma organized a party to search for me.

But—the thought came to me with chilling clarity—perhaps she wouldn't raise the alarm at all. Did Irma like me, or did she mistrust and despise me? I had no way of telling. She would often be kind, making sure that I had enough to eat, that I wasn't cold in my bed at night. She would willingly lend me her bike to go on private errands, or even for a spin down to Tedside. She never asked me for anything, apart from the cooking and cleaning I did for her. Then, sometimes, late at night, we would talk, and I was sure then that she wanted to talk to no one more than me.

But Irma also complained about me to Royal. And sometimes she would refuse to speak to me for a day or longer, when I had no idea why.

It was the same with Dennis; a gentle letter, with a touch of passion, would be delivered under my door just hours before he would reject me, refusing to eat with me. I kept thinking that one of these must be a lie, just for show, and it must be the notes and the intermittent warmth. By myself in my room, I cursed Dennis for being so two-faced.

But I was no longer sure that my accusation was correct; perhaps Dennis was being disconcertingly honest about the complexity of his emotions. One part of Dennis liked me, and another despised me. I remembered that he never signed his soft letters "Dennis," but "Sambo."

But if I fell from the canoe while hauling in a shark, who would be in the canoe with me, Dennis or Sambo? And would either of them feel moved to save me?

I saw the night come over the water, unrolling like a blanket. It approached quickly and seemed impenetrable, as if it might knock me off the wooden platform. But it just engulfed me.

The power must have been switched back on, because I could hear *"What's love . . ."* rising above the giant ferns by Tamanu, even though Nigger's neighbors could not. All I could see was the black of the trees below and the glint of the sea.

I grew afraid. But of what could I be frightened? Beasts? Strangers? Ghosts? The night itself? I wasn't frightened *of* anything, just as I no longer waited *for* something. I was just frightened.

# 13 · the uttermost part of the world

The film crew landed first. Three agitated and stringy young men, they walked backward in front of the clean-shaven, all-American Dr. Cunningham, holding the microphone close to his broad, beaming face. As he set foot on Pitcairn, Dr. Cunningham began to swing his large head from side to side very slowly, indicating that this was a historic moment, and held his hand out to the empty air, ready to be shaken. Following Dr. Cunningham were his wife and two blond children, who, until motioned to by the cameraman's assistant, had sat very upright in the launch, one hand on each gunwale, their apple-pie smiles cemented even through the heavy spray.

The Cunninghams' vessel, *Pacific Ruby*, was anchored two miles off Pitcairn, and although she was small—little longer than a good-size tug—

she was clearly visible from Bounty Bay. She was a mercy ship, crewed by volunteers from Youth With a Mission. An hour before her arrival, the second officer, a woman, had radioed to the island that they would be staying for several days—so there had been no need to rush and gather curios for trade—and that they had their own launch in which the passengers and crew could come ashore. There was, the officer said, a dentist and a doctor on board, who would perform operations. And we were very fortunate because YWAM's (which the officer pronounced *Why?Wham!*) International President Dr. Loren Cunningham and his family were sailing with them.

Why?Wham! began to infiltrate and organize Pitcairn. The doctor and the dentist—two petite, mousey, late-middle-aged men, barely distinguishable from one another—brought their equipment ashore: an operating table, suitcases of instruments and a futuristic dental chair, which moved all by itself in a robotic fashion. The chair and operating table were set up in the dispensary, and a list was drawn of who needed which operation. Ben had a recurrent hernia that ought to be fixed; Charlotte needed her leg seen to; and Kari had a peculiar bump on her nose. Most of the children would visit the dentist; none of the adults would bother to attend, as most had no teeth of their own, including Dennis and Nigger. Sets of dentures were shipped out from New Zealand.

The crew of *Pacific Ruby* were a mere fifteen, who, despite Why?Wham!'s promise of youth, were mostly late converts to the evangelical cause. They were joined on board by an equal number of mission workers. These troops were billeted to Pitcairn families, along with the crew. We were allocated Jessie, the unusually tall and thin Filipino first mate, who was ever so thankful for being taken into the bosom of our home. I would have preferred to have been entertained by Why?Wham!'s Pacific director, a mighty American Samoan, who had told Terry that he could break three concrete blocks in half in one swipe and tear up telephone directories, a talent that was wasted on Pitcairn, where there were none.

The island was soon transformed by the energy of Why?Wham!,

whose adherents far outnumbered the adult Pitcairners. They imported zeal; people began to talk about getting something done "by one o'clock," and to fix things that had been broken for years. And among all this purpose strolled Dr. Loren Cunningham, smiling and nodding, with a backward-walking film crew in front of him.

But the person who was most energized by this unexpected visitation was Rick. Dr. Cunningham's descent upon the island was, to Rick, what a call from the Queen would be to the staunchest royalist: the most honored visitor imaginable. And he was staying for three whole days, stretching over Sabbath, and would make a personal statement in the church. Rick arranged for an additional service to be held on Friday evening—the dawn of Sabbath—in honor of Why?Wham!.

Irma and Ben were getting dressed for the service. I sat on the veranda, waiting to walk down to the church with them. I was sipping a cup of milo and eating a slice of bread with fresh molasses on top, sticky and delicious, when I heard the sound of a bike coming down the road that led to Tedside. I instinctively looked up. Nigger rounded the corner, his eyes cast down toward the veranda. Our faces met, but neither greeted the other, and he roared on.

The church was packed. We had been promised that all the *Pacific Ruby's* crew would be there with the exception of the Captain, who was staying on board overnight for the security of his ship, and the mighty Pacific director. He had gone fishing, wearing nothing but a sarong wrapped around his waist.

I sat at the back, listening once more to Rick narrate the story of Ashlee falling down the cliff at Down Isaac's, the miracle. He seemed to be wiping away tears. Then Dr. Cunningham walked into the center of the church, where the preacher or the video screen usually stood.

Dr. Cunningham looked wise and serious, and tilted his dimpled chin slightly toward the floor. Then he raised his head, and slowly began to smile. His hands rose from his sides, I noticed, in exact synchronization with the edges of his mouth curling up. Then he began to speak.

"I have something on my heart to share . . ."

"I need to get *closer,*" spat the sound man from the film crew, who was standing in the aisle next to my pew.

Dr. Cunningham stated most emphatically that, as international president of Why?Wham! and president of the University of the Nations, Why?Wham!'s very own university, he had been to every country in the world—Every. Country. In. The. *World.*—*except* Pitcairn.

"The word that's on my heart today is that . . . everybody's got a destiny . . . a purpose even from your mother's womb. *I,*" and he placed emphasis on the *I,* "believe that is true for nations.

"Some would think about the mutiny as being an illegitimate birth of a nation. But I want to say that God has a destiny for Pitcairn. . . . He took the mutiny on the *Bounty,* turned it around and used it as a trumpet call to the whole world as a witness for Christ. As I see in history what God has done for this land, I get so excited to know that I'm on the very land . . . because God has given you a destiny."

I looked around at the favored few. They were all there, arranged by household: Mavis, Jacob and Meralda; Thelma, Len, Clarice and Nigger; Terry and his mother, Vula; Carol and Jay with Charlene and Darrylene; the crowd from Big Fence; Perry, whom I couldn't remember having seen in church before; Tom and Betty and their teenage daughters; Dave the Mouth with his wife; the schoolteacher's family; Kari and her two children. They were looking toward Dr. Cunningham, but not at him. There was a blankness in their faces, like children watching the teacher in a classroom, pretending to be paying attention but hearing nothing.

"He has given you a destiny that you can be not only proud of, but you must understand the tremendous weight of responsibility . . . When the word got back that the people here on Pitcairn had found God through the reading of the Bible, that caused people to listen in Europe and North America. . . . Your voice is so amplified that from the land of Pitcairn they hear about you throughout the world. . . . Every nation has its destiny, but there is no comparison to the destiny, the place in God's *program,* that he has for Pitcairn."

Dr. Cunningham adopted a technique of public speaking that emphasizes one word—no matter which—in each sentence.

"No other people can *do* what you can do. You *can* go to New York City and get on a TV program nationwide, *simply* because you're from Pitcairn. . . . *Why* is that? And why does it *count* after two hundred and one years? It's about *witness* that God has given you to be. It's the *trumpet* call that God wants to renew throughout this land—it could be the last call—to rise up missions to go to the end of the *earth*.

"In Jerusalem, when Jesus said go and preach to the uttermost parts of the world—mathematically, where people live, *this is* the most distant place in the world."

Dr. Cunningham relaxed his square shoulders a little, and began to talk about himself.

"This is my two hundred and *ninth* country to be in, in the world. Earlier this year I was where the *pygmies* are in Equatorial Guinea. I thought that was tough to get to! But it's *nothing* like getting to Pitcairn."

The shoulders squared up again.

"God has given you a voice that you must not squander. You must use it for his glory. You must *use* it for his praise. You have a destiny. *God* has given you a destiny."

For a moment, I thought that the doctor had started at the beginning of his mental notes all over again, by mistake, and we were going to sit through the entire speech twice. But then, he came to his most important point.

"Sometimes God brings somebody from afar just to remind you."

I wasn't sure whether or not to applaud, but the only sound was the whine of the film camera. Rick moved back into the center of the aisle, and made meaningful eye contact and exchanged sage shakes of the head with Dr. Cunningham.

We filed out, and I went to sit next to Alison on the bench in the Square, watching children being nudged in to see the dentist. The screaming was horrible.

"What were you doing at Nig's until five-thirty in the morning?"

Her freckled, girlish face didn't fit her expression, which was very adult, almost middle-aged, and I felt the younger of the two of us. *I* was the teenager whose misconduct had been uncovered by a prying, grown-up world who could see around corners and through windows. Who had told Alison that I was at Nig's? How did she know the exact time I had left?

"Talking."

"Talking about what?"

"Fishing."

Alison could do a very sardonic grin. "People on Pitcairn are only interested in the three *F*'s—fishing, food," she was counting on her fingers, "and fucking."

Dr. Cunningham, his wife and two children passed across the Square in front of us, the film crew scuttling backward in front of them. He gave Alison and me a royal wave. He seemed to be oblivious to the tremendous noise emanating from the dispensary.

At the other end of the bench Charlotte was leaning lightly against Irma, sobbing. She had never been to a hospital or had an anesthetic, and was worried about her operation, which was planned for later that day. For a moment, the film crew turned their lens on this elderly, vulnerable couple, before refocusing on the Cunninghams.

"I don't think Irma's much interested in any of those *F*'s," I said.

Alison smirked. "No. But Nig is."


The skipper of *Pacific Ruby* had agreed to give Perry passage to Tahiti.

Perry was convinced that he would soon be returning to Pitcairn. There had been a temporary hiccup, he had stayed with the wrong family, but next time it would all work out. I tried to understand exactly what had gone wrong at Tom and Betty's, and why Perry had had to leave, but I couldn't discover a reason, I couldn't pinpoint what had caused the rift. Perhaps it wasn't a single issue that you could put a finger on, but one so nebulous that it couldn't be named or explained. If it had been something particular, it could have been tackled and challenged; Perry could have mounted a defense. But something so indistinct was impossible to refute. He had simply had to leave Tom and Betty's, and now he was leaving the island. Only Kari was sad to see him go.

"He was good to talk to," she said.

I asked Kari what made her decide to stay.

"I like the isolation. I like the few people; wherever you walk along the street you meet people you know. Here, I am never scared. I know there are no strange elements. You can feel safe. To me, that is safety—it's not limitation at all."

She paused.

"I always knew this was just the place for me."

Jessie had proved to be a most obliging guest; he offered to help in whatever task I was doing, and was hugely grateful for any small service done for him. As I prepared food for supper, he pursued me around the kitchen, attempting to help me fetch, carry and cut, and engaging me in conversation. He stood behind me at the sink as I washed the dishes.

"God loves you, you know that."

The red cat skipped into the room with a rat between her teeth, the head and tail twitching. I picked up a broom and chased her outside.

"Just after I met my wife, I wrote a letter to her."

I moved sideways to the billy and embraced it, pretending to be absorbed in switching it on.

"I wrote that it was God's will that she should be my wife and the mother of my children."

I walked over to the fridge to get something, anything.

"She wrote a short note back: *I think God is wrong.* But now we are married and expecting our first child in December!"

I turned around to look at Jessie's face, which was grinning, triumphantly. I went out to the veranda, hoping he would be unable to sit down

with me for long, as his missionary zeal caused him to be in a state of
constant motion. I was surprised to find Terry already sitting there; I
hadn't heard him arrive.

For a while, we said nothing.

"What did you do last night, Tel? Watch a video?"

"Oh, yes."

"Which one?"

*"MacGyver."*

"Had you seen it before?"

"Oh, yes."

We said nothing for a while longer, then Terry took up a piece of
wood. Even when he carved, he made no more noise than a gecko.

A few yards away, the cat was playing with the mutilated rat, batting
it first with one front paw then the other, as if practicing a football maneuver. Then, the rat, which I had presumed dead, began to hobble off, by
moving its right legs and trailing its left legs after it. I should kill it, batter
it to death with the broom, I thought. But I couldn't. The cat playfully
chased the rat, and picked it up neatly in her teeth again, then let it go,
watching it drag itself away, its fur matted with blood. The cat picked it up
again, and came and dropped it at my feet, like an offering. Then, perhaps
seeing my horror, she took it away to eat. First she bit off the rat's head,
chewing very hard. I could hear her crunching on the skull, or perhaps the
teeth. She sat down, licking her lips. I rested back in my chair, but started
up at a terrible retching sound. The red cat was vomiting. She was vomiting up the rat.

It was not that, but the burr of a bike, which made Terry lift his
head, but the bike passed by.

Someone must have peered through Nigger's bedroom window that
night. It was someone very soft, their approach was so silent. We had
heard nothing but the sharp crack of a twig.

When I looked up again, Terry had gone.

·   ·   ·

Tom, sometimes known as Worree, was in a stew. Someone had stolen his alligator.

He was going around to all the homes in Adamstown, asking if anyone knew of its whereabouts. By the time he arrived at Irma's, he had already visited Mavis's, Carol's and Dave the Mouth's. All of them had made suggestions as to who might be responsible for taking it, but no one had firm evidence or had witnessed the theft.

This year, there had been only one alligator on the whole island. All the trees except Tom's had failed, and Tom's had only produced one fruit. Tom went to inspect the lonely pear every few days, hanging low on a tree on the road to Tedside, just past Brown's Water. Reports on its progress, which was unspectacular, this alligator being a very average specimen, were relayed around Adamstown by Tom, who was as proud of his product as if he had raised a rare pedigree dog.

It was difficult to imagine anyone stealing Tom's alligator and devouring it surreptitiously on the shore at Tedside. A Pitcairner would never enjoy eating alone; it would have been a miserable reward for their crime. But when, a couple of nights later, Royal was adding the shark teeth to her carving, she said, "I wonder what ha tief done with ha alligator." And it struck me that—of course—it might not have been stolen to be eaten at all, but as an act of spite against Tom. The thief could have just thrown the fruit into the sea at Tedside.

The alligator wasn't mentioned again for several days, until Royal, who spent even more evenings with us since Irma's illness, said, "Worree still mad as a hatchet," and I could swear she was looking straight at me.

In the whispering and gossiping, I had begun to hear things. I thought I was being accused. Whenever I overheard Irma and Royal chatting on the veranda, I was sure that they were talking about me. Once, I burst out of my room, where I had been pretending to be asleep, and shouted, "That's not true!" although unclear what crime I had just

---

*alligator*—the Pitcairnese word for avocado pear

heard—hadn't I?—being attributed to me. What was the truth on Pit-cairn? Whenever I tried to ask people what *really* happened—to Aden, with Dennis and Mary—there was no clear answer. Fact and fiction, real-ity and rumor were not just confused, but quickly became indistinguish-able. If something was believed enough, it was true.

It was so with their faith: the words of the Bible were embraced as literal, unalterable truth. And when Irma watched a movie on the video—a thriller, a romance—she would wonder at such goings on.

"But it isn't *true*," I'd say. "It's all made up!"

But for Irma, a documentary and a drama were the same. Realizing this, I saw the dismissiveness with which Charles's fantastic tales were greeted in a different light. Charles's crime was to make up stories so outlandish that they couldn't possibly be true, as if in doing so, he was deliberately exposing the elaboration within everyday conversation. But now, my own ability to distinguish between hurtful slander and harmless rumor was becoming blurred.


Ben was carried up from the dispensary on a stretcher after his hernia operation, Steve, Dennis, Terry and Trent taking a corner each. The make-shift bed on the veranda had been prepared for his convalescence, through which he was nursed by an energetic Irma. There was a constant stream of visitors, bringing dishes of food that I assembled in the kitchen and served to the guests. Dennis switched on the television; the whole of Ben's opera-tion had been captured on video. The patient was chirpy and delighted.

"Save me five hundred dollars!" he said, estimating what the opera-tion would have cost in New Zealand, had he been able to go there.

It was a rare Sabbath that Ben did not go to church, but, although able to limp about the house, he was still shaky, and both the short bike ride and the walk were only for the fit. Irma would come along at the last minute, so I walked up to the church by myself.

There was already quite a crowd, as most of *Pacific Ruby*'s mission workers were still ashore and more Pitcairners than usual had come to the service. Perhaps it was because we had a lot for which to thank God—and Why?Wham!. Nine operations and 117 fillings had been executed in just two days! Tomorrow, the *Pacific Ruby* would sail for Tahiti.

Trent was playing the organ in place of Irma. He was dressed entirely in black, from his shirt to his shoes, like a young Elvis Presley. While Irma's position before the electronic keyboard was always seated, stoic and straight-backed, modeled on the posture of an organ player in church, Trent hunched his shoulders and attacked the keys, throwing a smile toward his audience every now and then, as a star might do.

The words of the hymn shone down from the overhead projector.

> *If you're happy and you know it, clap your hands.*
> (Clap, clap.)
> *If you're happy and you know it, clap your hands.*
> (Clap, clap.)

I smiled and clapped, mouthing the words.

> *If you're happy and you know it*
> *Then you surely want to show it*
> *If you're happy and you know it*
> *Clap your hands.*

Clap. Clap.

# 14 · *the dispensary*

"How old's Meralda?" I was making idle chat with Ben as we worked on our curios.

"She se born three years after Grumps."

"But how old's Clarice?"

"She se born same winter Terry."

"When was that?"

"Three Christmases before the Mouth."

Everybody's age, it seemed, was measured against someone else's. What was important was not how many years you had, but how much older or younger you were than your closest cousin or neighbor. Clarice was also Olive's and Nigger's sister, Thelma and Len's daughter, Tom and Betty's niece, Trent's aunt, Sherilene's and Darlene's cousin . . . It was absurd for me to try and pluck Clarice out of this web. What aged her—what mattered—was her relationship to everyone else.

Whether someone was thought of as young or old—of the "young set" or of the "old set"—was also not a matter of arithmetical calculation. Nor was it, as in other places, about how self-sufficient someone was, how removed from the core of their family. On Pitcairn, people didn't unwind from each other as they grew, and age wasn't about separation. When a Pitcairner described someone as young, they meant in attitude; it was meant, in particular, that they drank and danced. Carol, a teetotaller, was of the old set; whereas Kari, who was in her late forties and several years Carol's senior, had always been counted among the young.

There was going to be a party for the young set at Tamanu; the scientists had radioed in to say that they were sailing to Pitcairn in a few days' time to collect supplies. Nothing grew on Henderson apart from coconuts, and on Pitcairn they could gather fruit, vegetables and fresh water.

Only the young ones would go to the party; the older ones were not invited, to avoid the embarrassment of having to refuse an invitation, which no Pitcairner could comfortably do. The pastor and his family, although far younger than most of the partygoers, were also left off the guest list.

"I'm glad me and Jenny haven't been invited," said Rick. "I can't take God into that situation. And where God can't go, I don't want to go."

"But people will be enjoying themselves." This was not an argument to win over Rick.

"Jenny and me wouldn't dance together—even in our own home. God comes before everything for us. That's explicit. Before our marriage. Before everything."

When I arrived at Tamanu the mood was subdued. A country and western song was drawling over the stereo, and people were leaning against the kitchen counter or draped on the edges of chairs, most with a can of

Carlsberg in their hands. The music was too loud to talk, so we just hung around, the scientists stroking their cans and rocking gently to the music to give the appearance of being in the swing of things. Halfway through a song, one of the Pitcairners would jump up and insist that it be changed for something better, so all we heard were snatches from harrowing tales of betrayal and unrequited love.

I waved a tiny finger-wave to the scientist who had asked me what I had hoped to find on Pitcairn. He was even more wiry and sprouting more facial hair than when I had seen him on Henderson; now his face was completely covered, apart from a button-red nose and two deep eyes.

"D-I-V-O . . ." The tape was popped out.

During the dispute between Darrylene and Dave the Mouth over which cassette to put on next—Johnny Cash or Tammy Wynette—the hairy scientist came over to me.

"How's your stress level, then?"

I tried to make it sound like a joke: "I've never been so stressed in my life."

". . . R-C-E." The Mouth had won.

Nigger was sitting close by the female scientist, trying to talk to her over the wail of the song. As Tammy Wynette died down, he went over to the stereo and inserted a new tape.

The music washed through the room like surf, lifting the Pitcairners from their seats so only the scientists were left sitting. The Pitcairners put their hands on their waists and swung their hips, at first gently, then wider and wider, forming a loose line across Nigger's big room. Then they took their hands and placed them on their knees, and their bodies started to buckle and bow in time to the beat.

*Ver-ruum, ver-ruum, ver-ruum . . .*

It was as if they had been possessed. They were bold, Polynesian people, thrusting and beckoning with their large frames. And I wondered what was here before Adventism came with its prohibitions, and pushed the pigs over the cliff. What was Pitcairn like in those years between the early deaths of the mutineers and the arrival of Captain Folger, when the only person who was not Polynesian was a man with no name?

Some of the scientists tried to join in the dance, but soon shrugged their shoulders and gave up; they were too thin and too brittle. Nigger thrust at the female scientist, who wiggled her hips a couple of lackluster times, then came and sat next to me. She had a boyfriend in Oxford, she bellowed in my ear, and was a committed Christian. What was she to do? I looked over to Nigger. Olive must have just told him a joke, as he laughed and threw his head back. He was enjoying himself, chatting to his sister among lifelong friends. If he looked toward us it was the female scientist whose eye he sought.

"What should I do?" she asked again. I advised restraint, and she nodded in agreement. Nigger was now dancing by himself.

The female scientist continued to shout in my ear, but I mimed, by shaking my head and pointing toward the stereo, that I was sorry but I couldn't make out a single word. I didn't want to dance—I couldn't dance, not like that—but I desperately wanted to get drunk. I went to get another can.

Steve staggered over to me. "What exactly are you doing here?" It wasn't a question; it was an accusation, to which I could no longer give a spirited defense.

When Steve offered to drive me home early, I accepted. Not until we had sped under the banyan trees, passed the graveyard where Jayden Jacob Norfolk Warren was buried and the *Bounty* cannon in Len and Thelma's garden, and reached the hill, did I look up, to see if the light in Irma's shack was still on. As we bumped upward, I wondered for how much longer I would feel the closeness of a Pitcairn night.

Royal came around earlier than usual the next morning. From my bed, I could hear her chatting with Irma. Irma had news for her sister-in-law: she had seen Toj's bike go up the hill just half an hour ago. Royal had news for Irma: she had heard Jay's bike this morning, heading in the same direction. There must be something going on.

Royal added, as if it followed, "Debbie come home last night?"

Irma must have moved to the back of the kitchen—probably to check the copper—as I couldn't hear her reply, just Royal's response.

"Might be she se gone out ha window."

My bedroom window was a good ten feet above the ground. I could not have leapt from it easily, if at all, and especially at night. I would have risked spraining my ankle, or even breaking my leg.

"I bin hear Mavis dog bark last night." Royal had the whole scene sharp in her mind. I had come home, just to deceive Irma, but left again shortly afterward, through my bedroom window. It was also clear where I had gone. I would have had to have walked past Mavis's to reach Tamanu.

I jumped out of bed, determined to interrupt Royal's filmic version of last night's events, so detailed that Irma would find it irrefutable. I walked from my room, greeted Royal and Irma—"Morning. Wut a way you?"—passed the open grate and went outside. Where once there had been just one, now there were two giant spiders, as big as my fist, copulating in the duncan.


There was another bit of gossip blowing about the island; Hollywood was going to make a new movie about the mutiny. And this time it would be filmed on Pitcairn.

The cast list had already been drawn up. Alec Guinness was playing Captain Bligh. As island magistrate, Jay should put him up, although they might need to install a ramp up the hill, as he was so old perhaps he couldn't walk. Roger Moore would be Fletcher Christian. Dennis said that he ought to stay with us, as our household were Christians, but Tom and Betty, also sixth-generation descendants and with plenty of room now Perry was gone, were already putting in a rival bid. Brooke Shields would be the leading lady, although in what role it wasn't quite certain. What was clear was where she would sleep.

"She be staying with Nigger," said Dennis.

Everyone was going to be employed as extras, with Vula, with her rolling body and classic elderly Polynesian looks, in particular demand. The Mouth suggested that the film crew would bring their own ship and the actors sleep in luxury cabins offshore rather than in the Pitcairners' simple weatherboard homes, but this was dismissed as a ridiculous idea, mere rumor.

Charles was most eloquent on the subject of the fictionalization of Pitcairn by film. He had seen most of the movies on video, and had particularly enjoyed the 1935 classic, with Clark Gable as a dashing Fletcher Christian and Charles Laughton as a sadistic, elderly Bligh. That, said Charles, was by far the most accurate portrayal of what really happened, and everyone agreed.

*Mutiny on the Bounty,* filmed off the coast of California and in Tahiti, had been an early Hollywood extravaganza with a simple moral message, portraying a clear-cut confrontation between tyranny (Bligh) and justice (Fletcher Christian). Metro-Goldwyn-Mayer had issued teacher's manuals to American high schools, encouraging children to act the parts of the men in the mutiny and discuss questions such as "Would you have clambered into Bligh's launch?" Within weeks of its release, six hundred thousand people had seen the film, one of the most successful of the decade.

But it was the next movie, made thirty years later, which was to become the most enduring image of the confrontation between the two men. Marlon Brando, cast as Fletcher Christian, claimed to have read one million words about the mutiny to work himself into the part. Tons of white sand were shipped from New Jersey to spill over the black, volcanic Tahitian beaches so that Paradise matched the moviemakers', and moviegoers', dream. Trevor Howard played a demented, demonic Bligh, but Brando was rather foppish, and the Pitcairners preferred to claim Clark Gable's swashbuckling heroism as their heritage.

"I like the most recent one best. The one with Mel Gibson." Everyone turned to look at me.

"Heap of shit," squawked Nola.

"Cack," said Charles.

"Piss," smirked Royal.

Charles elaborated. "Em got it wrong. Em make out Bligh good 'un."

"Well . . . not exactly." Anthony Hopkins's Captain Bligh was a tortured, not a torturing personality. His primary battle was not with Fletcher Christian, but within himself. This Bligh was, for the first time, a believable man.

"Shouldn't be allowed to make movies like that," said Charles. "Heap of shit."

And the portrait that had drawn me to Pitcairn was summarily dismissed.

We counted more than two hundred kingfish, and there were plenty more. Trent alone had caught seventy-four.

The day had begun slowly. Our phone was making strange noises, ringing all by itself, which was exhausting for Irma, who had to keep checking that it wasn't a garbled long ring. Trent came to sort the problem out; as trainee engineer, he was in charge of fixing the phones. Trent was supervised by his father, Steve, in his capacity of supervising engineer, and assisted by Terry, the electrician.

"I hear ha boat gwen fer fish this afternoon," said Trent. He sprayed the earpiece with oil and put it back on the hook.

"Who told you that?" Dennis was watching him fix the phone.

"I forget."

"I no hear," said Terry, offended. "Wha time?"

"I ka wa."

"I hear three o'clock . . ." And in this way, a decision was taken that we would all go fishing that afternoon in the longboat, with no one having to take the responsibility for making it.

At first, I had misread this method of ensuring that something took place. "They've been talking about doing that for *ages*," I'd groan. "It's never going to happen." But talking about it wasn't, as I thought, a symptom of procrastination, but the opposite: it was a way of making sure that something happened, and sooner rather than later. Like so many things on Pitcairn, talking about them made them real. And sure enough, that afternoon, we climbed into the longboat to go fishing. Some canoes joined us, and the fleet left for the far side of the island.

As soon as the lines were dropped, the kingfish began to bite, and bite, and bite. The bottoms of the canoes and longboat were shiny with fish. Trent seemed to have the luckiest line and Len, who was usually the most gifted fisherman, caught only five kingfish and one yellow fin, which would have been considered a handsome catch on any other day.

We were jubilant, rich with our catch. There were so many fish that they were counted and gutted down on the Landing and the debris thrown into the water. I borrowed a knife from Dave and started slitting them along the soft belly, from head to tail, reaching in for the warm yellow and red guts. The count reached three hundred, and everyone cheered. There was a small pile left. We all counted out loud—*"Three hundred and twenty-one, three hundred and twenty-two, three hundred and twenty-three."* Three hundred and twenty-three kingfish. No one could remember a day like it.

The longboat was still tied to the side of the jetty, and I jumped in to retrieve my waterproof, stepping onto a plank laid across the gunwales. The boat, from being a level platform, suddenly tilted violently on a wave, and I tumbled into the hold, hitting the back of my head on the plank as I fell.

For a few moments, I just lay there. But then I knew that I had fallen, and that there were people above me on the Landing, and that every now and then one of them would laugh, leer over, and a parcel of red guts would fly over into the bay. Everything had the look of being underwater; I could see the shape of those gutting, but couldn't make out who they were, and when they opened their mouths they seemed to be blowing bubbles rather than talking.

Perhaps no one had seen me lying there right below them, and I should shout for help. I made some sort of sound, but none of the fuzzy human shapes responded; they just flayed their blurred, bloodstained limbs.

"Dennissss . . ." Only a soft hiss emerged, but in my head I was screaming, *SAMBO. SAMBOOOOO.*

I lay for a while, I don't know how long, concentrating. I must get up, I had to get up. Slowly, I lifted my hand, grasped the plank and pulled myself to sitting. The surf had died down, but I was still rocking. I was going to vomit.

I was on my feet, clasping the gunwale, when a hand dripping crimson reached down from the Landing.

"You se capsize bad," said the fuzzy head. "Surf comen up."

I looked around for Dennis; I wanted to go home, to lie down. He was talking to the Mouth as he gutted. Perhaps he hadn't known that I had fallen. Perhaps the jubilant banter had drowned out my strangled cries.

I staggered over to the boat shed, slumped down on the concrete and waited for the afternoon's bloody work to end.


The next morning I went to the dispensary. My back ached and I could feel the inside of my head. I didn't want medication, I wanted reassurance. I wanted someone to tell me that the humming in my brain would be gone by evening, and that no permanent damage had been done.

Jenny sat behind a desk, as a doctor does, while Royal hovered to one side of her. Royal was wearing a green uniform—the sort of plain but well-pocketed ones that nurses have—and a serious expression. She was listening very intently to Jenny and me.

All consultations with the resident nurse took place like this, in one room that served as surgery and waiting room, and with Royal watching. What if a patient wanted to discuss an embarrassing condition? An emotional problem? And there was Royal, taking it all in. I had never heard anyone complain about this lack of medical confidentiality, nor had anyone seemed reluctant to go to see Jenny at the dispensary. Yet, with Royal listening, I was barely able to speak. I told Jenny I had a headache, accepted some pills and hurried home.

I was sitting on the veranda, recording my visit to the dispensary in my diary, when Irma came in from weeding the watermelon. She looked at me and said, "Writ-ing, dear?" but implying, "Spy-ing, dear?"

I finished the sentence and shut the book.

"One writer," said Irma. "He se write about Pitcairn. He larn one woman's children have no father."

I knew the journalist to whom Irma was referring. He had been careful never to mention the woman by name. But to Irma, whether an individual was identified or not made no difference: the name of Pitcairn was being slandered. Royal could watch you have your breasts examined, listen to you talking about the pain in your gut, and everyone else on the island could be informed about your most intimate examination within the hour. But an outsider couldn't report on it, even an outsider who took pains to conceal the patient's identity. They would be making public very personal things about a Pitcairner, and Pitcairn itself—the thirty-eight knitted souls—would feel offended and intruded upon.

I remembered that Kari had once said to me, "No one has a private life on Pitcairn," and at the time I had thought she meant it as a criticism. But now I saw that it had been intended as a comment upon how people live. In other places, people acted differently, dressed differently and spoke differently once they crossed the threshold of their home. But on Pitcairn, inside your weatherboard house was the same as outside; they were not two different worlds. There was no house with a door, yard with a gate, or field with a fence. The threshold over which a stranger was intruding on private ground wasn't the veranda, it was the shoreline, it was the sea.

Dennis was acting as if we were the best of friends. We had spent the morning collecting bananas, and I had tied a bunch to the back of his bike and driven it up to Chris at the schoolhouse, so she could dry them in her dehydrator. When I returned home, Dennis was having breakfast.

I asked him when the last trial was heard in the courthouse.

"For me!" he cheered.

Andrew Young, age ninety, who had died a few years earlier, had kept a table on top of Ship Landing Point, a peak to the northeast of Bounty Bay, where he liked to work on his carvings. One day, Dennis and some other young men had pushed the table off the peak. Andrew Young took them to court and Dennis was issued with a warning. He could not remember a time when anyone had been imprisoned. The very idea of a prison on Pitcairn seemed absurd. The island itself was such a natural fortress, entrapping all its inhabitants. Where would prisoners escape to? Tedside? Big Pool? Down Isaac's?

Nevertheless, to celebrate the 1989 bicentenary of the mutiny, the Pitcairn Islands Administration in New Zealand had come up with a project: Pitcairn, they said, needed a new jail. The men had been given paid work to construct a three-celled prison from hardiflex and corrugated iron. In each cell, there was a camp bed and a small window, just large enough to wriggle through, on which there was no lock. There was an outside duncan with two holes, just like Irma's. Since construction, one cell had been used to store boating equipment and the life jackets, which would have been more usefully stacked in the holds of *Tin* and *Tub*. The other two cells had never been used. To complete the bicentennial project, a signpost has been erected, TO GOAL, although I had reached it following Dennis's directions: "Se pass ha rose apple fer Bla Bla's."

Dennis and I were both in high spirits. The weather was warm and the sea calm, and in the afternoon the young set were taking out the canoes to go diving on the *Bounty*. The ship lay just off Bounty Bay, under only six feet of water. Her skeleton could be clearly seen if you leaned over the side of the canoe.

All the costly reconstructions made for the *Bounty* movies were of a mighty ship, but the shivering shape in the water was little bigger than a longboat. The *Bounty* had been very small for her time, only ninety feet long and twenty-four feet wide. There had been no superstructure, and all accommodations and facilities were cramped below deck. The great cabin, where the Captain should have lounged in splendor, had been appropriated for the preservation of the breadfruit plants, and Bligh had slept like a sentry in a small cabin to one side. The total cost of the extensive refitting had been four and a half thousand pounds, more than twice the purchase price. With the best quarters and first call on the limited supply of fresh water reserved for the plants, the *Bounty* had been redesigned with the greatest concern for the well-being of the seedlings and little consideration for her men.

On arriving at Pitcairn, the *Bounty*—the Admiralty's pride and hope—had been stripped. Her sails were first used as tents and then, when the wooden and thatch houses were constructed, as clothes. It is said it was only eight days after she anchored off the island that her gutted remains were set on fire, perhaps by Christian to prevent escapes or perhaps by Quintal, drunk. The supposed day of the *Bounty*'s burning—January 23—is a national holiday and hugely celebrated on Pitcairn, with a *Bounty* replica launched from the Landing and set alight.

There were half a dozen canoes out and Glen and Dennis were already in the water wearing snorkeling masks and flippers, as bright and lively as any rockfish. They would disappear for a few minutes, then pop up, pointing and shouting, although their words became indistinct over the water.

When I dived in, within seconds I was touching one of the *Bounty*'s ribs. I dived again, touched her backbone and pushed up to the warm air. Nigger's broad, dark shoulders broke through the water in front of me. I watched as he forced his fingers back through his wet hair, and saw how the movement made his shoulder blades rise and fall. Pitcairn was so tiny, so connected that it had been impossible not to know where he was, what he was doing, with whom he would eat his supper that night. Once, early one morning Tom had called Tamanu on the VHF and Perry had an-

swered, telling all Pitcairn that Nigger was still in bed. When I was pounding the dough on the kitchen table, his voice would erupt into the room
over the VHF, calling Dave or Steve. I could not escape hearing him, and I
would be within fingertip reach of him many days, yet we had not once
touched or exchanged words since he had issued me the driver's license.
Sometimes—especially when neither Irma nor Dennis were speaking to
me—I felt the torment of such distant closeness.

Nigger dived back down, embraced by the ocean.

That afternoon the phone went *long-short-long-short-long,* and Irma answered.

"Call fer Debbie at commercial radio station," she said. "You wan ha
bike?"

I jumped on and drove up to Taro Ground. At the commercial radio
station, Tom was sending a telegram urgently requesting the whereabouts
of Aden Butterfield, whose name I hadn't heard since Dennis had mentioned him at the schedule with Norfolk. Tom waved me toward the radio.
It was a simple system, with a foot pedal that had to be pressed when you
wanted to talk.

"It's Debbie. Over." I pressed the pedal. I couldn't hear any human
noise, just crackle. It was another futile attempt, another dead line. I tried
just once more.

"It's Debbie. Over."

He sounded farther away than I could possibly imagine, but I recognized his voice. It was my boyfriend.

"Kevin. Kevin. Is that you? Over."

Nothing.

"Kevin. Is that you? You have to say something, then say 'over.'
Over."

I could hear the form of a short sentence. The words were indistinct,
but the tone was clear. He was screaming.

"*Dead. Dead. Dead.*"

"What's dead? The line? What's dead? Over."

"*Dead. Dead.*"

"I can't hear. And say 'Over' when you finish. Over."

"Mum is dead. Over."

"Oh. Oh. Oh, Kevin." But I had forgotten to press the pedal. He hadn't heard me.

"Kevin. *Kevin!*"

He sounded as if he were being sucked away, as if he were drowning. The connection was lost.

I walked past Tom, who was reading out his telegram—since the departure of Aden Butterfield from this island, stated Tom, certain electrical equipment had been missing. I walked to the very edge of Taro Ground. I could see the ocean on all sides, on and on and on. It fell and rose, like an exposed lung, rarely breaking into whitecaps at the top. If it did break, everyone would comment, "Whitecaps today."

I began to weep uncontrollably, but not for Kevin's mother. I was crying for the hopelessness of communicating, and of comforting, across the watery gulf.

Then I saw her, a long, slow bulker, moving from west to east across the water. She was only a couple of miles off the island; Tom would be able to radio out to her. There would be an officer on duty on the bridge, who would answer our call.

I ran back into the radio station; Tom was still working on the telegram, in pursuit of his quarry.

"*A-D-E-N. Aden.*"

"There's a ship! There's a ship!"

Tom reached the window as she came into view. He took up the microphone.

"ZBP, Zulu Bravo Papa. Pitcairn Island Radio. This is Pitcairn Island Radio. Ship two miles off. Can you read me? This is Zulu Bravo Papa, Pitcairn Island Radio."

Tom tried again. "ZBP, Zulu Bravo Papa. Pitcairn Island Radio. Ship two miles off. Large bulker. Can you read me? ZBP. Zulu Bravo Papa. Pitcairn Island Radio."

"Why don't they answer?" I didn't understand. They could see the island, and must have been able to hear us.

Tom shrugged. "Some time jus don. Jus don wan talk."

Tom tried once more, and then we watched for a while until the bulker didn't look so very large.

My dough would have risen, and it was time to go back to Irma's.

## 15 · *a r r o w r o o t*

"*O*ur ring phone good fer nothing after em spray it," said Irma. It was not a good morning to be out of touch. The annual arrowroot dig might begin today, and we were all waiting on the call.

The arrowroot fields were spread over the island, but most were to be found in the direction of St. Paul's, before Down Rope. Each family had their own field, but each field was dug by the whole island, as everyone moved from patch to patch. This year, Charles and Charlotte's field would be the first to be dug. When the call came through after breakfast, everyone headed toward the east of the island, a snake of bikes bumping over the red paths tailed by the dogs.

No instructions were issued, and no one appeared to be in charge, but each Pitcairner set to work. The men took up pitchforks and began to dig up the roots. The women picked the roots up, knocked off the clingy mud and threw them into the ni'au baskets, except Clarice, who dug along with the men. It was a laborious process, and various attempts were made to speed it up and reduce the toil. When we reached Carol and Jay's field, a large patch, Jay suggested we fetch the tractor and plow up the earth to make it easier to pull out the roots. But the tractor plowed up the roots as well, breaking and reburying them under the freshly turned earth.

All day we moved seamlessly from field to field. The Pitcairners worked, not as a set of dedicated individuals, but as part of an organic whole. It was the same when they went out to trade on a ship, unloaded supplies at the Landing or hauled *Tub* into the boat shed. They moved as if choreographed, with the rhythm coming from within the group itself.

I had thought I had acquired most of the skills necessary to live on Pitcairn. I was proficient at basket-weaving, baked very good bread, could play a strong hand at canasta and climb confidently Down Rope. But the core skill to being a Pitcairner—to be part of a whole, not a whole in yourself—still eluded me. I was unable to shake off an unrelenting individuality.

I knocked mud off the roots and watched Reynold and Ben. The arrowroot was processed with no orders given but absolute order observed. But what I saw for the first time was that while everyone responded to each other's movements, they never touched. I couldn't remember having seen anyone hold anyone else, not even a mother her child. I was shocked that I hadn't noticed this before. Perhaps it was because the choreography was as intimate as actually touching that the absence of the brush of flesh against flesh had passed me by.

By the end of the day the fields were all dug. I gave Ben a lift down

---

*ni'au*—the leaf of the coconut palm, which is woven into rectangular, lidless working baskets by the Pitcairners, used for gathering vegetables and fruit, and for taking them out to the ships to trade. Ni'au baskets—genuine, working Pitcairnese items—are never sold as souvenirs.

from Big Grass on the back of the bike. He sat with his legs to one side, unable to straddle the wide saddle.

"Halfway and still alive!" he cheered, as we rounded the corner into Jim's Ground. I looked back; his shirt had flown open and his baseball cap had blown to the back of his head. His legs were kicked straight out sideways, to avoid getting tangled in the tires.

"Not far now!" He kept cheering as we negotiated each difficult corner. "Nearly there!" as we passed Carol and Jay's, just minutes from home.

The peeling began that night. The arrowroot was long and thin, like a large white penis, and the dark outer skin had to be removed, which the islanders called husking. There were so many to be husked that two tables were set up—one at Big Fence and the other at Len and Thelma's—onto which the roots were shaken from the sacks.

The peeling continued around the big tables all through the next day, and I joined the group at Big Fence. More timesaving methods were experimented with: Steve attempted to shortcut the peeling process by putting his arrowroot in the concrete mixer. It emerged mashed. Dennis experimented with a few roots in the washing machine, which had an abrasive tin tub that spun around and around. It worked, and he pulled out perfectly peeled but very wet roots, which could rot overnight.

The piles of arrowroot seemed insurmountable; I could not imagine why we needed so much. Nola and Reynold had dug ten sacks; although famed for her orange arrowroot pie, even Nola couldn't bake that many. Irma told me she still had some arrowroot flour left from the crop of two years ago, and that, if properly refined, it could keep up to twenty years as it didn't attract the bugs like ordinary flour. Royal said she ends up throwing half of hers away. But need on Pitcairn was not measured; you could never have an excess of anything. If there was an opportunity to gather yet more wood for carvings, barter more frozen foodstuffs from a chief steward, accept another donation of an electric kettle, then you grasped it, however many you already had or however large your stocks. Olive had asked the steward on a passing ship if he had any oil to spare.

"A bit," said the steward. "How much do you need?"

"How much have you got?" replied Olive.

"Seven gallons."

"I'll take them," she said. If he had said two or twenty, Olive's response would have been exactly the same.

The motivation wasn't greed, it was fear. Whatever you had now might have to last forever. There was no guarantee that any supply line would continue; there might never be another ship, and the weather might destroy all you had. The Pitcairners' hoarding was a well thought out and tested strategy in this struggle.

On the third day, the peeled arrowroot was pulped into flour. A large mill was set up in the Square, powered by the tractor. The men pressed the mushed arrowroot, known as mama, through a sieve, passing water over it all the time, which washed into a large oblong container called a cradle. The water slopped about and was sticky when it dried on your clothes and skin. When the arrowroot had been processed with two washes of water, the water was ladled, using buckets, through old pillowcases into large tin tubs.

At first the water in the tins was cloudy; but after an hour or more, it began to change color, becoming a glassy gray. This, Mavis told me, meant that the arrowroot had settled. The women then poured off the top water, to be used again for passing through the sieve. A hard cake of white sediment was left at the bottom of the tin, which we scraped out with wooden spoons. This was the flour.

After three long days' work, we were still nowhere near the final product. The white sediment was washed again, before being broken up and spread out on door-sized drying tables, erected in each home. Depending upon the weather, it took about three days for the flour to dry, turning it each day. Ben was in charge of the turning in our house, and set aside a certain time each morning to move carefully the white powder that had laid claim to the veranda.

---

*mama*—from "to chew" or "masticate" in Tahitian.

It had been a good week, and we had all worked hard. But I knew that the ease with which I sat at the table and drank my milo, chatting to Dennis about whether to make sweet or savory arrowroot biscuits, might not last long. I knew that I was wrong to have seen, and sought, acceptance as a straight line, from stranger through friend to good-as-family. I no longer expected to become more and more part of Pitcairn the longer I stayed. Acceptance wasn't like that; it worked a wandering, tortuous path, sometimes never reaching the place you hoped it would.

I turned to *Return to Laughter.*

It is an error to assume that to know is to understand and that to understand is to like. The greater the extent to which one has lived and participated in a genuinely foreign culture and understood it, the greater the extent to which one realizes that one could not, without violence to one's personal integrity, be of it. This importance of fidelity to one's own culture and one's own standards is mutual. That is what tolerance means: allowing each man his own integrity.

Dave the Mouth came around to show Dennis his great shark carving, almost as tall as himself. He was making it in case a French naval vessel called; "the Frenchies" liked their sharks big, and paid good money for them.

I left the others on the veranda and went to do the washing. The Mouth came and stood behind me at the sink, reaching over for a plate. I sensed the tip of his knife in the small of my back, and felt it twist. I swung around and the Mouth laughed, placing the weapon back in its sheath.

I was trying to write a letter to Kevin, which could not be sent. But I could take it to Dennis one Tuesday morning when the post office was open, and he would sell me the correct stamps and frank it for me, and I would feel, at least, as if I had done all I could to communicate. In the letter, I briefly mentioned that I had capsized the bike one day at the back of the island, when I had been out looking for bananas. I no longer dared to tell the Pitcairners of such small failings.

Now the arrowroot was dry and jarred, Dennis was no longer speaking to me. I had tried to tempt him with sweet coconut and arrowroot biscuits, but he was stubborn. I decided to go to the schoolhouse and read some old *Miscellany*s.

I was looking through issues from the early sixties, when I came across an article on William Brown, the gardener from HMAV *Bounty*. It was not surprising to learn that little was known about him, apart from Bligh's description of his magnificent scar, stretching down one side of his face from his eyelid to his throat. While the ship was anchored off Tahiti, Brown had busied himself potting hundreds of breadfruit seedlings. Although taking no active part in the mutiny, he had willingly thrown in his lot with Fletcher Christian and sailed to Pitcairn with his consort, Teatuahitea (Sarah). He was murdered about three years later, the last white man to be killed by the Polynesians, having fathered no children. The place where he found a well is still called Brown's Water. The article continued: "Although the name Brown is one of the four surnames in use on the island today, they are descended from a later immigrant to the island, not from the young horticulturalist-turned-mutineer."

Nigger Brown, son of Len and Thelma Brown, was not a descendant from HMAV *Bounty*. I turned over this news, and was surprised at my own reaction, and unsettled by it: I felt cheated. It became brutally clear why I had embarked upon, perhaps engineered, our encounter. I had wanted to be immersed in the myth of the mutiny, become part of it, to live inside the dream I had formed at the Elephant.

Now I knew: I could not be part of this organic whole, this Pitcairn. Until Nigger, I had been a tolerated, sometimes amusing outsider. But, in trying to get closer, I had abandoned that privileged status and become an aberrant insider. In trying to touch a Pitcairner, I had acted in a way in which a Pitcairner never would have.

I walked back from Up Pulau shadowed by a full moon. Earlier in the day, the tide had been so full down at the Landing that it had washed right over the jetty. There was hardly any wind, but the giant bamboos by the path to Tamanu still groaned, and the smaller sounds of the bush—the cracking of leaves under tiny padded feet—spotted the night.

In the rare quiet, I heard footsteps behind me. Perhaps it was Dennis. Or Terry. Or the Mouth. Something scurried away behind the mango, known for its bright red leaves. I took the road up Jack's Tatties, a longer route, but avoiding the banyan trees with their strange trunks, which a human could hide in. I walked past the turning for John Adams's Grave, thinking for a moment that I might see him wandering around the island while everyone else was inside, hiding from the dark.

As if refining this year's arrowroot crop hadn't been enough, the bell in the Square was rung to call people to paid work. Paid work was never popular, although you earned three dollars and twenty-five cents an hour. It was mostly painting—the courthouse, the school, the dispensary. No one was required to do it, but the jobs had to be done and it was expected that everyone would lend a hand.

The tin roofs on the dispensary and the courthouse needed to be repainted. A ladies' team of Carol, Meralda, Royal, Betty and I were appointed for the dispensary job. The men did the courthouse, which had a higher roof with a greater pitch. They had to tie a rope around their waists and work in pairs, counterweighing one another over the lip of the roof. Glen was in charge of repainting the notice above the door: THE COURT HOUSE was being renamed THE PUBLIC HALL.

The ladies had to climb up onto the dispensary roof and balance ourselves on the slope, a brush in one hand and a pot of aluminum paint in the other, working across and down until one patch was painted and we could move on to the next. We had to be very careful not to step on a part that had already been painted, which was difficult, as the fresh silver paint and the original paint were exactly the same color. But the fresh paint was very slippery, and if we trod on it we would have slid off the roof and fallen fifteen feet to the concrete below. It was awkward work, so chat was curtailed until we climbed down from the roof for a rest. Betty and I sat on the bench, shaded from the sun.

Of all the Pitcairners, Betty was the one who could have most easily walked along an English suburban high street and not turn a single head. With her little sharp nose, her light brown ringletted hair and her fair skin, she had little physical trace of her Polynesian ancestry. And when she spoke English, her long-voweled Pitcairnese accent was faint and she was discursive when she spoke, as I had found no other Pitcairner. Kari and Betty were close friends. Because of this, and Betty's familiar look, I asked her the same question I had asked Dennis and Terry at Christian's Cave.

"What do you feel like? Are you Polynesian?"

"I feel that we're from mutineers," said Betty. "I'm not ashamed of that like some people are. We don't know why things happened the way they did. Mutiny wasn't the right thing to do, but Fletcher"—she used his first name only, as if he were still alive and close to her—"felt he was doing right by doing what he did. You get to a place where you can only take so much."

When Betty and her family had been away, touring the United States as ambassadors for the Seventh-day Adventist Church, they had covered twelve thousand miles, giving two slide shows a day about Pitcairn.

"So many people wanted to touch us. 'Can I touch you?' 'Can I hug you?' 'Can I shake your hand?' As if coming from Pitcairn you were not a real human being, but someone special. You have to live up to some kind of standard, you have to be something you're not. So many times I said, 'We're just people.' "

Betty said: "There's no perfect person, no perfect community. It's sort of like the Garden of Eden. There was a serpent even there, which ruined a perfect place."

.   .   .

Dave the Mouth was building a new driveway up Bill's Ground. He wanted to be able to park his bike up the back, rather than in front of his home.

Because of the patchwork division of land on Pitcairn, Dave's plot was surrounded by other people's land. Bla Bla was to one side and Royal to the other, with Irma and Ben on the opposite side of the road— Dennis's first site for a house. But they were all family (Dave was Royal's nephew) and the land was not cultivated. He had been working on the new driveway since finishing his giant shark, clearing the ground and chopping down trees.

"Dem china es mine 'un," said Royal one morning. Chinas were the only privately owned banana trees on Pitcairn. Royal had come around straight after the dispensary had closed, which was always a sign that she had something important to impart.

"Mouth bin chop em," Royal snarled with all her face.

Irma fussed, tutted, shook her head and said, "Paan." But Royal's anger was quiet and inconsolable.

"Dem es my china," she said.

It wasn't until the next day that Royal's revenge was revealed.

"Power es-e-on," said Ben.

"Em nails outside Mouth's, in ha mud," said Dennis, chattily.

"Wha?" Irma, who was out the back at the bolt frying fishballs for the freezer, had sensed there was news.

"Royal put em nails in ha mud, outside Mouth's." Dennis held his finger and thumb wide apart. "Daa long. She stick em in, point up, and hide em under em leaf."

"But one of the kids could have stepped on them." No one paid any attention to my remark. Everyone here goes around barefoot, I thought. And if there's an accident, there's no doctor.

"Dave find two. Might be more some place," said Dennis.

Irma went back out to the bolt, shaking her head as she went.

"What's going to happen?" I asked Dennis.

He shrugged, and helped himself to some arrowroot pie.

"Nitho," he said.

"But . . ." But I went no further. It was inconceivable that Dave would go to his brother, Nigger, and ask him to arrest his aunt, Royal, and bring her before the island magistrate, Jay. There was no longer a courthouse to try her in anyway.

I walked through the bananas and down to the Square; there was no one around, and the long bench was empty. I saw some bikes along Main Road, and remembered that it was Thursday, and the shop must be open. Rick was leaning up against one of the pillars outside.

"Heard about the nails?" I asked.

He nodded. Of course, everyone had heard about the nails. Rick then told me a story of how, on the last trip to Oeno, a man had taken out a knife and attacked a woman with it. She could have been killed, and the man should have been charged, but no one would do it, not even Nigger, the police officer, whose job it was.

"They're frightened of retribution," said Rick. "They're scared that if they say something against someone they'll get back at them at some later date. You rely on everyone, every day, for your life—in the longboat, climbing the ladder. You just can't walk away from things here."

I imagined how a court case would be conducted on Pitcairn. What if someone was murdered? Stabbed? Allowed to lie where they had fallen? What if someone pushed me off the cliff Down Rope? Even if the crime was committed in front of a crowd, who would bear witness against another Pitcairner? Who would stand up and accuse? Who would defend, cross-examine and judge? Perhaps the Pitcairn Islands Administration in New Zealand could bring in someone from outside, to conduct an impartial inquiry and establish the facts. But who would refute the tale that I tripped and fell? Accidents were common on Pitcairn.


The wind rose up overnight, and all the flies on the island seemed to be taking refuge around my flashlight. Minute fruit flies, so small that they lodged in my eyes and made them smart; tickly spider flies, like mini daddy longlegs; flies that buzzed, mosquitoes that whined, silent dust-colored moths and hoards of breaknecks, which, if you slapped one as it landed on your throat, thinking it was a common fly, would leave a small, irritating blister where it had been crushed.

I opened my Afrique-Trunk and pulled out one of the presents, shaped like a slim book. I unwrapped the patterned gift paper; there was a star chart inside. It unfolded to show the southern hemisphere at night and wildly named constellations—the Chameleon, the Serpent, the Mariner's Compass. My friend must have gone to some trouble to find this in England.

I turned off my flashlight and took the chart to my window. The sky was clear, but the stars just pinpricks, light-years away. I had hoped that my friend's gift would be comforting, enabling me to reach out to home. But looking from the chart to the black sky, I saw the huge distance between myself and anything, anything at all.

## 16 · s h o o t i n g
## b r e a d f r u i t

The sound of gunfire thudded through the valley. It came from .22 rifles, which vibrated and smelled smoky when shot. Reynold kept his bullets in a tiny cardboard box, and emptied them out to me three at a time—one for the barrel, the other two to keep in my pocket. Our target was breadfruit; it was the season for their shooting, and at the next general party breadfruit would be a major item on the menu.

The wonders of the breadfruit have long been extolled. William Dampier, in his 1688 *Voyage Round the World*, pointed to its great economy—"as big as a penny loaf when wheat is at five shillings the bushel"—and how "soft" and "tender" it was, with a "sweet and pleasant" taste. As early as 1776, Dr. Daniel Solander, a Swedish botanist who had accompanied Cook on his first voyage, had praised it as "one of the most useful vegetables in the world." Once the skin was scraped off with the lid of a corned beef tin, pilhi could be made from its grated flesh, folded into a banana leaf; breadfruit chips were very tasty and breadfruit stew with coconut cream was filling. Meralda had held a bicentenary party at which everything was made of breadfruit, which the Pitcairners called bread, much as the Admiralty had hoped the West Indians would.*

Although the breadfruit is widespread throughout Polynesia, Pitcairn is the only place where it is picked by being shot at. The breadfruit is the size of a human head, but breadfruit trees are up to sixty feet high—many times higher than anything else on Pitcairn. The trick was to hit the stem that held the fruit to the branch so it fell to the ground whole. With my first shot, I scarred the skin with a fleshy wound. Then, with my second bullet, I hit the fruit in the center and it exploded, the juice falling like rain.

"Keep ha musket high," said Reynold. He was concerned about the waste of bullets and the loss of fruit, but also that I might kill someone. Although we were up in a valley behind the house, a bullet from a .22 could travel all the way down to the Square. Several people had been injured when breadfruit were being shot, and, once, a woman was said to have been hit in the arm while sitting inside her own home, working on a curio.

Dennis, Toj and the Mouth had already potted several fruit, and Dennis was rummaging for them in the undergrowth.

"Show me once more how to fire it, accurately," I asked Reynold, loading the barrel. First I sighted a low-hanging fruit. Then I moved the barrel across slowly until it was pointing straight up the valley, and I had first Dennis, then the Mouth in sight. I fantasized about defending myself. I knew how easily, how frequently, how inexplicably accidents happened

---

* *Bread* is the most common word for breadfruit, but *uru,* Polynesian for "breadfruit," is also used. This became popular after the Marlon Brando *Mutiny on the Bounty* film was shown on the island in 1980, as it is used frequently in the script.

on Pitcairn. I was now frightened *of* something, something particular. I was frightened of being shot.

That night I made breadfruit chips. First I boiled the fruit and scraped off the warty skin. Then I cut through its floury flesh, making sticks as long but twice as thick as my fingers. I popped them in the deep-fat fryer. They were delicious, and even Irma ate some before retreating into her radio shack.

"*Irma* is the handle. India Romeo Mike Alpha. On Pitcairn Island. What is your handle? Over."

Ben and Dennis were watching a 1950s musical on the video, the only sort of film Ben watched, but most of the songs were drowned out by Irma's radio talk.

"Thank you. That was a good contact. We hope to be meeting up again in the future. We'll say seventy-threes, VR6ID, and thank you for the contact. Over and out."

This scene was so familiar; for several months, I had been part of it. If anyone had parted the bananas and walked through the veranda, they would have seen Ben, Irma, Dennis and I, each idling or going about everyday tasks, elements in a Pitcairn home.

There was a long ring, and Irma answered.

"Yourley there? Yourley." Irma listened.

When she hung up, Dennis, Ben and I were gathered around her to hear the news. A ship had contacted Tom at Taro Ground; she would be passing Pitcairn, and hoped to stop offshore for a couple of hours. She was called the *Bow Star*. I determined she would be the ship on which I would leave Pitcairn.

More news was brought to us over the next day. *Bow Star* was a chemical carrier, of the same line that had brought me to Pitcairn, and the Captain had asked after me. He had heard from his colleagues on NCC *Najran* about an English girl they had dropped off a few months earlier. Terry said he recognized the Captain's name.

My emotions had become as confused as the Pitcairners'. I was scared on Pitcairn, so scared that even when I went out to the duncan at night I grabbed a broom handle on the way. Yet I felt pain at the thought of departing. I both feared and wanted this island, perhaps as Dennis both feared and wanted me. I asked Tom if the *Bow Star* had made contact with the radio station again, and to ask them where they were bound, and if I could be given a passage.

When the long ring came through that the *Bow Star*'s ETA was 0800 hours the following day, it seemed too soon. I went to see Kari, Up Tibi.

"Whenever I had to go back to being a radio officer again, it was terrible to leave. If I asked a ship to pick me up, I hoped it would be delayed or sail right on by," said Kari. "I felt that if this was the last time I saw Pitcairn, life would not be worth living."

Perhaps I would miss Kari. But most of all, I would miss the ocean. I heard it every morning when I woke; it was my first sound. Then I saw it before anything else, from my window. It was a sight and sound from which I could not escape. Only when I was asleep was the sea silent. And then I often dreamed of it. One night, I had dreamed that Pitcairn had lost its anchor and was floating across the ocean like a floe. We were making for New Zealand, from where I could catch a ship home.

On the last night, I had severe-weather nightmares. On the night of the long ring, there had been terrible gusting and the sea had been choppy with whitecaps in the morning. In this weather, the *Bow Star* might not stop. The next afternoon the wind was so fierce that the rhombic at Taro Ground was blown down.

Betty was reassuring.

"If God wants you to leave, he will bring fine weather," she said.

Repacking did not take long; most of what I had brought with me— my writer's life—had remained in my Afrique-Trunk. I tried to busy my hands. I made faniu brooms, stripping the coconut fronds and tying together their stiff ribs with a strip of pandanus. I gave one to Mavis, one to

Charlotte, even one to Chris, whom I was sure wouldn't use it. They were received with nods of recognition rather than gratitude. I was leaving; they had been so right not to invest any emotion in me. Because once I had gone, like anyone who went, I would never return. If someone had grown to like, or even be fond of me, how could we have coped with the pain of utter severance, as final as death?

We were just waiting. Dennis had opened the post office the night before, and had a basket of bananas ready to offer the Captain in return for taking the mail. Ben was working on a hand vase and Irma was re-arranging one of the freezers. She would need to make room for the goods from the share out of the *Bow Star*. My Afrique-Trunk was tied to the back of the bike. The bell in the Square rang—*dong, dong, dong, dong, dong*—and the bikes started up all over Adamstown. Somewhere, I could hear a roar.

Irma thrust a note in my hand, addressed to Ron in Buxley Green. "Could you get this to Ron, if you don mind, dear?"

It was such a small request. "Of course," I said.

Then Irma scribbled on the envelope, as if we could no longer speak directly to each other, "Kindly Delivered by Debbie."

The bikes had gathered down the Landing, and the baskets were being loaded onto *Tub* to trade. One by one, the Pitcairners hugged me, and as they did so whispered something in my ear. "It was good to meet you," "I'm glad to have known you," "It was fun," all in such correct English that the parting seemed like an official ceremony, each of us do-ing what was expected of us.

We scrambled up the ladder, my Afrique-Trunk was lifted on board by a rope, and the curios were spread out on deck to trade. I watched the Pitcairners as they rolled up their sheets, repacked the unsold curios and disembarked from the *Bow Star* as swiftly as they had boarded. Tom struck the first note of the "Goodbye Song." "Now one last song we'll sing . . ." Tomorrow, anyone parting the bananas and walking through our veranda would see a typical Pitcairn home—Irma, Dennis and Ben, and be offered a piece of arrowroot pie, baked by Debbie.

"She se gone," Dennis would say.

"She can cook ha arrowroot pie," Ben might have said.

"Paan!" said Irma.

The surf was coming up. I watched until the tiny longboat, lighter laden after an hour's good trade, entered Bounty Bay. I stood on deck, staring out at the deep green island, then went down to my cabin. After lunch, it was still there on the horizon, but gray. When I came out later, Pitcairn was gone. There was nothing but sea.

## 17 · the bounty

........................

Captain Beechey's chart of Pitcairn is pinned up above my desk. Because it is only of the island, without the surrounding sea, it disguises Pitcairn's single defining feature—its isolation. It could be any island, off any coast. It could be in the English Channel, not far from my home. Or off the coast of Spain, or in a Scandinavian archipelago, or lounging in the sea in sight of an African shore. But it isn't; it is farther away than now, at my desk, I can imagine.

I brought little back from Pitcairn—a couple of shark carvings, a T-shirt, my basket, a hattie leaf, and one of Ben's hand vases. Most of the things in my Afrique-Trunk are as they were put in there, unused. I have mailed Irma's note on to Ron.

He phones me occasionally with news from Pitcairn. The sun spot has moved, he says, and he has been able to make good contact with Irma. Going out to the *Maxim Gorky* in sixty-four-knot winds and a mountainous sea, the longboat's tiller had smashed Steve's ribs as he stood at the helm. The longboat had been unable to reenter Bounty Bay, and sought shelter overnight in the huge swells off Pulawana. Steve had had to be evacuated to a hospital in Tahiti on board the cruise ship. It was all due to El Niño, said Ron. Later he called to say that there had been a massive landslide Down Rope, and Pitcairn's only beach had been buried. The tiny country was still, little by little, shrinking. And, did I know, Kari had left Pitcairn.

I began to write about Pitcairn—I had a commission from an American magazine—retreating into the safe harbor of history and seeking out relics from the mutiny. John Adams's pigtail was in the possession of the National Maritime Museum at Greenwich, where the Admiralty had condemned three *Bounty* mutineers to be hanged.

"Relic, human: pigtail. Organic: hair. Length: 190mm. Width 16mm," read the catalog. It said that Reverend W. H. Holman, pastor of Pitcairn Island, had brought the pigtail to England on his return in 1853. It was not considered worthy of permanent display and was stored, the archivist informed me, in a warehouse in a suburb of London. I could make a special application to go on an escorted visit to view it. I might also be interested in seeing John Adams's tombstone while I was there.

"Ceremonial artefact. Tombstone. Organic: wood. Metal: lead." The catalog entry said that the tombstone had been brought to England in the 1850s. The tombstone on Pitcairn was not John Adams's at all; it was a cheap concrete marker, erected no one knows quite when. Even the only known grave of a mutineer was a fake.

When I inquired about going to see these relics, I was informed that they were on temporary loan to Gieves and Hawkes, a gentlemen's tailor in Savile Row, and I would be welcome to go and view them there.

Gieves and Hawkes was a splendid establishment, where the emphasis was on subdued sounds, whether created by the soft furnishings and deep-pile carpet or the whispers of the sales assistants. In the midst of this hush, between rows of brogues and barathea blazers, was a glass case in which lay a tiny blond pigtail, the length and width of a garden worm. More *Bounty* paraphernalia was displayed, with numbers attached; a major private collection of *Bounty* items was being auctioned, and the pigtail had been borrowed to accompany the display of the objects for sale. "Lot 60" was a collection of items recovered from the wreck of the *Bounty* on Pitcairn, including a glass bottle and several nails.

An impeccably dressed sales assistant acted as a guide to the display, pointing to portraits of Bligh peeping out from behind racks of pin-striped suits, and the gold-lettered spines of editions of his log resting between silk ties.

"Strange enough," said the assistant, "Captain Bligh was one of our customers. Gieves supplied to the navy; Hawkes to the army. We amalgamated twenty years ago."

As he spoke, his eyes rested at my chest level, and I suspected that he was inspecting the lie of my lapel. There was a button missing on my jacket, and I am sure he spotted it. I was also sure that Captain Bligh would never have presented himself so poorly.

I submitted my article on Pitcairn past and present to the American magazine. The fact checker phoned from New York to go over a few points with me. Exactly how far was Pitcairn from New Zealand? She had measured it on the map, and had made it three thousand three hundred miles, twenty more than I had written. And, the fact checker continued, where was the closest place to the south?

"Antarctica," I replied. "The South Pole."

"What about somewhere in between?"

"There's nothing in between," I said. "Just ocean."

I had quoted Ben and Dennis. The fact checker wanted to know their phone number, so she could confirm the quotes with them. This, she said, was nothing to worry about; it was the magazine's standard practice to follow up on sources.

"They're not on the phone," I said.

"Where's the nearest phone?" asked the fact checker. "We could arrange to call them there."

"Three thousand three hundred miles to the west in New Zealand or six thousand miles south at the South Pole."

The fact checker was getting worried.

"Fax?"

"Nope."

"How long does the mail take?"

"Six months—maybe. It all depends."

This was a new situation for the fact checker. She'd have to check with her superior that it was okay.

There were few people who could confirm what I had written. I called Tim; he answered the phone. "Hell-o."

"Hi! It's Dea. I'm back!"

"Hello?"

"Tim—it's Dea. I've just got back from Pitcairn!"

"This isn't Tim," said Tim.

"Aaach." I thought he was making a joke.

"This is Tim's brother," said Tim.

"*Tim?*"

"He'll probably be back later this month. He's away—on the *Macalau*. I'll tell him you called." And he hung up.

I remembered that Tim was writing a book about Pitcairn. I called up the publishers he had given me. They had never heard of Tim, and had no book about Pitcairn in the pipeline.

The absence of any record of Tim's visit in Jay's book; the fact that no one on Pitcairn could remember having seen a microlight flying from Taro Ground; and now Tim's refusal to speak to me on the phone: perhaps he had never been to Pitcairn.

Tim had been able to describe his experiences on Pitcairn in such detail because there had been no way of checking him, either. He could describe the beautiful valleys and paths, the close friends he had made, the brave deeds he had enacted. Pitcairn was the only place where he could keep that fantasy alive, the only uncheckable place in the world. Then I came along, and proved him false. I was the destroyer of his dream.

We all hold a place within our hearts—a perfect place—which is in the shape of an island. It provides refuge and strength; we can always retreat to its perfection. My mistake was to go there. Dreams should be nurtured and elaborated upon; they should never be visited. By going to Pitcairn, I had vanquished the perfect place within myself.

At eight o'clock one Sunday morning, which would have been the end of Sabbath on Pitcairn, Ron called to say that Ben had died. He had suffered a stroke and been unable to recover. He had been buried the day before, on Sabbath, because the pastor and his family were leaving the next day on the *African Queen* for new pastures in Papua New Guinea. Anyway, it's best to bury a body swiftly in a subtropical climate. And did I think any of the national newspapers would be interested in an obituary? Ben had been island secretary for twenty-five years, after all.

I contacted an editor, who was happy to have an obituary of a fifth-generation descendant of mutineer Fletcher Christian. I wrote about Ben's contribution to his small community, his hard work and good humor, and detailed his award of the British Empire Medal for services to Pitcairn, of which he was immensely proud. When the heavily rewritten obituary was printed, it read as a brief history of the mutiny on HMAV *Bounty*, with more information given about his great-great-great-grandfather than about Ben himself. It omitted all details of his public service and did not mention the medal. Even in death, Ben could not escape being part of our fantasy.

The new issue of the *Pitcairn Log* arrived, and I read that the American chapter of the Pitcairn Islands Study Group had established a Pitcairn Island website, although it could not be accessed on Pitcairn. At the same time, another newsletter informed me that a computer forum called "un-

Holy Island" was being set up. "UnHoly Island is a slab of unrock in the middle of nowhere," said the newsletter. "On it, writers and other artists will meet and chat. They'll create and build with words, images, manipulated photographs, sounds. They'll create landscapes, roads, towns, villages, cities, streets, homes . . . to collaborate on constructing an imaginary place." It sounded just like Pitcairn.

Pitcairn had, almost since anyone knew of it, been more an idea than a geographical entity. But such tiny islands have not only been promises, but also prisons. The most notorious penitentiaries—Alcatraz, Robben Island—have been surrounded by water. Islands are places upon which we can become trapped. Pitcairn had begun as my escape, but I had ended by escaping from Pitcairn.

When my article appeared in the American magazine, several letters arrived each day, forwarded from the editor and always marked "Personal." A single mother, "teacher 4th grade," wanted me to call her collect in California and let her know if Dennis and Terry would be the "only options." The great-grandson of a missionary requested the address for Pitcairn; next to "Personal" on his envelope was written, "If Your God Is Dead—Try Mine. He Lives! I Know, I Talked With Him Today." A thirty-page fax arrived from Hollywood; Johnny V. Baron, President of BIP FAB, wanted to make a movie about Pitcairn. "I have a feeling that you are also a DESCENDANT OF THE BOUNTY MUTINEERS," he wrote. "I sometimes feel I am, too." He provided exhaustive details of proposed financing and distribution, and included a cast list; there was no Brooke Shields. He signed off, "Wishing I was on Pitcairn, now, at this moment, I remain . . . Johnny V. Baron."

Ron called again. "I want to talk to you. Is Kevin there?"

"No."

"Good. It's about Irma's letter."

"That's okay. It was no trouble forwarding it."

"No. It's not that. She says something about you and Nigger in it."

I recalled Irma handing me the letter just before I straddled the back of Dennis's bike on my last trip down the Hill of Difficulties: "If you don mind, dear." I had seen the scribbled note of thanks on the envelope. I had carried it back with me all the way from Pitcairn; it had never occurred to me to look inside. I had innocently brought the evidence of my own transgression home with me, and handed it over to Ron. In the indirect method of Pitcairn, I was being condemned by Irma.

"It's not true. Just rumor," I heard myself saying to Ron.

"Well, Irma is not pleased. But it does sound *ridiculous.*"

"You know how Pitcairn is," I said. "They love to gossip. Mountains out of molehills . . ."

Ron was relieved. "I thought it was rubbish," he said. "Just Irma."


I walked down to the seafront, where there was the amusement park and the ride called The Bounty. The replica of the mutineers' vessel was swinging violently against a backdrop of a beautiful isle—palm-fringed, girthed by golden sands—on which lounged a flutter of garlanded Polynesian girls. The picture-book green sea against which the *Bounty* swung had whitecaps, and the sky was an unnatural blue. Just yards beyond this backdrop was our sea, the Channel, gray under a dull sky. The Bounty is a popular ride.

Summer was ending, and next week the ride would shut down for the season. When I climbed on board, there was a father with three children on the bench stretched from gunwale to gunwale in front of me, and a teenage courting couple behind.

The swinging began gently, then became wilder. The children began to scream, clinging to their parent. I saw the perfect palm trees, the sea-lapped golden sand, the beautiful maidens with their sweet smiles flit past me as we swung toward the gray sky. On the way down, I captured it again, fleetingly, the image of Paradise.

# *a p p e n d i x*

............................

*Plants and Trees*

| | |
|---|---|
| breadfruit | *Artocarpus altilis* |
| candlenut | *Aleurites moluccana* |
| coconut | *Cocos nucifera* |
| Elwyn grass | *Sorghum halepense* |
| Jack fruit (paw paw) | *Carica papaya* |
| Job's tears | *Oix lacryma-jobi* |
| lantana | *Lantana camasa* |
| miro | *Thespesia populnea* |
| pandanus | *Pandanus pitcairnensis* |
| rose apple | *Syzygium jambos* |
| tau | *Cordia subcordata* |
| tee | *Cordyline fruticosa* |

*Birds, Fish and Animals*

| | |
|---|---|
| Galápagos giant tortoise | *Testudo elephantopus* |
| Henderson rail (chicken bird) | *Nesophylax ater* |
| nanwe | *Kyphosus cinerascens* |
| Noddy | *Andus tenuirostris minutus* |
| Polynesian rat | *Rattus exulans* |
| tern (white bird) | *Gygis alba* |
| wahoo | *Acanthocybium solandri* |

thanks to:

Royal Mail International, who sponsored the project and gave me a purpose that must have seemed impossible even to them.

The Francis Head Bequest, for coming to my financial aid in time of need.

Jim Russell, for sharing his unique knowledge of the island.

Jan Pedersen of Odfjell Tankers, who gave me passage, and the captains who not only took me there and brought me back, but did so with great humor and hospitality.

Timothy Waters, Bountyana supremo, and Greg Dening, expert of the legends surrounding Bligh and the mutiny.

Anders Källgård, who has extensively researched "Pitkern."

Captain Graeme Cubbin, for yet again correcting my nautical errors.

The Amazonians, for debates, ideas, networks.

Georgia Garrett and Liz Knights, who believed in Pitcairn even when I didn't.

My friends and family—Toolises and Birketts—who were always there, even when I wasn't. Kevin Toolis and Storme Toolis, in particular, for reluctantly sharing sustaining bowls of pasta.

This journey, as many others, began in books. I was inspired by and took advice from:

Ian M. Ball, *Pitcairn. Children of the Bounty* (London: 1973)
Jean L. Briggs, *Never in Anger* (Massachusetts: 1970)
Rachel Carson, *The Sea Around Us* (New York: 1951)
Irma Christian, *Pitcairn Island Cookbook* (Hawaii: 1986)
Greg Dening, *Mr. Bligh's Bad Language* (Cambridge, UK: 1992)
Anders Källgård, *Fut Yoli Noo Bin Laane Aklen?* (Goteborg: 1991)
*Sir Peter Scott Commemorative Expedition to the Pitcairn Islands 1991–1992. Expedition Report* (Cambridge, UK: 1992)
Sven Wahlroos, *Mutiny and Romance in the South Seas* (New York: 1989)
Meralda Warren, *Taste of Pitcairn* (Pitcairn Island: 1986)
Simon Winchester, *Outposts* (London: 1985)

about the author

Dea Birkett grew up in the south of England and was educated in Edinburgh, London, and the United States. She works as a freelance writer; her articles have appeared in newspapers and magazines throughout Britain and America. She is the author of *Spinsters Abroad: Victorian Lady Explorers* and *Jella: From Lagos to Liverpool—A Woman at Sea in a Man's World*, both of which were published in the United Kingdom. She lives in London.